THE DIRECTOR OF PUBLIC PROSECUTIONS

THE DIRECTOR OF PUBLIC PROSECUTIONS
PRINCIPLES AND PRACTICES FOR THE CROWN PROSECUTOR

An inquiry carried out at the Centre for Criminological Research, University of Oxford

GRAHAM MANSFIELD AND JILL PEAY

Foreword by
Sir Thomas Hetherington
KCB, CBE, TD, QC
Director of Public Prosecutions

Tavistock Publications
London and New York

First published in 1987 by
Tavistock Publications Ltd
11 New Fetter Lane, London EC4P 4EE

© 1987 Graham Mansfield and Jill Peay
Foreword © 1987 Sir Thomas Hetherington

Phototypeset by Rowland Phototypesetting Ltd
Bury St Edmunds, Suffolk
Printed in Great Britain at the
University Press, Cambridge

All rights reserved. No part of this book may be reprinted or
reproduced or utilized in any form or by any electronic, mechanical or
other means, now known or hereafter invented, including photocopying
and recording, or in any information storage or retrieval system,
without permission in writing from the publishers.

British Library Cataloguing in Publication Data

Mansfield, Graham
The Director of Public Prosecutions:
principles and practices for the Crown
Prosecutor: an inquiry carried out at the
Centre for Criminological Research,
University of Oxford.
1. Great Britain. *Department of the
Director of Public Prosecutions*
I. Title II. Peay, Jill
354.41065   KD8348

ISBN 0-422-60000-8

CONTENTS

Acknowledgements	vii
Foreword	ix

1 PROSECUTION STANDARDS – PAST, PRESENT, AND FUTURE — 1

An Independent Prosecution Service for England and Wales: Germination and Evolution	3
The DPP: Functions and Workload	7
The Reasonable Prospects Approach as a Prosecutorial Standard	10
Lawyers Acting as 'Filters as to Fact'	16
Prosecutors Acting as Arbiters of The Public Interest	26
The Need for Research	42
An 'Independent' Prosecution Service?	45
Postscript: The Reasonable Prospects Test – A Basis for Revision	52

2 PRE-TRIAL DECISION-MAKING — 61

The Research Approach: Questions and Context	61
Case Findings and Analysis	70
Conclusions	108

3 THE PROCESS OF PROSECUTION — 113

Introduction	113
I Pre-Trial	116
II The Trial	131

4 IS THE REASONABLE PROSPECTS TEST AN ATTAINABLE STANDARD FOR THE CROWN PROSECUTION SERVICE?	188
I The Expository Approach	189
II The Contextual Approach	202
5 CONCLUSIONS	215
The Critique of the Reasonable Prospects Test	217
Restructuring the Public Interest Element of the Reasonable Prospects Approach	225
Accountability	230
Bibliography	237
Name index	242
Subject index	243

Tables

1	The likely characters of prosecution witnesses (re: 'involvement')	139
2	A check-list for prosecutors (re: attack on their witnesses)	140
3	Case outcomes and principal defence strategy	158
4	Potential pitfalls for prosecutors	160

ACKNOWLEDGEMENTS

Our principal debt of gratitude is due to the Director of Public Prosecutions, Sir Thomas Hetherington, and to the staff of his office for their co-operation and interest throughout the research. This debt extends so widely that individual acknowledgements would be too numerous to include here, although Tony Woodcock's considerable assistance with the preparation of the manuscript merits a special thanks. We would also like to stress that the warmth with which we were received at the DPP's office, and the hospitality afforded us, went well beyond the call of duty.

Other prosecution agencies also afforded invaluable support and stimulation to the research at various stages: Sir Barry Shaw and his staff at the DPP's office in Northern Ireland; Bill Chalmers, former Crown Agent, and his staff within the Procurator Fiscal Service; the Prosecuting Solicitors' Society; numerous prosecuting solicitors' departments and police forces.

We should like gratefully to acknowledge the financial sponsorship of the Home Office Research and Planning Unit, and the advice we received from a distinguished Consultative Committee established by the Home Office.

Our colleagues at the Oxford Centre for Criminological Research deserve particular gratitude. Andrew Ashworth, then Acting Director of the Centre, supervised the research. He not only provided invaluable encouragement and advice throughout the research but also read what must have seemed to him endless drafts of our manuscript. Roger Hood similarly gave us most helpful comments on his return to the directorship of the Centre. Several people have worked on the production of the manuscript: Carol McCall, Hilary Prior, and Michelle Hicks; but Janet Larkin deserves credit for bearing the brunt of the work.

The views expressed in this book are ours and should not be taken to represent the view of any of the individuals and institutions to whom we are so indebted.

G.M.
J.P.
July, 1985

AUTHORS' NOTE

We should like to stress that no reference is made here to the Code for Crown Prosecutors published in the summer of 1986, which sets out the principles upon which the Crown Prosecution Service is to exercise its functions. Such an inclusion, at the time of writing, would have required the skills not of researchers, but of clairvoyants.

FOREWORD

In 1982, the Home Office funded the Centre for Criminological Research at the University of Oxford to conduct research into the prosecution system in England and Wales, and Dr Jill Peay and Dr Graham Mansfield were asked to undertake a 'warts and all' study into the workings of my department. It must have been a daunting prospect for them, and I, too, must confess to some trepidation at the thought of such scrutiny at the hands of researchers of their experience and perception. They set about their task with industry and an engaging enthusiasm. It was indeed a pleasure to work with them. They have now produced a book worthy of their efforts. It charts with accuracy the complexities of decision-making in the prosecuting process and is, I think, a valuable contribution to the debate on the criteria that the Crown Prosecution Service should adopt from its inception in 1986.

Sir Thomas Hetherington, KCB, CBE, TD, QC
Director of Public Prosecutions
25 July, 1985

CHAPTER 1

PROSECUTION STANDARDS – PAST, PRESENT, AND FUTURE

'The qualities of a good prosecutor are as elusive and as impossible to define as those which mark a gentleman. And those who need to be told would not understand it anyway. A sensitiveness to fair play and sportsmanship is perhaps the best protection against the abuse of power.' (Douglass 1977: 4)

The distinction between prosecution and persecution may be easier to draw for those who prosecute than for those who are prosecuted. From the professional side of the fence prosecution requires a combination of technical legal skills with an ability to portray an event for people who were not there, but who have to decide the truth or otherwise of the prosecution's case. The process of prosecution requires the prosecutor to engage in a series of tasks. First, since laws are framed in general terms, the prosecutor has to decide whether a particular act or omission by the accused might reasonably be said to fall within the ambit of the criminal law. Once this has been established, the prosecutor has next to decide whether to prosecute, or whether the case may be more appropriately dealt with by means of a caution, or, indeed, by taking no further action at all. In these pre-trial decisions the prosecutor exercises considerable discretion; a discretion which becomes subject to judicial review only in those cases where a prosecution commences.[1] The prosecutor's third task in making out a case is to persuade the court that all the necessary technical elements of the particular criminal offence were present in the behaviour and state of mind of the accused. This has to be established to the satisfaction of either a judge in the Crown Court or, in the Magistrates' Court, either lay justices or Stipendiary Magistrates, if the case is to get beyond 'half-time' and the accused is to be called upon to present his defence.[2] Fourth, if the prosecution is to result in a conviction the case also needs to be presented in a form that is both comprehensible and capable of being persuasive, beyond reasonable doubt, to lay assessors, whether magistrates or jurors. Finally, the prosecutor has to curtail the content and presentation of his case in accordance with the rules of evidence to prevent those lay assessors from being unreasonably persuaded that the accused is guilty. The supposed justifications for these evidential restrictions are the need to prevent the courts from acting on 'unreliable' evidence and the need to protect the rights of the accused. Thus, the prosecutor is constrained in his telling of the story.

'Telling a story', though, is precisely how many accused persons would regard the presentation of the prosecution case. For them, prosecution may appear as a game played by a series of rules which they may neither know nor understand. They may dispute that their behaviour was in any way illegal and, even if it was wrong, they may challenge the particular charges brought against them. They may feel frustrated at not being able to speak when they want to, at having their case put for them by a lawyer, and at hearing their case presented in court in a way which conflicts with their 'certain' knowledge of what occurred. For them, the process may feel inherently unfair. Yet it is precisely because of the need to ensure that the game is played by the rules that the contestants are lawyers, the referee a judge, and the ultimate arbiters 'peers' of the accused. Even where the defendant feels marginal to the proceedings, prosecution cannot be equated with persecution if it is conducted by the rules and without enmity.

In contrast with the decision to prosecute, the decision to convict rests primarily with lay people, whose minds may not be hardened by the experience of crime or cluttered by the technicalities of the law. But, if 'morality' is to be assessed against a background of 'legality', these lay individuals require the case to be presented to them by those who do understand and can apply the law. So, lawyers should prosecute in the spirit of 'ministers of justice' and not as if in pursuit of a verdict.[3]

At the office of the Director of Public Prosecutions (DPP) the prosecutors act as gatekeepers, making decisions as to which cases will go forward for prosecution and which will not.[4] This book addresses the question of how the DPP's lawyers go about their job as prosecutors: what principles underlie their decision-making, and how this affects the process of prosecution. Prosecutorial responsibility falls into two parts: first, the decision as to *whether* to prosecute; and secondly *how* to prosecute – the manner of the prosecution. The maxim of 'prosecution without persecution' should apply to both stages.

A recurrent theme throughout the book is the tension between prosecutorial *theory* and prosecutorial *practice*. The first chapter begins by reviewing why the DPP has become the focus for an independent prosecution service; it examines the role of the DPP and it explains the nature of the 'reasonable prospects' approach to prosecution. Following this, there is a more detailed analysis of two of the elements of a prosecutor's role as envisaged by the reasonable prospects approach: first as an 'arbiter of facts' and secondly as an 'arbiter of the public interest'. This theoretical framework is criticized as providing an insufficient guide for prosecutors keen to emulate the DPP's approach to prosecutions; the problems likely to arise out of it lead into an explanation of the need for the empirical research undertaken – distilling theory from practice. Finally, the question of what amounts to practical as opposed to theoretical independence is addressed. As a postscript to the chapter, a possible revision to the 'reasonable prospects' test is briefly presented for the reader to reflect upon in the course of the subsequent chapters.

AN INDEPENDENT PROSECUTION SERVICE FOR ENGLAND AND WALES: GERMINATION AND EVOLUTION

In 1981 the Royal Commission on Criminal Procedure reported that 'the present arrangements for the prosecution of criminal offences in England and Wales defy simple and unqualified description' (1981: para 6.1). Indeed, it deliberately refrained from describing the arrangements as a 'system', since they were neither uniformly organized nor did they rest on a single legislative foundation. However, the Royal Commission did note that the great majority of prosecutions were brought by the police and that these police prosecutions were locally based, with each of the forty-three separate police force areas organizing their own prosecutions under the control of the local chief constable and the police authority. It also noted that the arrangements could be characterized, at least so far as police prosecutions were concerned, 'by the unitary nature of the investigative and prosecutorial functions, with primacy of responsibility for the decision on prosecution being vested in the police and not in the legal profession' (para 6.6).

Within these arrangements the DPP was exceptional in that he acted on a national basis handling all cases of certain types (see pp. 7–10). But two further features of the DPP's approach were singled out by the Royal Commission. The first related to the question of who gets prosecuted (the prosecutorial standard), and the second to who takes that decision, and how the case is subsequently conducted ('independence').

The prosecutorial standard

The Royal Commission distinguished the DPP from local prosecutors on the basis of the standard of evidence required before a prosecution could be launched. At local level, prosecutions would routinely be brought where a *prima facie* standard of evidence could be established, namely where there was 'evidence, upon the basis of which, if it were accepted, a reasonable jury or magistrates' court would be justified in convicting' (Royal Commission on Criminal Procedure: 1981 para 8.8).[5] At the DPP a more stringent criterion was employed in that prosecutions would only be brought where there was 'a reasonable prospect of conviction'. This requires a standard of evidence which makes it more likely than not that a conviction will be returned. Over and above this evidential requirement, a prosecution would only be brought by the DPP where it was considered to be 'in the public interest'. Thus, prosecutors at the DPP had both to satisfy the reasonable prospects *test* which required weighing of the evidence, and then to apply the reasonable prospects *approach*, which amalgamated this assessment of evidential sufficiency with public interest considerations. The difference between these two apparently similar terms must be stressed here, since it is central to discussions in this book. The reasonable prospects approach includes the reasonable prospects test, the latter being simply the evidential part of the wider approach.

Thus, if the prosecution process is likened to a conveyor belt, the essence of the Royal Commission's recommendations with regard to the prosecutorial standard was that fewer of the cases which end in acquittal should be placed on the conveyor belt at all. Instead of the prevailing presumption, namely that where the *prima facie* standard could be satisfied the case should be 'put to the court', all prosecutors were now enjoined to exercise a discretion to prevent cases from joining the otherwise natural progression to court. Such a progression has been termed the 'prosecution momentum'.

Independence

The second distinguishing feature of the DPP was his independence from those conducting investigations into crime. As a prosecutor the DPP acted neither for nor at the behest of the police but 'for the public [and] in the public interest' (Hetherington 1980b). Other lawyers, acting as prosecutors for the police, did not share this independent standing but acted within a solicitor–client relationship: the prosecutor as solicitor acted upon the instructions of the police as client – he could offer advice but the police were not bound by that advice. The Royal Commission considered this to be deficient. Those who investigated the crime, namely the police, should not also have the responsibility for prosecuting because their objectivity might be impugned. Thus the Royal Commission sought to ensure that the functions of prosecutors of crimes should be separated as far as possible from those of the investigators of crimes.[6] It recognized that there was an extent to which this objective had already been realized in some police authority areas, where prosecuting solicitors' departments provided a permanent prosecution service for the police, but that the situation varied from area to area. More importantly it maintained that mere demarcation of the prosecutors' role from the investigators' role would not constitute a sufficient reform. It would, however, be a necessary precondition for the attainment of its second objective, the abolition of the 'solicitor–client' relationship. The Royal Commission opined that this relationship 'is not precisely defined, and much depends upon the co-operation and understanding of the individuals concerned' (1981b: para 143). But, if overall responsibility for prosecutions were to shift from the police to lawyers, then the prosecutor's independence must be assured and not left to the vagaries of individual relationships. Hence, the prosecutor was to be able to stand back from the conveyor belt and judiciously examine the merits of allowing a case to proceed to prosecution.

The Royal Commission's recommendations

The Royal Commission criticized the existing prosecution arrangements on the basis of three standards: fairness, openness and accountability, and efficiency. Its major recommendation was that a Crown Prosecution Service should be established, with the conduct of prosecutions becoming the responsibility of a service staffed by individuals with legal qualifications who were not identified with the investigative process. The Royal Commission further recommended that in line with this transfer of responsibility the new Crown prosecutors should adopt a higher evidential standard, namely the reasonable prospects test.[7] Its underlying rationale for this wider application of the evidentially more stringent test was that someone should not be put on trial if it could be predicted with some confidence that he was more likely than not to be acquitted, since this is 'both unfair to the accused and a waste of the restricted resources of the criminal justice system' (1981a: para 8.9).

Although the Royal Commission never explicitly characterized its proposed Crown Prosecution Service in terms of its 'independence', the Government's response to the report was to recognize a strong case in principle for 'an independent prosecution service'.[8] Independence was to become the keyword in the subsequent publication in October, 1983 of the White Paper, *An Independent Prosecution Service for England and Wales*. It can be argued, however, that the prosecutorial standard and independence are not strictly separable: since adoption of the reasonable prospects test may in itself entail some adjustment to the traditional solicitor–client relationship existing between the lawyer and the police. In dealing with professional conduct generally, and duty to the court specifically, the solicitor is exhorted in a Law Society publication not to mislead the court but: '*He ought not to forsake a client* on mere suspicion of his own as to the case or *on any view he might take as to his chances of success*' (Lund 1973: 54; emphasis added). Since the DPP's 'prospects of conviction' is not dissimilar from 'chances of success', and since this test was to provide one of the foundations for a revision of prosecutions, the solicitor–client relationship was clearly an impediment to the Royal Commission's proposals.

Similarly, adoption of the higher prosecutorial standard may help the prosecutor to ensure that his view of how a case should be handled prevails over that of the police and of counsel at trial. First, each case referred by the police to the prosecutor, presumably still on the basis of *prima facie* evidence, will require active reassessment to determine whether the reasonable prospects test can be met. The presumption of proceedings where *prima facie* evidence exists will therefore be challenged. Secondly, in a system in which cases and specific charges are only proceeded with if the prosecutor has decided that there is a reasonable prospect of conviction, there is significantly less scope and incentive for prosecution counsel handling the case to engage in plea negotiations than in a system where cases are brought merely on a *prima facie* standard. If plea negotiation amounts to one of the ways in which the prosecutor's control over the course taken by a case may be undermined, it is less likely to occur where the prosecutor employs reasonable prospects in his decisions. This is because he is less likely to 'overcharge' in the first instance.[9] It would be logical to infer that both the early need actively to review an initial decision by the police to prosecute and the reduction of the later scope for plea negotiation will protect the prosecutor's independence.

Thus, it is not surprising that the prosecutorial standard became the first focus for reform. Early in 1983 the Government affirmed its commitment to the spirit of the Royal Commission's recommendations when the Attorney General sent a circular to all Chief Officers of Police, which provided guidance on the criteria for prosecution (Attorney General 1983).[10] These criteria are similar to those employed by the DPP, in that they incorporate guidance on the meaning of the reasonable prospects test and emphasize the public interest element in the decision to prosecute. Not only is the DPP's approach to prosecutions to be promulgated throughout the Crown Prosecution Service, but the subsequent White Paper also specified that the Director is to head the new service, with his department forming its central headquarters.[11] The DPP is to become the linchpin of the proposed service.

THE DPP: FUNCTIONS AND WORKLOAD

The post of Director of Public Prosecutions was created by statute in 1879; its historical development has been fully explored by Edwards (1984) and will not be reviewed here. The essential functions of the office have not altered substantially in the ensuing 100 years.[12] At the time at which the research was conducted there were some fifty-nine professional officers (POs) at the office of the DPP, working in ten divisions each headed by an Assistant Director (AD). Two Principal Assistant Directors (PADs) oversaw their work, with the Deputy Director and Director at the apex of the department.[13]

The fundamental role of the DPP is to undertake prosecutions in cases of importance or difficulty, and to offer advice to the police when such advice is sought. The DPP operates under the Prosecution of Offences Regulations 1978, with a consolidating statute in 1979. Section 2 of the Prosecution of Offences Act 1979 states:

> 'It shall be the duty of the Director, under the superintendence of the Attorney General to institute, undertake and carry on such criminal proceedings and to give such advice and assistance to Chief Officers of Police, Justices' Clerks and other persons concerned in any criminal proceedings respecting the conduct of those proceedings as may be prescribed, or as may be directed, in a special case, by the Attorney General.'

Subsection (2) stipulates that: 'The regulations shall provide for the Director's taking action in cases which appear to him to be of importance or difficulty, or which for any reason require his intervention.' The DPP thus has a duty to prosecute and advise in prescribed cases and the discretion to take action in any case he deems appropriate.

However, this role limits the DPP to a small proportion of indictable cases. In only 3 per cent of all indictable offences is the decision to prosecute taken by the DPP, and in a further 5 per cent advice on prosecution is offered to the police. This small percentage is not evenly spread across the criminal calendar: the DPP is responsible for dealing with all cases of certain types, for example all prosecutions of police officers and all murders. The caseload consists chiefly of cases tried at the Crown Court. The DPP's officers are responsible for the decisions as to whether and how to prosecute in a particular case, and for the conduct of the pre-trial stages of a case – up to and usually including committal to the Crown Court. However, the case is conducted by counsel at trial.[14] In this sense, the responsibilities of both barristers and solicitors employed at the DPP may be likened more to those of advisers than advocates.

For DPP cases tried at the Central Criminal Court the Director can nominate Treasury Counsel to conduct the case for him. At the time that the research was conducted there were 7 senior Treasury Counsel and 10 junior Treasury Counsel plus a supplementary list of 27, all appointed by the Attorney General.[15] The Treasury Counsel system has two main advantages. First, the DPP has priority in calling upon counsel of the requisite calibre and experience who are familiar with his approach to prosecutions. Secondly, counsel can be available to offer advice to the DPP during the earlier stages of a case – sometimes even before the decision to proceed has been made. However, there is the possible drawback that Treasury Counsel lose the benefits said to accrue from handling defence cases too (see p. 51 and letter to *The Times*, 10 August, 1984).

The 'consent' cases

Criminal proceedings for certain offences may only be taken once the consent of the law officers (Attorney General or Solicitor General) has been given; more than sixty statutes require the DPP's consent, either exclusively or in substitution for either of the other law officers.[16] Although there is no obvious pattern in the consent provisions, Parliament appears to have included the requirement where otherwise there would be a risk of prosecutions being brought in inappropriate circumstances. Since it is not always possible to define precisely the intent of the legislature in passing a particular statute, the inclusion of a consent provision may help to ensure that prosecutions are restricted to those cases where the spirit as well as the letter of the statute is contravened – examples are sexual offences such as incest, buggery, and gross indecency (restricted for the latter two to categories where one of the parties is under 21), and the theft of, or damage to, the property of a spouse. These consent provisions can assist in securing consistency of practice, prevent abuse through recourse to vexatious private prosecutions, and enable account to be taken of mitigating factors which may not be susceptible to statutory definition.[17] Consent provisions are also included where there is likely to be considerable public concern about the decision to prosecute – either because the law deals with matters that are particularly sensitive or controversial, such as race relations or censorship, or because there are important considerations of public policy such as may arise in relation to official secrets, corruption, or explosive substances. Thus, the consent provisions apply to offences varying from quite minor to very serious cases which may have national or international repercussions. Although only the consent of one of the law officers is required before proceedings may be instituted,[18] the more serious cases will also tend to be retained for prosecution by the Director's department itself, rather than being referred to the police to prosecute once consent has been granted.

The 'regulations' cases

A number of other serious offences have to be reported to the DPP under Regulations 6(1) and 6(2) of the Prosecution of Offences Regulations 1978. The prosecution of these offences is invariably handled by the DPP. They include homicide, some offences under the Offences against the Person Act 1861, large-scale conspiracy and fraud, robbery using firearms, cases involving EEC law, and multiple rapes.[19] A provision under the 1978 Regulations enables the DPP to vary the list of reportable offences as the pattern of serious crime changes. Another empowers chief officers of police to seek the DPP's advice in any case.

The 'police' cases

Under Section 49 of the Police Act 1964 the police are required to refer to the DPP any complaint against a police officer unless the chief officer of police is satisfied that no criminal offence has been committed. On an annual basis these cases account for over half of the DPP's incoming caseload. However, a substantial proportion of these relate to Road Traffic Act offences, with the remainder being made up principally of allegations of assault.[20] In contrast to all the other cases coming into the DPP, where a *prima facie* case has to be made out by the police, allegations against police officers may come into the DPP on a much lower standard of evidence, since the existence of *any* evidence should be sufficient to prevent the chief officer from being positively satisfied that no offence has been committed. The corollary of this is that many of these allegations against police officers fail to meet the DPP's evidential standard and consequently do not go forward for prosecution.

It is axiomatic that none of the categories of case that come to the DPP could be described as 'routine'; rather, they represent areas of specialism or sensitivity.[21] They are numerically small in contrast with the local prosecutor's daily diet of theft, handling, and criminal damage. Hence it is advantageous that decisions about proceedings in these unusual cases are made on a centralized basis, by individuals who can stand back from the immediacy of those crimes. The DPP asserts that the advantage that accrues is uniformity in proceedings – it might equally be characterized as facilitating 'justice for minority criminals', on the basis of experience in handling comparatively rare cases within a particular category of offence.

THE REASONABLE PROSPECTS APPROACH AS A PROSECUTORIAL STANDARD

The criteria which the DPP applies in deciding whether to prosecute fall into two categories. First, is the evidence sufficient to justify proceedings? Second, does the public interest require a prosecution? The prosecutor should satisfy himself as to the first question before moving on to the second. Although the two stages have been described at length elsewhere (Barnes 1975; Royal Commission on Criminal Procedure 1981: Appendix 25; Attorney General 1983), their constituent parts and some problems arising will be briefly reviewed here.

Sufficiency of evidence

There are two issues at this stage. First, the DPP has to be satisfied that it is *possible* to proceed. Hence, there is a need to establish that there are no insuperable legal or jurisdictional obstacles to the success of the prosecution. In assessing whether the essential legal underpinnings of a case are present, for example admissible evidence of each element of the crime(s) charged, the lawyer as prosecutor requires technical competence. The second issue, and that which has attracted the most publicity, is whether there is a reasonable prospect of conviction. This entails weighing the adequacy of the evidence which the prosecution are in a position to present, in order to decide whether a conviction is more likely than an acquittal before an impartial jury properly directed in accordance with the law. Thus, the prosecutor acts as a sort of socio-legal pundit, attempting to 'second guess' the jury.

This means that in determining whether there is 'sufficient' evidence the prosecutor has to assess both objective and subjective factors. Objectively, he has to examine the availability, credibility, and credit of the witnesses, and whether there is any conflict between witnesses – or any unusual lack of conflict which may indicate collaboration between them. Furthermore, he has to consider the potential admissibility and reliability of evidence such as confessions. In essence, the prosecutor has to explore thoroughly the strength of the prosecution's case as it appears on paper. Subjectively, when assessing reasonable prospects, the prosecutor has to predict whether the witnesses are likely to 'come up to proof' in court and how persuasive the jury is likely to find the evidence. Finally, he has to consider any facts that are likely to make the jury sympathetic to the accused (Royal Commission on Criminal Procedure 1981: Appendix 25). Thus, he has to make a subjective prediction of the subjective perception by jurors of objective facts that may or may not be assessed in an 'unreasonable' fashion! 'Reasonable prospects' is both a subjective test which the prosecutor attempts to apply in an objective manner and an objective test applied, inevitably, on a subjective basis.

Public interest

Once the evidential limb of the decision has been satisfied, the prosecutor must consider whether the public interest requires a prosecution. This will entail reviewing both the provable facts and all the surrounding circumstances; and asking whether it is incumbent on the Crown to prosecute or whether the prosecutor might proceed by some other route, for instance by offering a formal police caution. Thus, at this stage the prosecutor asks whether he should or must proceed. In this respect the prosecutor acts as both a barometer and an evaluator of society's interests. As set out in the Attorney General's *Criteria for Prosecution*, these public interest criteria concern mitigating factors: the accused's age, physical or mental infirmity, or good character; the triviality, staleness, and prevalence of the offence; the complainant's attitude, and that of the local community. A more detailed analysis is presented later in this chapter.

A reasonable prospect of a conviction?

Why should the Royal Commission have considered the reasonable prospects test to be evidentially more stringent than the prevailing *prima facie* standard? It adopted two working definitions of the *prima facie* standard. The first is the less stringent assessment: 'evidence upon the basis of which, if it were accepted, a reasonable jury or magistrates' court would be justified in convicting' (Royal Commission on Criminal Procedure 1981: para 8.8); this version requires a sufficient quantity of evidence and leaves the determination of quality to the court itself. The second, 'enough admissible evidence to prove all the necessary elements of the offence and evidence that does not appear to be so manifestly unreliable that no reasonable tribunal could safely convict upon it' (para 6.10) is a more stringent test in that it requires the prosecution both to be satisfied that there is a sufficient quantity of evidence and to make some minimal assessment of its quality. Evidence which is available but, in the prosecutor's opinion, patently unreliable may fail to satisfy this latter definition of the *prima facie* standard. The reasonable prospects test may be contrasted with the *prima facie* standard in that it does not just ask the prosecutor to assess whether the jury *could* convict (*prima facie* 1), or even whether they *should* convict (*prima facie* 2), but whether it is more likely than not that they *will* convict. However, this predictive element creates problems for the prosecutor in assessing the likelihood of a particular outcome.

First, to what extent should the prosecutor address himself to issues that do not appear in the papers but will be influential at trial – namely, any gaps in the prosecution's evidence and, most importantly, the defence case? The Fisher Report recommended that it should be the prosecutor's duty to

> 'analyse and evaluate the totality of the evidence in a critical way, not confining his attention to the question of whether there is evidence to support the charge, but considering also whether further police enquiries should be made before the case should be allowed to proceed, and whether there are any other reasons why it should not continue.'
> (Fisher Report 1977: para 2.52(c))

On this view, the prosecutor should assess the 'strength and weakness of the prosecution's case in an objective way' (Fisher Report 1977: para 2.45).[22] The Royal Commission on Criminal Procedure also believed that the prosecutor needed 'to assess all the available information, including any explanation or further information forthcoming from the prospective defendant' (1981: para 8.8). That the DPP does attend to the likely strength of lines of defence has been suggested in relation to individual cases,[23] but this policy is not spelt out in the more general guidance emanating from the DPP about its approach to prosecutions.[24] Indeed, there is little reference to the strength of lines of defence as opposed to characteristics associated with the defendant or his offence which may induce the prosecutor not to proceed.

Secondly, what tribunal should the prosecutor have in mind when making his prediction of the likelihood of a conviction? Reference to an 'impartial jury' does not necessarily exclude consideration of other tribunals (Attorney General 1983). In the memorandum prepared in 1980 for the House of Commons Select Committee on *Deaths in Police Custody*, the present Director stated: 'The first consideration is whether the totality of the available evidence is of such a quality that a reasonable jury (or magistrate in respect of summary offences) is more likely than not to be satisfied beyond reasonable doubt that the accused is guilty of the offence charged.' This not only suggests that the reasonable prospects test incorporates the standard of proof to be satisfied – beyond reasonable doubt – but that it may also take into consideration the level of tribunal. Would either of these factors in practice make a difference to the quantity or quality of evidence required to satisfy the reasonable prospects test?

If the premise is adopted that juries may less readily be convinced of an accused person's guilt than magistrates, it is evident that the prosecutor who takes his cue from the magistrates may be prepared to proceed (since he believes he has a reasonable prospect of conviction) on a lesser standard of evidence than that required to take the case before a jury. If such a twin-track system of justice exists between the lower and higher courts, could not the prosecutor, by adopting a jury-based reasonable prospects assessment for all of his cases, help to 'iron out' such differences? Adopting the higher standard and not proceeding unless it was satisfied could effectively prevent magistrates from returning convictions on the basis of evidence that might be more likely to result in acquittals in front of juries.

Even if the lack of clarity of the reasonable prospects test on this point can be overcome, is the essence of the test stable, static, or standard, or are there officially recognized situations when it may be varied? For certain types of offence an even more stringent evidential standard might be applied by the DPP where an acquittal would or might produce unfortunate consequences.[25] For instance, in obscenity cases, account might be taken of the publicity received by a book as a result of prosecution, if its sales are likely to be enhanced in consequence. Similarly, where a defence witness is subsequently acquitted of perjury this may cast doubt on the original conviction of an accused. The consequences of an acquittal in trials that are abnormally long or expensive, and where the offence is not especially grave, may also cause the DPP to require a higher standard to be satisfied before the prosecution proceeds. Thus, in some cases the prosecutor may take the view that the risk of the effects of an acquittal outweighs the arguments in favour of proceeding even where the 'reasonable prospects test' is satisfied.

Do cases proceed where there is less than a reasonable prospect of conviction? Can the standard shift downwards because of the consequences of a decision not to proceed? This may occur in very serious cases where the impact on the prosecutor of the certain knowledge that a suspect, potentially guilty of murder, will not stand trial (because, despite the existence of *prima facie* evidence against him, the evidence does not satisfy the reasonable prospects test) outweighs the risk of an acquittal – so a prosecution ensues. Recognition of this dilemma in official sources is somewhat equivocal. The Royal Commission on Criminal Procedure (1981) stated: 'It does not follow that no case where the prosecutor has doubts about its strength should be prosecuted. We accept . . . that in such doubtful cases the prosecutor should "let the court decide"' (para 8.9). But the Report goes on to suggest that cases where there is no reasonable prospect of conviction can hardly be described as 'doubtful'. The Attorney General's *Criteria* states that 'the graver the offence the less likelihood there will be that the public interest will allow of a disposal less than a prosecution'. This hints at a greater difficulty with serious crimes, but still apparently assumes that the reasonable prospects test has to be satisfied before moving on to considerations of the 'public interest'. Finally, may the nature of the consequences that follow from a *conviction*, for example hospital treatment being obtained for a mentally disordered offender, or an incestuous father being separated from 'at risk' daughters, influence the DPP's thinking when he calculates whether the reasonable prospects test has to be satisfied? Whether the anticipation of 'beneficial' consequences arising out of a conviction influences the prosecutor will be examined empirically; strictly applied, the theory of reasonable prospects should not permit this.

Does the evidential standard also vary according to the nature of the offender? A previous Director, Sir Norman Skelhorn (1981), has asserted that where there is adequate evidence prosecutions should be brought without fear or favour. Yet the DPP has been subject to criticism for its prosecution decisions in relation to particular groups of offenders and specific individuals. For example, because so few prosecutions are brought against police officers, the suggestion has been made that a higher standard of evidence is required before the DPP will proceed – namely, a very reasonable prospect of conviction. This has been strongly denied by the DPP. The low prosecution rate may be partly explained by the number of cases that come to the DPP which fail to satisfy the *prima facie* standard, let alone the reasonable prospects test. But even where cases are prosecuted there is a comparatively low conviction rate. Might this even be taken as an indication that the DPP prosecutes too readily in police cases? Probably not. When explanations are sought for the relatively high proportion of acquittals, it is clear that juries have a tendency to believe police officers (as defendants), particularly when the evidence against them comes from individuals with previous convictions. Thus, the acquittals are not attributed to the quantity or quality of the evidence, but to jurors' assessment of its quality. If this assessment, and the presumption that it will occur, is built back into the prosecutor's decision-making on whether the reasonable prospects test is satisfied, fewer cases should be prosecuted than on an assessment of the strength of the evidence as perceived by the prosecutor. If this presumption is ignored, fewer convictions might be anticipated as a proportion of the total numbers of cases proceeded with.

It has been suggested that such allowances are made for defendants other than police officers (Barnes 1975). Whether there is a reasonable prospect of conviction may depend not only upon the probative value of the evidence as such, but also upon the status and character of the accused. Evidence that may be strong enough to convict defendant A may not be strong enough against defendant B. For example, if a High Court Judge were accused of trivial shoplifting the DPP would require very strong evidence of *mens rea*, because if a defence of absent-mindedness seemed likely, the prosecutor might legitimately believe that the jury would be unlikely to convict a person with such a status and financial standing.

Thus, the standard of evidence required to satisfy the reasonable prospects test may vary for different groups of offences and offenders. However, this may be defended as a legitimate aspect of a test that separates the quantity of evidence (which may remain the same across all of these groups) from how it is likely to be perceived by a jury. Thus, the same standard may be differentially applied in relation to the non-legal predictive element of the reasonable prospects test.

LAWYERS ACTING AS 'FILTERS AS TO FACT'

It has already been established that the prosecutor occupies a strategic and sensitive position in the criminal justice system. He stands between the police and the courts, striving for a balance between ensuring the conviction of the guilty and ensuring the acquittal (or rather, anticipating and pre-empting the acquittal) of the innocent. Under the reasonable prospects approach the prosecutor's criteria for reaching the decision to prosecute are clearly intended to be more stringent than those of the police (*prima facie* evidence) but inevitably less so than those required for the jury to convict (evidence which establishes a case beyond reasonable doubt). But precisely where should he pitch his standards between these two extremes? For the prosecutor to adopt the jury's criterion would be unfair to society: some doubts may legitimately be resolved in the course of trial; for him to maintain the same criterion as the police would be unfair to the defendant: the prosecutor would take into account none of the humanitarian and economic arguments advanced by the Royal Commission against the prosecution of 'weak' cases.

Other developments have made the prosecutor's role as a 'filter of fact' of central importance. First, since 1967 examining justices have had the power to commit an accused for trial without considering the evidence against him (Magistrates' Courts Act 1980: Section 6(1)). Since the vast majority of Crown Court defendants are now committed for trial via this 'paper committal' route, there is no independent assessment of whether the evidence against them satisfies the *prima facie* standard.[26] Only where an accused chooses the 'old-style' committal route and the prosecution is obliged to present sufficient evidence, usually by calling witnesses to give testimony, to establish at least a *prima facie* case, will there be any means of filtering 'weak' cases out of the process prior to trial (Magistrates' Courts Act 1980: Section 6(2)). Hence, the prosecutor's assessment of the sufficiency of evidence is crucial. Secondly, it will be argued that the *Galbraith* judgment in 1981, which is discussed in detail below, has curtailed the discretion allowed to judges in directing that there is 'no case' for the defendant to answer, i.e. that the facts adduced by the prosecution against the accused are not capable of being sufficiently persuasive for the jury to convict. It is ironic that this judgment, that less discretion should be allowed to lawyers who are judges, should have been delivered almost simultaneously with the Royal Commission's recommendation that more discretion should be conferred upon lawyers who are prosecutors. It will be argued that this misalignment of prosecutorial standards with the evidential requirements of the courts may, in practice, lead to inefficiency and tensions between prosecutor and court.

These twin developments, which have reaffirmed the role of the jury at trial but have strengthened the prosecutor's hand in avoiding trials altogether in some cases, reflect a more general ambivalence towards juries. The reasonable prospects test places emphasis on the jury as a point of reference for prosecution decisions, yet in applying the test the prosecutor may in practice avoid putting the case before the jury. What role is left for the jury when the prosecutor adopts the reasonable prospects test and assesses the persuasive weight of the evidence? By so doing, he effectively curtails the jury's role as to decisions on the facts. But, it is only the jury's role as 'acquitters' that is eroded. Their role as 'convictors', in cases either where the prosecutor predicts a conviction is likely or where one hangs in the balance, will not be eroded.

This tendency to bypass the jury may reflect the simple point that responsible prosecuting necessitates that only worthwhile cases be put before a jury. Alternatively it may be regarded as symptomatic of a decline in the importance attached to juries. Another example of this would be the suggestion, emanating from, among others, the Lord Chief Justice, that jury trials should be abolished for certain categories of cases, such as lengthy and complex fraud cases.[27] Even if this can be justified on the grounds of good sense (i.e. preventing juries from reaching the wrong decisions because they are unlikely to understand the relevant issues – or where it is impossible to present the relevant issues in a comprehensible form), it amounts to a departure from the principle of the right to trial by jury. Although the reasonable prospects test might be regarded as contributing to an erosion of the jury's role, alternatively it can be presented as just another illustration of the sensible constraints placed on the jury within a criminal justice system which remains wedded to the concept of jury trial but which recognizes its fallibility. Under reasonable prospects the jury's role is less than paramount in respect of some cases, and more than symbolic in others. The question of whether the prosecutor, when exercising his discretion not to proceed, acts as quasi-judge or quasi-juror will be a recurrent theme. It will be argued that neither represents a clearly appealing model.

The following discussion will examine what cues are available to the prosecutor in determining the standard of evidence he should seek before making a decision to prosecute. For current purposes the areas of potential dispute in relation to the assessment of facts fall into three categories. First, sufficiency: can the necessary *quantity* of facts be established? Secondly, credibility: are the facts *capable* of being believed? Thirdly, persuasiveness: are the facts *likely* to be believed? The reasonable prospects test requires the prosecutor to make assessments within all three categories. It will become clear that others who have to weigh facts in the Crown Court, the Court of Appeal, and the Magistrates' Court do not.

Galbraith and the Crown Courts

There is a cardinal premise in criminal justice that questions of law are for lawyers whereas fact-finding is a lay function. The reasonable prospects test, which urges the prosecutor to make some preliminary assessment of the persuasiveness of the facts rather than just adducing them, evidently goes against this premise. Similarly, although a conventional form of summing up by the judge at the end of a trial includes some statement along the lines that 'the law is for me but the facts are entirely for you, members of the jury', this is an oversimplification.[28] The judge, in determining whether there is a case for the defendant to answer, will have already made an assessment of the quantity of facts and will have made some assessment of their quality. Galbraith clarified the extent to which trial judges are entitled to assess the quality of facts given in evidence. The judgment concerned the circumstances in which the judge may direct the jury to acquit. Where there is no evidence the court anticipated no difficulty: the judge would stop the case. The difficulty arose, however,

> 'where there is some evidence but it is of a tenuous character, for example, because of inherent weakness or vagueness or because it is inconsistent with other evidence: (a) where the judge concludes that the prosecution evidence, taken at its highest, is such that a jury properly directed could not properly convict on it, it is his duty on a submission being made to stop the case; (b) where, however, the prosecution evidence is such that its strength or weakness depends on the view to be taken of a witness's reliability or other matters which are generally speaking within the jury's province and where on one possible view of the facts there is evidence on which the jury could conclude that the defendant is guilty, then the judge should allow the matter to be tried by the jury.' (1981: 73 Crim. App. R. 124)

At first sight, the *Galbraith* judgment may look like a classic exposition of an idealized model of decision-making. The judge's and the jury's minds are presented as being in a symbiotic relationship; the experienced legal mind decides upon the potential of the evidence, then 'fresh' lay minds decide what actual reliance to place upon it. It seemingly accords well with Devlin's characterization of the parameters of the jury's role, by what might be called a 'minimax' principle: the rule that 'there must be a certain minimum of evidence to justify a verdict and a certain maximum that the jury must not disregard' (1956: 92). By this he meant that there must be sufficient evidence to justify a conviction and that the conviction must not be against the weight of the evidence. However, Devlin recognizes that it is the judge who initially decides whether reasonable men *could* return a verdict on the evidence offered, rather than the jury having a free hand as *ex officio* reasonable men.[29] A judge may withdraw a case or a defence from the jury if this evidential minimum is not, in his view, attained. Thus, as Devlin recognizes, the rule can be restated in its true terms: the verdict cannot be supported unless a *reasonable lawyer* thinks there is evidence upon which reasonable men could convict. He defends this by reference to consistency: 'there must be a minimum of evidence as weighed by the judge . . . estimated by one of a body of men who think alike and are guided by precedent' (1956: 111). In Chapter 5 this concept of 'lawyers judging lawyers' will be more fully examined.

But how are judges to interpret *Galbraith* when deciding whether a case should be left to the jury? *Galbraith* will bear at least two interpretations. First, the judgment may have been aimed only at flagrant judicial encroachments into the jury's province. This interpretation would be supported by the comment that, 'there will of course, as always in this branch of the law, be borderline cases. They can safely be left to the discretion of the judge' (1981: 73 Crim. App. R. 1062). However, even if flagrant cases were the real target, surely it is 'borderline cases' which would require regulation, not those obviously lying at either side of the margin?

The alternative interpretation is that *Galbraith* did more than just pay lip-service to juries, and in fact signalled a fundamental reaffirmation of jury sovereignty. Early in his reasoning Lord Lane, CJ, identified two schools of thought: '1. That the judge should stop the case if, in his view, it would be unsafe (alternatively unsafe/unsatisfactory) for the jury to convict; 2. that he should do so only if there is no evidence on which a jury properly directed could properly convict' (1981: 73 Crim. App. R. 1061E). Since the court preferred the second school of thought it might be suggested that in future trial judges were not to look beyond the *prima facie* criterion in deciding whether a case should continue.

Common sense would suggest that the true purpose of the *Galbraith* judgment lies somewhere between the two interpretations offered. Indeed, it could be argued that it is only the *expression* of the exercise of the judicial discretion that was altered, from pessimism about what the jury might believe (the high-water mark of judicial discretion) to a lack of optimism – a preparedness to leave cases to the jury (the low-water mark of judicial discretion).

To return to Devlin's analysis: although the experienced legal mind of the judge decides upon the potential of the evidence, this assessment has largely to do with the quantity of the evidence. The prosecutor may therefore be left without 'cues' he might adopt from the judge when it comes to making some preliminary assessment of the evidence. Lord Lane, CJ, apparently intended, in *Galbraith*, to lead judges to strike a balance between the danger of usurping the jury's functions and the danger of unjust convictions. An independent prosecutor may be seeking to attain a similar balance, but *Galbraith* does not appear to be of immediate help.

Furthermore, the ruling in *Galbraith* on the role to be adopted by the judges may be taken to weaken the defendant's position to an extent inconsistent with the presumption of innocence. Glanville Williams has defined the object of a submission of 'no case' as being twofold: 'To avoid the risk of perverse jury verdicts and to protect the accused against a prosecutor who has failed to make out a *prima facie* case and hopes to make good the deficiency by cross-examining the witnesses for the defence' (1963: 82). Pattenden (1982b) further argues that the accused needs protection just as much against unsound evidence as he does against insufficient evidence. Although Lord Lane may have been reasserting the sovereignty of the jury, he failed to refer expressly to the right of the defendant not to have to prove his innocence.[30]

As Wood (1961) pointed out there is a practical shift, 'however slightly', in the burden of proof on to the defendant after 'half-time'. Wood asserted that even if the prosecution evidence is strong, the usual standard of proof – beyond reasonable doubt – should apply in any assessment at the close of the prosecution case. Although the tolerance in practice of a lesser standard may be indicative of a natural desire to establish the truth, it does blur the adversarial concept of the duty of the prosecution to prove its case beyond reasonable doubt. It can be argued that the *Galbraith* judgment has contributed to Wood's practical shift in the burden of proof by affording the defendant even less protection against weak cases 'coming good' after half-time because of the limitations placed on the judge's discretion.[31] Thus, prosecutors wishing to pre-empt jury acquittals and spare defendants unnecessary and unjustified suffering would have to look beyond the Crown Courts for their prosecutorial cues.[32]

The Court of Appeal

The Court of Appeal (Criminal Division) shall allow an appeal against a conviction on the grounds that under all the circumstances of the case it is unsafe or unsatisfactory (Criminal Appeal Act 1968, Section 2, as amended by Section 44 of the Criminal Law Act 1977). Lord Widgery has detailed how this test should be applied by the Court:

> 'In cases of this kind the Court must in the end ask itself a subjective question, whether we are content to let the matter stand as it is, or whether there is not some lurking doubt in our minds which makes us wonder whether an injustice has been done. This is a reaction which may not be based strictly on the evidence as such: it is a reaction which can be produced by the general feel of the case as the Court experiences it.'
> (*R. v. Cooper* (1968) 53 Crim. App. R. 82)

This standard is patently broader than that advocated in *Galbraith*. Could it be said that in applying the reasonable prospects test to weigh the evidence, the DPP is acting quasi-judicially on the same basis as the Court of Appeal? There are significant difficulties with this argument. First, the Court of Appeal reviews evidence given at trial, which may be regarded as fixed and certain. The DPP relies upon witness statements, which may be regarded as speculative (the witness may not 'come up to proof', or even come to court). Thus the DPP reviews the potential of the evidence, the Court of Appeal its actuality.

Secondly, the Court of Appeal looks at the whole of the case, so that evidence presented by the defence may be weighed against – or sometimes with – that offered by the prosecution.[33] Yet, if the DPP is truly an anticipatory agency, why should this interim part of the case be ignored? It might be argued that a failure to consider the defence case does not matter, since the Court of Appeal will. But such a response hardly sits comfortably with the general ethos of the DPP, which recognizes the human and economic costs of prosecutions as a justification for filtering cases out of the criminal justice system. Indeed, since the reasonable prospects test is based on jury predictions, it might be said to require a prediction of their assessment of the defence case.

None the less it can be maintained that the two approaches have one essential difference which validates the DPP's primary preoccupation with the prosecution's side of the case. The Court of Appeal is clearly retrospectively saying that the jury got it wrong. The orthodoxy of the DPP's stance is that it prospectively filters out only those cases where juries would acquit if given the chance.[34] In this sense, when exercising the discretion not to prosecute, the DPP gives juries the benefit of the doubt, assuming that they will get it right, rather than giving them the benefit of actually trying the case.

Third, only a small minority of Court of Appeal decisions quash convictions on the grounds that they are unsafe or unsatisfactory: the most common ground of appeal is some form of misdirection or non-direction, and those cases provide no evidential cues for the DPP.

The Magistrates' Courts

The position on a submission of 'no case' in the Magistrates' Courts may be contrasted with that in the Crown Courts. In 1962 in a Practice Note issued by Lord Parker, CJ, it was stated that, 'a submission that there is no case to answer may properly be made and upheld: (a) when there has been no evidence to prove an essential element in the alleged offence; (b) when the evidence adduced by the prosecution has been so discredited as a result of cross-examination or is manifestly so unreliable that no reasonable tribunal could safely convict on it.' ([1962] 1. All E R 448 (D C))

Thus, if a submission was made, the decision should depend not so much on whether the adjudicating tribunal (if compelled to do so) would at that stage convict or acquit, but on whether the evidence was such that a reasonable tribunal might convict.

The *Galbraith* judgment probably does not alter the Practice Note of 1962, so magistrates may continue to weigh the evidence on half-time submissions from the defence (unreported Queen's Bench Division Case, 21 December, 1983, co/650/83 *ex parte Luciano Petrone*). The rationale for this is, of course, that the magistrates constitute a joint tribunal of law and fact. Once they have directed themselves on whether the evidence is legally capable of bearing the weight of a conviction, they can then assess factually whether it does. This means that the Magistrates' Courts may witness the embarrassing situation put forward by Williams where the defence has such confidence in its submission of no case that it offers no evidence even after the submission is refused (see Note 31). The beyond-reasonable-doubt standard then comes into play with the magistrates considering whether they find the credible evidence sufficiently persuasive. However, to the public gaze at least, the magistrates might first rule that there is a case to answer and then, almost immediately afterwards, acquit.

Where magistrates are asked to hold full committal proceedings they should not weigh the evidence but rather commit the case where the *prima facie* standard is satisfied. To do otherwise would pre-empt the jury function held sacrosanct in the Crown Court. But in summary trials they are entitled to weigh the evidence. Considerable confidence in the magistracy is demanded by the flexibility of thought processes dictated by this divided position resulting from the Practice Note in 1962 combined with *Galbraith* in 1981.

Practical consequences of the prosecutor's anomalous role as arbiter of facts

What is likely to be the effect of these differing evidential criteria on the prosecutor? Unlike the magistrates, he is expected not to adjust his approach according to the case route. It is clearly anomalous that the prosecutor employing reasonable prospects can exercise a discretion in weighing the persuasive burden of the evidence, but trial judges, in considering submissions of no case, cannot. This means that the DPP, without the benefit of testimony, can assess evidence as being insufficiently cogent for a successful prosecution without seeing the witness, whereas the judge, who hears and sees them, cannot. Where the case proceeds by the old-style committal route, and the prosecutor is able to assess the persuasiveness and credibility of his witnesses first-hand, the further anomaly may arise that at precisely the same time that the prosecutor decides there is no reasonable prospect of conviction, the magistrates may commit the case on a *prima facie* basis, thereby tying the prosecutor's hands to go on with the case.

So how can the conscientious prosecutor, whose view of a case may be revised when it varies in strength as it proceeds, sustain his independence against opposition from the court? There are three avenues open to him to ensure that cases, once in the hands of the court, do not proceed. First, cases may be withdrawn. This does not mean that there is an acquittal (and may therefore prevent the award of costs to the defendant) and it requires the permission of the court. Secondly, there is the *nolle prosequi*, which postpones a prosecution *sine die* without fixing a future date. This does not equate with an acquittal either: theoretically the case may be reopened, although in practice it never is. This measure is the exclusive prerogative of the Attorney General and can only be used in the higher courts. Historically it was used to terminate technically imperfect proceedings or to prevent vexatious prosecutions. Now it is used principally on humanitarian grounds. Thirdly, the prosecutor may 'offer no evidence'. This does mean that automatically an acquittal verdict is entered on the order of the judge. As a matter of courtesy the prosecutor should ask for the permission of the court; it is not clear whether he needs this permission.[35] The power was discussed in the case of *Broad* (1979), which suggested that the courtesy practice of asking for the court's permission before offering no evidence had not only become customary but also that permission need not be granted automatically. The judge insisted that the case proceed; a conviction resulted. The defendant unsuccessfully appealed on the question of judicial authority to override the prosecutor's decision. It was noted that prosecuting counsel's assessment of the case might be 'quite unrealistic'. However, this retrospective judgment of *technical error* did not settle the point satisfactorily. The leading case of *Turner* (1978) is more helpful. Turner's accomplice, Saggs, was given immunity from prosecution and gave evidence against Turner, who was convicted and sentenced to seven years' imprisonment. Turner sought a 'revenge' private prosecution against Saggs. The DPP intervened, by taking the case over, and then offered no evidence. Turner subsequently brought an action for abuse of process against the DPP, which was refused (*Broad* (1979) 68 Cr. App. R. 281 and *Turner* v. *DPP* (1978) 68 Cr. App. R. 70; see also p. 31, *DPP* v. *Brown and others* (1975 unreported)).

This decision appeared to uphold the independence of the DPP in general, and in particular his attainment of it through the process of offering no evidence. It was widely assumed that even the present local prosecutors enjoyed the same particular freedom in respect of the courts despite their comparative general lack of independence. This assumption was called into question in *Littlewood* (1983), the 'naked ballerina' case. When the prosecuting solicitor (for the Metropolitan Police) sought to offer no evidence, the judge insisted that the case proceed to trial; a conviction for assault on the police resulted.[36]

All three measures are likely to ventilate the jurisprudential issues underlying the differences between the way in which the courts approach cases and the way in which the prosecutor does – with his greater latitude for 'filtering out'. To date there are only a few cases where such conflict occurred. These have been largely confined to the DPP cases. However, once his independence and decision-making criteria are spread through the new prosecutions system such cases are likely to multiply, particularly since the police are to retain the power to charge on what might amount to only a *prima facie* standard of evidence.[37] Before the case reaches court, the prosecutor is clearly to enjoy the power to 'uncharge' defendants. But, whether the courts will readily accede to requests by the prosecutor to withdraw cases, once such requests become more commonplace, is unclear.[38] If the 'legality' principle this implies is not clarified, some of the fundamental objectives of the new prosecution system, including sparing defendants unnecessary anxiety and avoiding directed acquittals, may be endangered.

Is the criminal justice system out of step with the DPP?

Discussion so far has focused on the question: what is the legitimacy of the DPP's prosecution standard within the surrounding legal context? The correctness of the DPP's stance has been treated as problematic; although defensible on humanitarian and economic grounds, it may be 'out of step' on narrower legal grounds. Aside from reference to the Court of Appeal as partial authority, there is no longer a judicial precedent to support the DPP's exercise of discretion with regard to the weight of the evidence. By process of elimination this means that the DPP is acting as quasi-juror. This is not a surprising conclusion, given that the reasonable prospects test is expressed as a jury prediction, but, in the wake of *Galbraith*, it runs counter to characterization of the DPP as 'following the courts not leading them'.

Perhaps this emphasis should be reversed. Are other parts of the criminal justice system out of step with the DPP? It appears ironic, against the contemporary background wherein the Royal Commission concluded that the *prima facie* test provided an inadequate basal level from which to launch prosecutions (necessary but not sufficient), to find the Court of Appeal advocating the continuance of prosecutions on the grounds that a standard closely approximating to *prima facie* is both necessary and sufficient for a case to be left to the jury.[39]

It seems not only in keeping with the spirit of the times that weak cases should be filtered out rather than allowed to run their course, but also good sense to allow trial judges to exercise discretion over the weight of the evidence, since they have the opportunity to see the prosecution witnesses. The humanitarian, economic, and legal perspectives might be reconcilable if the trial courts were permitted to act as a more effective filter as to fact. They should not invade the purview of the jury lightly, but *Galbraith* perhaps pushed the line back too far.

PROSECUTORS ACTING AS ARBITERS OF THE PUBLIC INTEREST

A review of the sources of legal guidance available to the prosecutor in the previous section tentatively concluded that prosecutors might 'take the lead' rather than emulating the courts in respect of the criteria making up the evidential limb of the reasonable-prospects approach.

This section takes up the same themes – of possible sources of guidance and of where responsibility should be located – in respect of the second limb of that approach, namely the public interest. However, there is an important preliminary question: what is the justification for considering the concept of public interest when it comes to applying – or not applying – the law in particular cases? What legitimacy is there in lawyers applying 'extra-legal' considerations in relation to prosecution decisions?

A rigid view of the law is that it should be fixed and certain: if it is broken it should be enforced. Mandatory prosecution ensures that all individuals against whom there is a minimum of *prima facie* evidence are tried by the courts; the court then becomes the selective enforcer of the law, if the law is to be enforced selectively at all. A more flexible view of the law is that it provides guiding principles for the regulation of behaviour, which are highly developed but do not, because they cannot, anticipate every eventuality and every variation in circumstances. Such an approach in turn requires significant discretion to be vested in those making the decisions about whether to set the law in motion.[40]

The 'rigid' view of the law is on relatively firm ground when offences such as murder are under discussion. But the scope for disagreement over the moral imperatives underlying the law becomes more acute as the conduct it prohibits shifts to wider social issues. In areas such as environmental protection or the control of material deemed to be obscene, where the harm done may be less tangible than murder, and there is room for differences of opinion, the rigid view of the law becomes less appropriate. Hence, even where criminal sanctions are provided, such areas of the law are characterized by relatively low rates of enforcement, with flexibility and negotiation instead of rigidity and penalty. These 'open-textured' laws recognize competing interests which the prosecutor has to take into account. Once it is conceded that laws are not automatically applied in every situation they cover, some justification must be advanced to legitimize abstentions.

Decision-making on grounds of public interest recognizes that competing values within any complex society must be reconciled. Thus the prosecutor's extra-legal considerations involve the balancing of different types of harm: the harm done, or avoided, as a result of prosecutorial action or inaction. The balance striven for may be characterized as pursuit of a society's 'net interest' in whatever issue is under consideration (Barry 1967). Some particular interests may override others but all interests should be considered in the cost-benefit analysis. In what types of cases do these extra-legal considerations apply? The DPP can assert that they may apply in *any* case, since the quasi-judicial exercise of a discretion as to whether and when he takes steps to enforce the criminal law is one of the DPP's explicit duties.[41] This general constitutional position has been specifically recognized for certain categories of the DPP's caseload – namely the consent cases – where the legislature has conceded the impossibility of drawing a precise line of criminality to regulate some forms of behaviour. The need for extra-legal discretion at the edges of the law is implicitly acknowledged in such cases as wasting police time, where the potential for harm resulting from over-zealous prosecutions (for example discouraging even 'dubious' rape complainants) could outweigh the harm to be minimized by penalizing thoughtless or malicious uses of a vital public resource. For other categories of offence, for example Official Secrets Act cases, the DPP's extra-legal criteria are more covert – as one might expect in such cases – but are present none the less. The DPP is advised by experts on the consequences of different types of prosecution action or inaction, then reaches a quasi-judicial decision. Even if such cases come to trial, the jury will frequently only hear aspects of the evidence which the prosecution has in its possession.[42]

What link is there between serious official secrets and less serious consent cases? Both types of case require the prosecutor to determine what course of action, if any, best serves society's net interests. Once this common thread is recognized it becomes clear that any discussion of the public interest in prosecutions which is confined to the 'high-visibility' offences is too narrow. Such cases represent only the tip of the iceberg of decisions which involve weighing up 'net interest' on behalf of the public.

However, it is appropriate that extra-legal considerations as applied in Official Secrets Act cases should be termed the 'national interest' and thereby distinguished, even if only terminologically, from those constituting the 'public interest' as applied in the more day-to-day consent cases, since the public's involvement in Official Secrets Act cases is confined to jury deliberations in the few cases which proceed to trial. It might be argued that the public, through their decisions to report criminal activity in other spheres, play a role in determining the limits of what behaviour they will not tolerate and which thereby becomes subject to review by the prosecutor applying an interpretation of what is in the public interest. However, it will become clear that this role is limited since it confines public interest to the question of *whether* to prosecute. The application of public interest by the prosecutor, as will be illustrated in the empirical chapters (Chapters 2, 3), highlights the subtleties of the prosecution process and the importance of the exercise of discretion along the way, i.e. not only *whether* law is invoked but also *how* it is invoked.

If considerations of the public interest in relation to prosecutions are treated as still problematic but resolved in the sense that they enjoy some legitimacy, two other fundamental issues remain for discussion. First, should lawyers be the arbiters of what constitutes the public interest? (And if so, *which* lawyers?) Are they qualified for the task? The answer seems to be that prosecutors as lawyers undertake this role by default, partly because prosecutors are strategically placed, and partly because the alternative candidates – the public, the police, the courts – have never been required to articulate the way in which public-interest considerations influence their decisions.[43] Secondly, what safeguards are there – or should there be – against legal expansionism or arbitrariness in decisions?[44] These questions lead into a discussion of accountability. But, since the argument will be advanced that public-interest criteria have not been adequately articulated, and that the route to more comprehensive expression lies in a study of practice, this discussion is deferred until Chapter 5.[45]

The DPP and the public interest

The DPP has said of his role, 'I am a public officer, acting in the public interest, . . . and "the public" consists of the community of private individuals' (Hetherington 1980a: 12). In exercising the discretion to prosecute, the DPP tries to reflect the public interest as a whole; but any decision to prosecute invariably involves only a small number of offenders and victims. How are their interests, immediate in their appeal, to be weighed against the interests of the wider, but more removed public?[46] It will become apparent that attempts to articulate the public interest have reflected the immediacy of individual interests, in that they have found expression in prosecution criteria – in contrast with neglect of the wider but less easily identifiable issues.

It is clear that the Director has these wider considerations at heart when he speaks of the need to 'balance' the public interest. Thus, society's interest in enforcing a criminal law intended to protect the public has to be weighed against factors tilting the 'other way' (see Hetherington 1980b). But wider considerations are not adequately represented in the authoritative criteria on prosecutions issued by the Attorney General. With the extension of the DPP's approach to prosecution decisions, the questions addressed in this section are:

what does the DPP mean when he states that he prosecutes 'in the public interest'? and how is this criterion *likely* to affect prosecutorial decision-making? The practical impact of public interest criteria on the DPP's decisions will be reviewed in Chapters 2 and 3.

A historical perspective

In describing the DPP's approach to prosecution decisions, and particularly the role of public interest considerations, importance has been attached to a Parliamentary speech by Lord Shawcross when Attorney General in 1951. This clarified the principles on which both he and the DPP then exercised their discretion as to whether or not to prosecute. Lord Shawcross noted that 'law and order are not necessarily promoted by prosecution in every case', because account has to be taken of a variety of considerations, all of them leading to the 'dominant consideration' of whether a prosecution was required in the public interest. He stated:

> 'Usually it is merely a question of examining the evidence. Is the evidence sufficient to justify a man being placed on his trial? . . . It is not in the public interest to put a man upon trial, whatever the suspicions may be about the matter, when the evidence is insufficient to justify his conviction, or even to call upon him for an explanation.'[47]

Two features distinguish this approach from that currently advanced in the Attorney General's *Criteria for Prosecution*. First the need for a case to be one where a conviction is more likely than not requires considerable confidence from the prosecutor; Lord Shawcross did not speak of the likelihood of a conviction, only of the need for one to be justified. Secondly, although it was *not* in the public interest to prosecute where there was 'insufficient evidence', the then Attorney General went on to discuss the variety of other wider considerations which may influence the decision as to whether or not to proceed, including 'the effect which the prosecution, successful or unsuccessful as the case may be, would have upon public morale and order'. Since Lord Shawcross had stated that public interest was the dominant consideration, were evidential questions one aspect of the public interest assessment, rather than a prerequisite to the public interest being raised as a separate matter? If so, this contrasts with the present approach, wherein 'having satisfied himself that the evidence itself can justify proceedings, the prosecutor must *then* consider whether the public interest requires a prosecution' (Attorney General 1983: para. 4; emphasis added). Although this implies a two-stage model of prosecutorial decision-making, in that the reasonable prospects test has to be satisfied *before* consideration is given to the public-interest component, the Attorney General's criteria for prosecution also apparently endorse Shawcross's presumption that public interest is the dominant consideration.

In practice, these two perspectives may be irreconcilable. The reasonable prospects test rests upon predictions of how a jury will assess the evidence. Under Lord Shawcross's approach it is the prosecutor's assessment of whether there is sufficient evidence to put a man on trial which is the determining factor. Under reasonable prospects it is possible for cases to arise where there is a strong public interest in prosecuting, but if the prosecutor believes that the jury will more likely than not acquit, the supposedly 'dominant' public interest consideration should not be raised, let alone be influential.

It will be argued that spelling out the constituent parts of the overall approach to prosecution decisions, as advocated by Lord Shawcross, has resulted in an unwarranted simplification of the decision-making process. This, in turn, has resulted in too rigid a demarcation between evidential and public interest considerations. Has the outcome been a subtle shift in the balance between them from the dominance of public interest to the dominance of the reasonable prospects test? If such a 'retreat from Shawcross' has occurred it may affect the nature of cases going forward to prosecution. This will be examined in the empirical chapters. Finally the possibility of a 'return to Shawcross' will be reviewed in the concluding chapter.

The courts, the prosecutor, and the public interest

In respect of non-evidential questions, the DPP formally enjoys an almost unfettered discretion, applying whatever criteria he may deem appropriate, subject to being answerable to Parliament through the Attorney General. The DPP is not answerable to the courts. This was confirmed by Viscount Dilhorne in *DPP* v. *Brown and others* (1975):

> 'I am wondering to what extent it is right for any court to give directions as to how he should conduct his business. The DPP works under the Attorney General; he does not work under any judges at all and any directions he receives as to the way in which he does his work must surely come from the Attorney General. I would have thought it quite wrong for it to come from any judicial authority at all. *He may be*

condemned for what he has done but he must not be told what he has to do in the future.' (emphasis added)[48]

The DPP thus enjoys constitutional autonomy.[49] How does his exercise of a public-interest-based discretion compare with the role of other participants in the criminal justice process?

The courts have no power to apply public-interest considerations in their decisions. Once the courts are seized of a case they may only dismiss it prematurely on evidential grounds; there are no opportunities for acquitting or filtering the case out of the system on public interest grounds.[50] Only when a conviction has been returned may the courts, through their sentencing function, give expression to public interest considerations, either through mitigation of sentence or through the use of exemplary sentences. In addition, the granting of an absolute discharge or a refusal to award costs to the prosecution may imply that the prosecution was not in the public interest (Practice Direction, 5 November, 1981; see also Wilcox 1972). This is not to say that public interest plays no part in the earlier proceedings; judges may covertly apply public interest criteria in their discretionary functions, for example in summing up and accepting pleas, but this process is not formalized. Thus the judges are unlikely to be of much help in clarifying public interest criteria for the prosecution. On the other hand, juries may apply public interest considerations when reaching their decisions. Yet this is primarily a matter for speculation. Where juries return verdicts against the weight of the evidence, how can it be known whether these decisions are perverse (i.e. have been influenced by public interest considerations more properly left to the judge or prosecutor)[51] or whether the jury simply reached the wrong decision? Where perverse convictions are returned there is the right of appeal. This procedure may assist in producing a body of knowledge about the influence of public interest factors at the trial stages of the criminal justice process but, as yet, it has failed to do so.[52] However, where the jury return a perverse acquittal this situation cannot be rectified.[53] Thus, unless the judge sees fit to give more direct expression to his views,[54] the prosecutor is deprived of guidance as to prosecutions which it is not in the public interest to bring.

Even if the prosecutor could distil juries' views of 'the public interest' in a systematic fashion there is the more fundamental difficulty that juries' views are more likely to represent public opinion than public interest. This is because, even allowing a romantic notion of the jury as a 'microcosm of society', they suffer from imperfect knowledge. The rules of evidence ensure that juries do not have access to all the information in the hands of the lawyers; if they did, it might unduly prejudice their role. Furthermore, where juries acquit against the weight of the evidence they may do so on an assessment of that case in isolation. They cannot be expected to assess the case against the wider context of crime, nor will they necessarily appreciate the ramifications if that isolated perverse acquittal were to form the basis of a policy of non-prosecution on public interest grounds by prosecutors. Hence, jury verdicts are 'one-off' decisions and should be consigned to public opinion, not public interest. But, although they are not interchangeable, public opinion may constitute an element of the public-interest criterion and thus help to keep those applying the law abreast of political reality.

Aside from the occasional absolute discharge or a string of jury acquittals, the prosecutor may gain little guidance from the courts; in defining the public interest, he is clearly on his own. In this respect the characterization of the DPP as 'following the courts, not leading them' (the judges) and the assertion that the DPP 'should not lead society, but should reflect public opinion' (the jury) are both at odds with reality. They imply deference to views extending beyond those held by the prosecutor, but in practice there are few sources for such views. There may, in contrast, be good justification for the DPP acting as a social pundit and leading, not following, the courts in this difficult arena. It can be argued that it is the public interest element of the prosecutorial decision that enables a flexible response to breaches of the law; if the law is not to remain static and thus become outmoded whilst society's morality evolves, some such responsiveness is necessary. Since there is no readily available barometer, the DPP has justifiably invoked his own.

Public interest and the Attorney General's criteria for prosecution

Although enjoying considerable discretion to define what is in 'the public interest', the DPP has apparently chosen to promote a comparatively narrow interpretation, giving prominence to criteria that are among the easiest to articulate. Despite this criticism, the DPP has taken the first step in defining what cannot be denied is an elusive concept.

In discussing the public interest in an interview in *The Times* (11

May, 1981), the DPP, Sir Thomas Hetherington, stated that attention was directed to the following factors: a) those associated with the offender – these would include the Attorney General's guidelines on youthfulness, old age, or infirmity, and mental illness or stress; b) those associated with the offence – the likely penalty, staleness, sexual offences where there may be no real victim, and the complainant's attitude if one existed; c) general policy factors such as the need, for instance, to exercise discretion according to 'reason and justice after paying due regard to the intention of the legislature and where appropriate to the climate of public opinion' (Barnes 1975). Finally the prevalence of the offence in the local community, the opinion of the police, and the good or bad character of the accused might be thrown into the scales. The Attorney General's criteria largely mirror these, while further advising that if a decision is still in the balance the case should be placed before the court.

Four aspects of the Attorney General's 'criteria' should be noted. First, they are primarily couched in negative terms – setting out the reasons why it may be possible either not to prosecute or to offer a caution when there is a reasonable prospect of conviction – rather than giving the reasons for prosecuting. The guidelines only help the prosecutor to identify cases where prosecution may *not* be necessary, rather than detailing what the public interest *for* a prosecution amounts to. This contrasts both with Shawcross's perception of the public interest as the 'dominant consideration' and with the preamble to the *Criteria for Prosecution*. These suggest that, given evidential sufficiency, the prosecutor should consider whether the public interest requires a prosecution. Secondly, the nature of the criteria is largely one of mitigation, in that the prosecutor is anticipating the court's likely view of the factors that might permit a fairly low sentence to be imposed on an offender. Thirdly, following this emphasis on mitigation, the effective sphere of influence for 'negative' public interest criteria is comparatively narrow and principally confined to more 'trivial' offences[55] or to the extreme personal characteristics of defendants. Finally, some of the criteria overlap with considerations that the prosecutor assesses in determining whether he has a reasonable prospect of conviction. For example 'staleness' may affect witnesses' memories and therefore also whether they will 'come up to proof'; a complainant who is reluctant to give evidence may not make a convincing prosecution witness; a defendant with a criminal record may discourage a defence challenge to confession evidence or any attack on the characters of the prosecution witnesses.

The criteria are not wholly narrow, for they recommend that the prosecutor assess the merits of a prosecution in the context of that case – what would be the risks and benefits associated with a particular course of action in the circumstances? Yet a truly wide appreciation would entail prosecutors assessing the individual merits of a case in the context of crime and society generally – the most difficult interests to articulate. However, just spelling out these issues might obviate some of the more commonplace prosecutorial dilemmas.

First, for instance, should an offender be prosecuted, given that there is a reasonable prospect against him, if, by using him instead as a prosecution witness, a conviction is made more likely against another offender accused of a more serious offence? That there is scope for disagreement is plain. The police may adopt a limited cost-benefit analysis and recommend prosecution of only the more serious offender, thereby increasing the likelihood of a conviction in his case.[56] The prosecutor may adhere to the view that society's net interest in obtaining convictions against both outweighs the risk associated with failing to convict both. But where would he look for support for this view?

Secondly, although, as a general proposition, it is the case that the DPP takes the view that it is in the public interest to prosecute only where there is a reasonable prospect of conviction, some prosecutions are brought where the prosecutor is not wholly convinced that a conviction would be merited. For example it has been said in response to the suggestion that a person's public position may make him less likely to be subject to a prosecution that there may in fact be a temptation for the DPP to prosecute because a man is well known (Havers 1984: 110).[57] Public figures may thus have some right to clear their names where the publicity attracted to a decision not to prosecute would be more damaging to them than the effect of an unsuccessful prosecution.[58] Hence the notion that a prosecution may be merited in the public interest even though a conviction would not necessarily be so (see the civil case of *Goldsmith v. Pressdram Ltd* (1977) QB 83; (1977) 2 All ER 557). The criteria do not address this departure in practice from the tenets of the reasonable prospects test. Spelling out such positive criteria for prosecuting runs the risk of highlighting those cases where reasonable prospects may not be satisfied. As such, it is not surprising that the DPP has largely refrained from doing so.

It should be noted that this reticence may also be located in the third and general difficulty with regard to greater openness in prosecution policies. In cases where it is decided not to prosecute, public justification may be problematic. The DPP may wish to protect the confidentiality of witnesses, there may be a desire to avoid a further public 'trial' in the press and to ensure that there is some finality in the Director's decisions. There may also be some reluctance, 'to risk it becoming known that certain offences of medium or minor importance can in fact be committed with relative impunity' (Barnes 1975). Herein lies the irony of the term 'public interest' as applied to prosecutions. For these policies may be more likely to survive intact if they are kept *private* within the confines of the prosecutor's office. If publicized, strong sectional interests may emerge, such as the shopkeepers' lobby which is vocal whenever some decriminalization or diversion of shoplifting from the criminal justice system is canvassed. In these circumstances the prosecutor may find it more difficult to pay regard to alternative, but less strongly pressed, views.

The fourth difficulty which the guidelines do not explicitly address is that it is not clear whether the 'mitigation criteria' are to have the same impact irrespective of whether the case is tried summarily or on indictment. The prosecutor is advised to pay attention to the likely penalty. Where an offence is not particularly serious yet is still triable on indictment, and the likely penalty is no more than a conditional or absolute discharge, he is further advised that it would normally be in the public interest to prosecute. Should the prosecutor proceed if he anticipates summary trial? This would avoid the criticism that scant regard had been paid to cost effectiveness. But what should the prosecutor do if the defendant then unexpectedly chooses trial on indictment? Should he reassess the public-interest considerations?

The fifth difficulty concerns *how* to proceed, once it has been decided to prosecute. For example, public interest considerations are involved in the question, 'when is it proper to accept a plea to a lesser offence?' In the light of research demonstrating both the extent and importance of this practice the guidelines should have dealt with it (Baldwin and McConville 1977; Moody and Tombs 1983). The fact that plea negotiation may be both controversial and/or unpalatable does not justify ignoring it. Either it should be expressly condemned, or if it is to be countenanced, an attempt should be made to structure these significant decisions rather than leaving them to local or individual practices. For the prosecutor employing the reasonable prospects approach, with its more stringent evidential standard, the question has particular relevance. By pitching his charges at a level lower than that which might more properly reflect the gravamen of the offence and the offender's culpability, the prosecutor may both increase his prospects of conviction, and increase the likelihood of an offender offering a plea of guilty – thereby achieving a considerable financial saving.[59] If the public interest is the dominant consideration, how should the prosecutor avoid the dilemma of appearing to invite a plea (in contravention to the spirit of the reasonable prospects approach) and yet still bring charges that satisfy both elements of the reasonable prospects equation? Strategies have developed within the DPP to curb any easy resort to plea negotiation, for example by ensuring that pleas to lesser offences cannot be accepted without the authorization of a member of the DPP with at least the status of Assistant Director. Although the policy was expressed in a letter from a previous Attorney General (Sam Silkin) to all circuit leaders and Treasury Counsel, there is no mention of it in the Attorney General's *Criteria*.

Such limitations within the public-interest criteria are likely to encourage inconsistency in prosecutorial practice since, in a wide variety of situations, the prosecutor can expect no help from the guidelines. The nuts and bolts of prosecutorial decision-making involve choices about whether and whom to charge, at what level charges should be pitched, and whether pleas are likely or acceptable. Public interest considerations may affect all of these day-to-day choices, but the guidelines cover little of general prosecutorial practice.

There is one final and overriding difficulty with the Attorney General's criteria: namely that the two stages of the prosecutorial decision-making model may not be genuinely distinct. It has already been asserted that the criteria that make up the quality element of the reasonable prospects test may cover similar ground to that subsequently labelled 'public interest'.[60] That some factors might be taken into account twice is not in itself a problem, provided that the prosecutor distinguishes the separate effects of the same criterion at each stage of his decision-making. Problems will arise, however, where the prosecutor anticipates the effect of public interest before resolving the evidential questions. The first concerns cases where the prosecutor does not believe a prosecution to be merited in the public interest. For example, in the case of an elderly, confused, first-time shoplifter the prosecutor might feel a caution is appropriate. Cautions should not be offered unless the prosecutor is satisfied there is sufficient evidence of the offender's guilt. Having to apply the 'reasonable prospects' approach instead of the *prima facie* standard may tempt prosecutors to recommend a caution in cases where, because of the very features of the case that make a caution appropriate, there may be difficulty in establishing that there is a 'reasonable prospect'. How should the prosecutor then respond if the offender declines the caution? The recently published Home Office guidelines on cautioning recognize this dilemma and recommend that, if such an eventuality occurs, no further action should be taken. However, if this policy were to be become widely known it might be open to exploitation (Home Office 1984).[61]

The second source of confusion between the evidential and public interest components of the reasonable prospects approach arises out of the inclusion in the Attorney General's criteria of the need to consider the effect of the prosecution on public morale and order. If it is accepted that public morale can be affected by prosecutions, how should its climate be assessed?[62] It has been noted that the DPP looks at jury conviction rates. But is that assessment only as good as the last prosecution? Public opinion will be influenced by the prosecutor's reasonable prospects predictions; those predictions were influenced by the jury's (public) opinions. Thus, jury decisions are influential at both stages of the prosecutorial test: once predictive and once retrospective. Can the prosecutor really be expected to distinguish two separate and possibly contradictory influences deriving from the same source?

Finally, what should a prosecutor do when he believes, with all sincerity, that a prosecution is in the public interest, but he cannot satisfy the reasonable prospects test because he believes that a jury may be influenced by extraneous or illogical considerations and therefore not share his assessment of the strength of the evidence? One solution would be to adopt the concept of an 'impartial jury', allowing the prosecutor to assume that the jury *will* share his view of the evidence. But this would raise further problems. How is the prosecutor to decide when he will adopt the 'impartial' jury test as opposed to incorporating a genuine prediction of the jury's likely assessment of the case? If he routinely assumes that the jury will share *his* view of the evidence, does this not defeat the purpose of a jury-based test?

This theoretical analysis of the Attorney General's criteria would indicate that the combination of narrow public-interest criteria with a two-stage model of decision-making is likely to pose a series of irreconcilable dilemmas for prosecutors. These dilemmas may, in practice, be resolved by departures from the necessary evidential prerequisite. Such departures will negate the spirit of reasonable prospects; 'weak' cases may still proceed to trial because of overriding, but unarticulated, public-interest considerations.

The likely consequences of the Attorney General's criteria: an empirical view

Moody and Tombs's study (1982) of the exercise of prosecutorial discretion by the Procurators Fiscal provides some insight into how the guidelines may be applied. Only two of the prosecution criteria described in that study could be described as non-evidential in a sense that is comparable with the DPP's 'public-interest' criteria. They were whether the offence concerned was of sufficient importance to be made the subject of a criminal prosecution and whether there was sufficient excuse for the conduct of the accused to warrant the abandonment of proceedings against him. This latter criterion is much the same as the DPP's 'mitigation criteria', in that it enabled Procurators Fiscal not to proceed where there were unusual characteristics associated either with the alleged offence (for example in domestic assaults, minor sexual offences, or where the offence was unusually 'trivial') or with the offender, 'for example, mental instability'. However, the research as a whole indicated that Scottish Procurators Fiscal regard the option of not prosecuting as a marginal issue with little relevance to the processing of most criminal cases. The average annual rate for 'no proceedings' was 8 per cent and the researchers considered this to be surprisingly low, particularly because it also included cases filtered out of the prosecution system on evidential grounds. They conclude that Procurators Fiscal were failing to make extensive use of their discretionary powers.[63] The important question remains 'why?'. They identified two principal reasons, both of which have implications for the likely operation of public interest discretion under a revised prosecution system. First, the Fiscals remain dependent on the quality and flow of information from the police. Sanders (1985: 4–19), on the basis of empirical research conducted into local prosecution arrangements in England and Wales, has similarly suggested that prosecutors are likely to remain dependent on the police, despite their future theoretical independence. According to his research, this is because the Attorney General's criteria are vague, and consequently manipulable by the police. In addition, the public-interest factor can be rendered largely irrelevant by the charging process. Indeed, this latter effect may be exaggerated in England and Wales, in contrast with the Scottish system, in that it is proposed that under the new arrangements the police will retain the decision to charge (Home Office 1983). The potential implications of this are profound, in the light of the DPP's view that 'of all the decisions which have to be made by those with the responsibility for the conduct of criminal cases, by far the most important is the initial one as to whether or not a charge should be preferred' (Royal Commission on Criminal Procedure 1981: Appendix 25). Withdrawing a case from the court on public interest grounds may prove extremely difficult (see pp. 92–5).

Moody and Tombs's second explanation for the failure of Procurators Fiscal to reflect their widely held image as *discretionary* decision-makers derives from the apparent presumption by Procurators that most cases are routine, and that it is only exceptional cases that require closer consideration.[64] Thus, the exercise of the discretion not to prosecute is perceived as being limited to a small number of unusual cases. This position contrasts vividly with the Dutch prosecution system where the prosecutor's working presumption leads him to look for a justification for proceeding rather than not proceeding; prosecution rates are correspondingly lower (Van Dijk 1983).[65]

Drawing upon these empirical findings it is suggested that the public-interest criteria in the Attorney General's guidelines are unlikely to facilitate the exercise of a widely used 'public-interest' discretion. This is because the criteria represent a classic compromise. Although the introductory tone of the guidelines is in terms of the need to justify proceeding, the small print encourages prosecutors to proceed unless they find features in a case that would enable proceedings not to be brought. As a result, will the prosecutors' principal attention be directed towards the small numbers of cases where the limited circumstances detailed in the Attorney General's *Criteria* may be met, rather than critically re-examining the major bulk of his cases with the question, 'what is the merit in a prosecution?' As a means of structuring discretion the Attorney General's criteria are too general. Finally, the guidelines advise placing cases before the court where doubt cannot be resolved – hardly a recipe for a rigorous appraisal of the merits of a case.

Redrawing the boundaries of public interest

This appraisal of what is meant by the 'public interest' in the DPP's approach to prosecutions has indicated three criticisms of the existing position. First, in the process of articulating the public interest, the model of decision-making employed has become oversimplified. Furthermore, there has been a theoretical shift from a general presumption against prosecuting unless it is in the public interest, to a presumption that there will be a prosecution unless certain specified criteria are present: at least, sufficient emphasis has not been given to the need to justify a decision to prosecute. It has been suggested that the narrow and principally negative appreciation of the public interest will curtail the scope for 'public interest' to influence the exercise of discretion. Secondly, it has been suggested that the two-stage model of decision-making is unworkable, necessitating an artificial suspension of judgment by prosecutors on questions of evidential sufficiency if they are to make public-interest decisions 'in the real world'. Finally, the criteria fail to offer guidance on a series of prosecutorial dilemmas that arise out of the 'nuts and bolts' of prosecutorial practice. Thus, this model of decision-making will probably lead to both explicit and covert departures from the criteria specified, to the inconsistent application of public interest criteria, and to a reluctance to clarify those criteria any further.

In a sense the DPP has 'undersold' its reasonable prospects approach. Rather than simply dismissing the concept as a 'short catchphrase embracing the fundamental conceptual problems of political interests, representation and policy formation' (Sorauf 1962), the DPP has recognized the desirability of spelling out its approach. It has taken the first step in relation to the enormously difficult task of defining the public interest, but in so doing, it may have served to mislead outsiders about the reality of public-interest decision-making. Local prosecutors who are keen to incorporate concepts of public interest into their decision-making, and thereby adhere to the recommendations of the Royal Commission for a more humane prosecution system, may do so at the price of consistency, fairness, and efficiency if they treat the guidelines as exhaustive. Even if the DPP's decisions in practice adhere to the spirit of Shawcross's approach (a question which is addressed in the next two chapters), there is no guarantee that local prosecutors, as the future arbiters of the public interest, may be able to do likewise on the basis of the limited explanations of the criteria at present available.

THE NEED FOR RESEARCH

This theoretical analysis of the constituent parts of the reasonable prospects approach has suggested that, in its present form, it invites inconsistency. Is the approach worth retaining? The Royal Commission made out a strong humanitarian and economic case for the adoption of this higher evidential standard. They believed that the process of prosecution and trial can cause great anxiety to defendants who are in effect 'punished' by the experience, even if acquitted. Cases which appear insufficiently strong to be left to jury by the judge should be weeded out by the prosecutor employing reasonable prospects. More controversially, the reasonable prospects test also seeks to anticipate and avoid jury acquittals, by requiring the prosecutor to predict such acquittals.

Aside from these humanitarian and economic arguments there are other reasons why 'reasonable prospects' may represent an improved approach to prosecutions. There is no clear criminological evidence that proportionately more prosecutions, convictions, and sentences result in the commission of proportionately fewer offences, but there is some evidence that the process of criminalization, especially when followed by a custodial sentence, may have deleterious effects on the offender and his behaviour. In these circumstances diversion away from the criminal justice system becomes a more attractive option if the overall reduction of crime is a major priority. The reasonable prospects approach, with its emphasis on public interest, may be taken to result in just such a form of diversion. Finally, from the legal perspective, it has been argued that reasonable prospects may represent a more effective form of protection for the defendant's rights than does proceeding on *prima facie* grounds and relying on the protection afforded by the judge in allowing a submission of 'no case'.[66]

There are numerous possible practical advantages which may attach to the reasonable prospects approach. First the exercise of discretion by the prosecutor necessarily demands professionalism and a rigorous code of ethics. The new approach ought to prevent cases from being pushed forward to the courts, propelled by a general 'prosecution momentum', without a thorough examination of each case by the prosecutor; the 'buck stops sooner'. Second, transplanting a generally 'higher' form of justice from the Crown Court to the lower courts (which a jury-based reasonable prospects assessment might be said to represent) may help to even out an arguably 'twin-track' system of justice. Third, the exercise of the prosecutor's discretion ought to have a reductive effect on an overstretched criminal justice system. This should result in shorter delays and more time to achieve a better quality of justice for those cases remaining. Fourth, a prosecutorial filter for weak cases is particularly important where some clerks to the magistrates show marked reluctance to hold, or are otherwise obstructive in relation to, 'old-style' committals.[67] Finally, the implications of the prosecutor's role for other actors in the system should be considered. Consistent decision-making by prosecutors might reduce the disparities which are sometimes said to exist in judicial rulings and jury verdicts. Similarly, although the difficulties for the police in working alongside prosecutors who exercise discretion have been extensively canvassed,[68] it may also be argued that the necessarily close working relationship which reasonable prospects entails may be more educative and informative for the police than simply having cases kicked out by the courts when they prove insufficiently strong.

Despite all these advantages, the adoption of the higher prosecutorial standard is not unproblematic, particularly with reference to the goals of openness, fairness, and accountability which the Royal Commission sought to attain. Endowing the prosecutor with greater discretion not to proceed legitimizes the exercise of 'justice behind closed doors' at a crucial stage in the criminal process. The prosecutor's exercise of discretion is not open to external review. The grounds for a decision not to proceed cannot be subject to public debate. No one would wish to see trial by the press without the protection afforded by trial by jury. Nor would the prosecutor necessarily wish to disclose information that might discourage witnesses from coming forward in the future. Where a decision to proceed is made the case will be *sub judice* and therefore cannot be subject to comment until after the trial. If an acquittal results the prosecutor may publicize his rationale for proceeding by explaining why he 'got it wrong'. But if a conviction ensues there may be no impetus for the prosecutor to explain his actions: either he got it right, in which case the details may be of no consequence, or he got it right for the wrong reasons, in which case he may prefer not to have the matter discussed. Therefore, it seems generally unlikely that prosecutors will be in a position to inform the public, on those occasions where they act as good/effective prosecutors, of the humanitarian, economic, criminological, or legal rationales for the exercise of their discretion. This hardly serves the end of greater openness in the criminal justice process.

Secondly, with regard to fairness, the reliance of the reasonable prospects test upon prosecutors' predictions of jurors' perceptions of the evidence is likely to introduce elements of malleability into the test – and hence inconsistency in its application. At the DPP such inconsistency may be minimized through the restriction of decision-making to 'a small coterie of senior staff' imbued with the Director's ethos (as implied by Edwards 1984: 405–13). But the extension of reasonable prospects through a series of prosecution guidelines such as the Attorney General's criteria may fail to capture the subtleties of the practice of the DPP's approach. How can consistency in decision-making be guaranteed if a malleable test is to be promulgated to prosecutors throughout the country without this practical context? Without consistency, how can the revised system be fair?[69]

Thirdly, there is the question of accountability. At one level it is apparent that accountability cannot be a realistic goal in the absence of detailed knowledge of *how* prosecutors exercise their discretion since there are no criteria against which to measure their 'performance'. Further discussion of this issue will thus be set aside until the empirical basis of the DPP's decisions has been reviewed. But something can be said about the procedures for introducing elements of accountability proposed in the White Paper. This rejected the Royal Commission's recommendation that the new prosecution service should be locally based and accountable to a local supervisory authority. The new prosecution service is to be accountable for its policy to the Attorney General and subject to the guidance issuing therefrom. It is regarded, in these circumstances, as not conducive 'to sensible and efficient management of the new service' (para. 10) for the local authority to be responsible for the finance and manpower of the system. Accountability for policy locally was regarded as 'not appropriate', and neither workable nor consistent with the independence of the service. Thus, the Government proposed that there should be a single line of accountability to the DPP for both decisions on cases and the management of resources. While the Attorney General was to be accountable to Parliament for his general policy, he was not to be held accountable for decisions in specific cases except for that tiny proportion in which either he or the Director was directly responsible. To do otherwise might result in 'excessive centralisation' (para. 8).

In conclusion, the Royal Commission's recommendations in relation to the adoption of the higher evidential standard certainly do not further, and may actually jeopardize, the goals of openness, fairness, and accountability which it sought for its new prosecution system. The rhetoric of these goals may have become divorced from the reality of prosecution practice. Indeed, it had never even been established that the reasonable prospects test made a real, as opposed to a theoretical, difference to the quantity and quality of cases going forward for prosecution. Although the ensuing chapters will demonstrate how complex a judgment that would be, it might have been advantageous had the Royal Commission addressed this issue, before recommending the widespread adoption of the reasonable prospects test. Herein lies a justification for the research. If the prosecutor's private exercise of discretion is to be guarded against capriciousness and is to attain given standards, these standards need to be spelt out; this requires detailed knowledge of the prosecutor's working practices, not merely a theoretical guide to the reasonable prospects approach.

AN 'INDEPENDENT' PROSECUTION SERVICE?

One issue remains – that of independence. From whom or what is the prosecutor to be independent? Implicit in the Royal Commission's Report is the assumption that separation of the investigative and prosecutorial functions will 'improve' the quality of decisions about prosecution; the White Paper assumes that independence will be a by-product. But this neglects two crucial issues. First, independence for the prosecutor may not be created simply by demarcating the role of investigators of crime and reallocating responsibility for the decision to prosecute. Secondly, in focusing on the question of 'who gets prosecuted' in the early stages of the prosecution process, the Royal Commission neglected the questions of how prosecutions are conducted and of the prosecutor's independence from unacceptable influences arising at the trial stages of the prosecution process. These two areas, pertaining to the prosecutor's relationship with the police and with counsel respectively, will be examined separately.

The discussion which follows is based on a series of visits to various prosecuting authorities. It has already been noted that the nature of prosecuting arrangements at a local level within England and Wales varies considerably. Therefore these visits included large centralized and smaller divisionalized prosecuting solicitors' departments. In the latter, the coterminous arrangements of prosecutors with police divisions facilitates closer mutual contact. One of the few remaining police authorities without a prosecuting solicitors' department, where the police are reliant on *ad hoc* use of private solicitors, was also visited. In addition, visits to Scotland and Northern Ireland provided illustrations under different jurisdictions of arrangements where prosecutors already enjoy independence from the police. All this pilot fieldwork was conducted prior to the major study at the DPP, and provided a 'grass roots' context for the subsequent research of prosecution problems.

Two questions arise. First, do prosecutors who lack theoretical independence within the existing 'solicitor–client' relationship achieve practical independence in their decision-making? Secondly, will conferring theoretical independence on the prosecutor necessarily enhance whatever actual independence they currently enjoy? Discussion of these questions leads to a shift in emphasis: the critical issue becomes not 'whether independence', but where and at what stage independence can most effectively be located. This proposition derives from a recognition that if independence is equated with distancing the prosecutor from prejudicial influences, this may in turn bring prosecutors closer to other prejudicial influences, or distance them from beneficial influences. Thus, the discussion may generally be conceived in terms of tension between detachment (which the prosecutor requires for objectivity) and isolation (which he wishes to avoid if his decisions are to be in keeping with the spirit of the times).

The prosecutor and the police

It has already been noted that, under the Crown Prosecution Service proposed for England and Wales, and outlined in the White Paper, the police are to retain the initial decision as to whether to charge (and obviously what offence to charge in the first instance), whether to caution, or whether to take no action. The DPP regarded as crucial the decision as to whether charges should be preferred and the case proceeded with (Royal Commission on Criminal Procedure 1981: Appendix 25). To leave either decision with the police might significantly impair the independence of the new prosecutor, and subsequently create difficulties for him in court.

McConville and Baldwin also highlighted the centrality of the police role in the prosecution process in England: they noted that the police 'dominate the process, they take most of the key decisions' (1981: 189). Even where prosecutors, as in Scotland, retain complete discretion over the decision to charge and the decision to prosecute, the prosecutor remains dependent on the police for the informational basis of the case. Moody and Tombs (1982) note that it was this retention by the police of the power to present information to the Fiscal and the manner of the presentation which effectively curtail the Procurator Fiscal's prosecution options.[70] Thus, if in the quest for independence, the prosecutor becomes too distanced from the police, he is liable to suffer the disadvantage of not being aware when the information he is presented with is partial. The tension between detachment and isolation may be crystallized in the choice between being objective about incomplete information or risking taking partial decisions on 'full information'.

The prosecutor who is physically distanced from the police may be peculiarly disadvantaged when applying the reasonable prospects test. In order to make such an assessment he requires information which the police may not record in sufficient detail in routine cases. Thus, the police may have to abandon the 'short-form' procedure for reporting cases, a 'cost-effective' procedure which entails only minimal information being recorded and used primarily where guilty pleas are anticipated in less serious cases. Alternatively, the prosecutor will have to ensure that he is in a position where if necessary he can supplement officers' written reports with verbal assurances – principally as to the witness's likely credibility at court. Otherwise, it is hard to see how the prosecutors' discretion to review police decisions will make any difference to the number and nature of cases going forward for prosecution.

The extent to which the prosecutorial conveyor belt can be either slowed or stopped altogether by referring a case to a lawyer should also be considered. The summonsing procedure undoubtedly creates greater options for the prosecutor as to whether and how to proceed than does arrest-charge, but Sanders (1985) has noted that there may be a preference amongst busy police forces to adopt the arrest and charge procedure rather than issue summonses since the former procedure entails significantly less paperwork. This does, however, make it almost impossible for the prosecutor to reverse that process. Similarly, it was noted by Sanders that where the police do not have prosecuting solicitors, a decision not to proceed has to be referred to a more senior level within the police hierarchy, that is to a chief superintendent, than would a decision to proceed, which can be dealt with by a chief inspector or inspector. This may encourage a tendency for cases to be referred to the prosecutor, where ultimately a decision not to proceed may be taken.[71]

Whether any significant increase in the volume of cases handled by local prosecutors is likely to reduce the consideration cases receive is open to speculation. It may be argued that pressure of work may incline the prosecutor similarly to pass the case on to the courts.

Aside from distancing the prosecutor from the police other strategies have been employed to increase the objectivity with which decisions are made. In both Northern Ireland and at one prosecuting solicitors' department it was noted that there was a division of labour among prosecutors: some would act primarily as advisers, making the decision as to whether there should be proceedings, and others would act principally as advocates, taking those cases to court and following the decisions of the 'prosecution advisers'. Like all other arrangements this had its drawbacks. It is suggested that this separation of functions may actually contribute to the prosecutorial momentum of a case.[72] A prosecutor who knows he has the responsibility for presenting his case is arguably more likely to make realistic assessments of its prospects of success than one who merely instructs another to prosecute the case. This finds expression in the prosecutor's dictum that 'nothing concentrates the mind so wonderfully as having to get up on one's hind legs'.

A number of strategies have also evolved that enable prosecutors to maintain a harmonious working relationship with the police, whilst still being sufficiently distant to challenge effectively their view of a case. In prosecuting solicitors' departments that have been 'divisionalized', some prosecutors work centrally, dealing with the more difficult cases, and others are based at the police divisions, working more closely with the officers involved in the cases. This arrangement permits the prosecutor to be sensitive to local issues without necessarily being subject to local influence, since cases may be referred centrally for advice where such problems are anticipated.[73] Another strategy is to ensure that the prosecutor who has to work directly with the police is not necessarily the one who brings unwelcome advice. Although some cases are ostensibly referred to counsel for an opinion, careful selection of a particular barrister may ensure that the opinion will concur with that of the solicitor. Under the present system, however, resort to such 'rice paper opinions' may not always succeed in diverting the police from a particular course. A third strategy is for prosecutors to arrange an old-style committal, similarly with the expectation that the magistrates will not commit, on the advice of the clerk when the decision clearly turns on a matter of law. Through these mechanisms the prosecutor may exert influence over the police, yet still divest himself of the direct responsibility for the decision.

If it is possible for the prosecutor to achieve some measure of practical independence within the existing prosecution arrangements, does this flexibility imply that reform of the prosecutor's underlying relationship with the police proposed by the Royal Commission is unnecessary? The answer is no. This is because, at one extreme of these gradations of independence, situations occur where the solicitor is dependent upon the police for continuing employment. In one police authority the solicitors were requested by the police to prosecute some cases regardless of the merits and evidential strength of the case. These 'requests' were supported by remarks such as 'if a solicitor puts his ethics before his employment duty what have you got? – you've got an unemployed solicitor'. Similarly, regret was expressed that it was no longer possible to employ local private solicitors. This had enabled the police to 'sew up' prosecutions because, through patronage, they could maintain control over both prosecution and defence solicitors. These sorts of remark were by no means commonplace but they illustrate why it has been considered necessary to change the basic relationship between the police and the lawyers.

Distancing the prosecutor from the police may thus have the advantage of allowing the prosecutor to reflect upon the merits of the case in an objective and measured manner, but there are concomitant disadvantages. In the police authority visited without a prosecuting solicitors' department – ostensibly perhaps the most extended form of distancing between police and lawyer – it was apparent that although private solicitors were employed to prosecute in certain cases, it was very rare for their advice to be sought early in the proceedings. This effectively deprived the lawyer of any opportunity to increase the awareness of the police of his needs as lawyer-cum-prosecutor. If, under the Crown Prosecution Service, the police and the prosecutors are to act harmoniously, there is an obvious advantage to be gained from their working closely together. Such harmonious relationships require the police not only to acquiesce in the prosecutor's exercise of discretion but, most importantly, to provide him with the kind of information he needs, for example accurate assessments of the likely credibility of witnesses, so that he can make a judicious assessment of the prospect of conviction.

In conclusion, it remains an open question whether leaving the decision to charge with the police, in combination with their retention of control over the informational basis of cases, will significantly erode the prosecutor's new-found 'independence'.

The prosecutor and counsel

It might be argued that in the Crown Court, where the conduct of cases has always been handled by an independent Bar, there is no need for a Crown Prosecution Service since there is already an injection of independence at the latter stages of the prosecution process. Even if the police control the prosecutor, the prosecutor as solicitor can only instruct counsel and 'the conduct of the case at trial is for them'. But this would conveniently ignore the fact that the vast majority of prosecutions are conducted in the Magistrates' Courts, where solicitors are primarily responsible for conducting the case, so that even this late injection of independence would not take place. Furthermore, counsel's influence, if exerted at all, comes largely at the relatively late pre-trial stages; several decisions will have been made still earlier which have profound consequences for the defendant, determining both whether he is placed on the prosecution conveyor belt and whether he remains there. An independent Bar may be able to ensure that defendants 'get a fair ride' in court, but it cannot routinely control which cases are placed in its hands. Finally, counsel may be subjected to pressures at trial, for example to agree to pleas of guilty to lesser charges. Backed up by a prosecutor with independent standing, counsel should be able to resist these pressures and hence sustain charges properly considered to reflect the gravamen of the offence. Thus, an independent Bar is not sufficient, of itself, to ensure independence in the prosecution process.

What degree of control should an independent prosecutor have over a case once it has passed into the hands of counsel for trial? The prosecutor's relationship with counsel is as important in the quest for independence as is his relationship with the police. The White Paper makes no mention of the role of counsel under the revised arrangements, but the report of the Working Party on Prosecution Arrangements does. It states that: 'In cases going to the Crown Court, Counsel would be briefed on the same basis and would have the same independent standing as now. There would therefore be no greater tendency for counsel to be engaged exclusively on prosecution work nor an increase or polarization of the Bar into prosecutors and defenders' (Home Office 1983: Appendix para. 3). Proponents of the independent Bar claim that if barristers alternate between defence and prosecution work, it will ensure that defences are conducted vigorously and that a healthy scepticism is maintained in respect of prosecutions, since the advocate sees 'both sides of the fence'. The argument conveniently ignores two difficulties. The first is that many summary cases are already conducted by full-time prosecuting solicitors. Although they may have previous experience of defence work, they will not have the case-by-case 'balance' that is claimed for some barristers. Secondly, the barrister's 'poacher-cum-gamekeeper' role may conversely induce scepticism toward defendants and a vigorous approach to prosecutions.

Furthermore, although the absence of statistics makes it difficult to be precise, it is clear that there is some tendency for the criminal Bar to divide between prosecuting counsel and defence counsel. On the defence side some firms of solicitors and law centres clearly favour particular counsel or sets of chambers. Thus, there is an enclave of barristers who habitually take defence cases. On the prosecution side the position is somewhat clearer. In London, the DPP instructs both Treasury Counsel and those on the supplementary list. Instructed by the Metropolitan Police Solicitors' Department is the Commissioner's list of counsel. All these counsel specialize in prosecution work, although they retain their independence, and many also defend. Outside London the position varies: in some areas the prosecution generally use a particular set of chambers, thus enabling them to sustain counsel loyalty; in other areas there is a commitment to sharing briefs around. One prosecuting solicitors' department visited exerted an element of control over which barristers were briefed, and for which cases, through the use of a grading system – a sort of 'Michelin guide' to the local barristers. In other areas there was less control; counsel had a free hand on such activities as plea negotiation and only telephoned the prosecuting solicitors' department 'when in trouble'. If the prosecutor is to retain effective control over the case once it reaches court his relationship with counsel clearly needs to be close. In the subsequent hurly-burly of the court room this can also be an advantage to counsel, who may be able to resist improper pressure from the court by using his instructions as the impetus for placing the responsibility for accepting pleas back with the prosecutor.[74]

Thus, the relationship between barrister and prosecuting solicitor is clearly symbiotic. Are there any drawbacks where this symbiosis is combined with the alternation of barristers between defence and prosecution work? On either side, prosecution or defence, the barrister's own inclinations are obviously an important determinant of the kind of practice he or she builds up. 'Reputations' form a key element in a barrister's career. In the context of a combative criminal justice system there is a tendency to ascribe the way in which cases are 'won or lost' to identifiable causes.[75] There is, of course, nothing unusual or wrong in the 'horses for courses' principle. But are there any limits placed upon the way in which it may affect patronage? Thus, where defence counsel vigorously attacks the evidence or integrity of a police officer, does he jeopardize the likelihood of his receiving further briefs from prosecuting solicitors acting for, or in future with, the police? Similarly, full-time prosecuting counsel may run the risk of being assessed in terms of their 'conviction rates'.[76] Thus, are 'independent' decisions more likely within the context of a secure post, where prospects of promotion are not dependent on counsel's record of success?

POSTSCRIPT: THE REASONABLE PROSPECTS TEST – A BASIS FOR REVISION

When applying the reasonable prospects approach, the prosecutor has to be satisfied both that there is sufficient evidence to comply with the reasonable prospects test and that a prosecution is in the public interest. This postscript provides an argument for revision of the reasonable prospects *test*. At this stage, the reasonable prospects *approach* (that is, the combination of evidential and public interest considerations) is not challenged.

The reasonable prospects test amounts to a prediction of what will take place in court and what the outcome of a case will be. In that sense it requires accurate assessments to be made of, first, witnesses' credibility, secondly, the persuasiveness of likely lines of defence, and, thirdly, predictions of jury decisions, if cases are to be weeded out where convictions are unlikely. The practice of reasonable prospects might be characterised as requiring a 'belief in the impossible', for all three features may be inherently unpredictable from the prosecutor's current position. Thus, although the spirit of the reasonable prospects test may be defended, its present expression has been criticized and requires some revision.

Arising out of the research at the DPP, recommendations will be made for amending the reasonable prospects test, whilst still adhering to its objectives. The essence of this proposed revision is presented here, to enable readers to assess the current practice of reasonable prospects presented in the following chapters in the light of an alternative test.

This proposal may not be as heretical as it appears at first sight. Some support may be gained from a previous Director for the view that although the reasonable prospects approach may be sacrosanct, the elements that go to make it up may not be. Sir Norman Skelhorn gave the following explanation of the reasonable prospects test: 'Our acid test was whether, on the evidence *before us*, if that evidence stood up in court and was *not eroded*, there was in our considered opinion a likelihood that a conviction would result' (1981: 80; emphasis added).

Does this imply that when the 'totality of evidence' was assessed, it was unnecessary to predict whether it would prove persuasive to the tribunal, and sufficient to assess the evidence available to the prosecutor at that stage? It would obviously be unwise to place too great a reliance on this interpretation of the passage, but it does provide a useful pointer as to how the reasonable prospects test might be revised. Instead of trying to predict twelve laymen's perceptions of the content of a trial of which the prosecutor's knowledge is both partial (no defence case) and imperfect (no knowledge of how persuasive witnesses will be on the day), might his predictions be more realistic if he were to focus his attention on the strength of the prosecution case of which he has knowledge, and assess its persuasiveness both to himself as a lawyer and to another lawyer, namely the trial judge?

Further support for relocating the prosecutor's attention might be gleaned from two features of the situation in Northern Ireland. Here closer attention is paid to directed acquittals (judge-based acquittals) than to jury acquittals. There are two reasons for this. First, some trials take place in the absence of juries (in the Diplock Courts) and, secondly, in others, unlimited opportunities to challenge jurors without cause can result in juries of a skewed sectarian nature. As a consequence of this, the concept of an impartial jury is, in Northern Ireland at least, recognized by some to be a legal fiction.

The Royal Commission also pointed to the rates of directed acquittals in support of their recommendation that the reasonable prospects test should be adopted. Inasmuch as directed acquittals stem from the prosecution's failure to establish a *prima facie* case their occurrence suggests that in some cases prosecutors proceed where even those minimal evidential requirements are not met.[77] Obviously, not all directed acquittals imply that the original decision to proceed was mistaken, because a proportion of these cases may fail where the evidence weakens substantially between the decision to proceed and the case coming to trial. Adopting the reasonable prospects test may reduce the number of directed acquittals by raising the initial evidential requirement and thereby making the prosecutor more careful. But it fails explicitly to address the question of why proceedings are brought in some inherently weak cases. If the Royal Commission had pointed to the substantial proportion of ordered acquittals or jury-based acquittals they might have found more relevant support for adoption of the reasonable prospects test.[78] It is these acquittals which better reflect the scope for disagreement between the decision to prosecute (as addressed by lawyers), and the decision to convict (as addressed primarily by lay people), that reasonable prospects seeks to reduce.

If a principal justification for revising the prosecutor's test is to ensure that weak cases are not proceeded with, might the prosecutor be better advised to focus his attention on *that* issue, i.e. avoiding directed acquittals, rather than seeking to achieve that end as a likely by-product of raising the evidential standard and taking his cue from the jury? This is the essence of the revised test. It seeks to focus the prosecutor's attention on avoiding directed acquittals; the term 'reasonable prospects' would be retained but without reference to jury outcomes. This could be achieved by adding a subtext along the following lines:

> 'When deciding whether to bring proceedings the prosecutor will normally only have access to the prosecution case; therefore his attention should naturally focus on the close of the prosecution's case at trial. He will wish to satisfy himself that there is no rational expectation of a directed acquittal. The prosecutor will nevertheless have regard to any lines of defence which are plainly open to the accused.'

It will become apparent that even this test is problematic, and would require some adjustment to other parts of the criminal justice system. These are discussed further in Chapter 5. However, it may represent a more realistic way forward for prosecutors keen to aspire to the goals of openness, fairness, and accountability set for the new prosecution service by the Royal Commission, rather than rigid adherence to a test that requires prosecutors to possess qualities more akin to soothsayers than lawyers.

NOTES

1 A decision not to prosecute may, in rare cases, become subject to either Parliamentary review or review by the Attorney General. Similarly, such decisions could be the subject of adverse press comment. However, judicial review of a decision not to prosecute would only arise where fresh compelling evidence emerged.

2 The vernacular term 'half-time' is used to denote the close of the prosecution case.

3 See Compton, J., in *R.* v. *Puddick* (1865) 4 F. and F. 497, 499 approved in *R.* v. *Banks* [1916] 2 KB 621; 12 Criminal Appeal Report 74 in which Avory J. stated 'counsel for the prosecution throughout a case ought not to struggle for the verdict against the prisoner, but they ought to bear themselves rather in the character of ministers of justice assisting in the administration of justice' (p. 76).

4 The unusual nature of the DPP's caseload (primarily serious, complex, or sensitive cases concerning 'death and dirt') means that their cases are largely dealt with at the Crown Court where counsel presents the case on behalf of the DPP. See also Ashworth (1984: 65–87).

5 See p. 12 below for an alternative definition of what constitutes a *prima facie* standard of evidence.

6 It should be noted that the Royal Commission believed that since the investigative and prosecutorial roles overlapped and intertwined in practice, it would be difficult to achieve a total separation. Indeed, they noted that 'the pure theory of separation could not work in practice' (1981: para. 6.31).

7 Whether the Royal Commission were equally enthusiastic about the wholesale adoption of the DPP's public interest criteria – the second limb of the approach – is less clear. A minority of the Commissioners wanted the prosecutor to confine himself to questions of evidential sufficiency, leaving 'other aspects of the decision' (i.e. the public interest) to the police; a consensus prevailed, however, through agreement that the two limbs could not satisfactorily be separated in order to operate in this way (para. 9:2).

8 Home Secretary, House of Commons, 27 July, 1982. It should be noted that with the publication of the Prosecution of Offences Bill 1984 the term 'Crown Prosecutor' was reintroduced, with the new service to be known as the 'Crown Prosecution Service'.

9 It might be argued that prosecutors are frequently motivated by expediency (for example, a heavy caseload or important witnesses not being available) and rarely convinced by the defence that a lesser charge would be the correct charge, so that introduction of the reasonable prospects test will not noticeably affect negotiation practices.

10 In that these criteria were sent to the *police* it remains unclear as to the precise evidential basis on which they will refer cases to the prosecutor; presumably *prima facie* will remain the base line, but some cases may not be referred on to the prosecutor even where this standard is met if the police further apply the Attorney General's criteria.

11 It should also be noted that under the proposed national integrated prosecution system the DPP was also to be responsible for the 'formulation and promulgation, under the superintendence of the Attorney General, of policy on prosecution' (Royal Commission on Criminal Procedure: 1981: para. 14); i.e. the DPP is to be absolutely central in establishing and maintaining standards for prosecutorial practice.

12 See Hetherington (1980b).

13 There were also approximately 150 non-professional staff providing supporting services. By 1985 the professional staffing at the DPP had increased. It then comprised the Director, the Deputy Director, four Under-Secretaries (PAD/Metropolitan, PAD/Counties, Fraud Controller and Principal Establishment and Finance Officer), 12 Assistant Directors, one of whom is at the Law Officers' Department, and 61 Senior Legal Assistants and Legal Assistants. The Divisions had become East, West, Fraud A, Fraud B, Fraud C, Metropolitan, Police A, Police B, Special Casework, and Crown Prosecution Service Planning Division.

14 With the exception of the small number of summary trials conducted by the DPP's professional officers.

15 It is worth noting that Treasury Counsel are not exclusively retained by the Attorney General or the DPP. Their status remains that of independent members of the Bar and they may defend cases. The numbers of Treasury Counsel have subsequently been cut significantly.

16 The Assistant Directors, Principal Assistant Directors and the Deputy Director are also authorized by the Home Secretary to carry out the duties of the Director, in accordance with the various statutes.

17 Home Office Memorandum (April, 1972), 'On the control of prosecutions by the Attorney General and the DPP'. (Extracted from written submission to Departmental Committee on Section 2 of The Official Secrets Act 1911, Cmnd. 5104.)

18 In *R. v. Elliot* (*The Times*, 13 February, 1984, p. 21) the Court of Appeal noted that proceedings were only instituted when an accused came to court to answer the charge. Thus, the consent of the law officers is not required before the police can charge an accused with an offence for which the Attorney-General's fiat is required (judgment delivered by Brown, LJ).

19 More than one victim with one defendant and/or one victim with several defendants.

20 For example in 1977 9,068 cases were received concerning complaints against the police; 4,442 concerned road traffic offences, 2,888 assault, 596 theft, 448 conspiracy or perjury, 112 corruption, 55 sexual offences and 527 'others' (evidence to the Royal Commission by the DPP).

21 It should also be noted that the DPP receives a mixed bag of other cases. First, those on which it acts as the Attorney General's solicitor, for example contempt cases, and secondly, cases which are not strictly 'consent' cases, but which are criminal matters, for example, Representation of the People Act cases.

22 The Devlin Report (1976) had similarly advocated that the police should act in a quasi-judicial spirit, conducting their inquiries 'as much with the object of ascertaining facts which will exonerate as of ascertaining those which will convict' (para. 5.98).

23 For example, Dr Leonard Arthur was acquitted at Leicester Crown Court on 5 November, 1981 of attempting to murder a 3-day-old Down's Syndrome baby by withholding proper medical treatment and administering an improper drug. The original charge of murder was dropped after a direction by the judge. The Director stated: 'If the prosecution had known in advance of the expert evidence to be produced by the defence, it might have changed the whole course of the trial. We might not have charged murder in the first place' (*The Daily Telegraph*, 15 February, 1982).

24 For example, Attorney General (1983).

25 See Royal Commission on Criminal Procedure (1981: Appendix 25) and Attorney General (1983).

26 Although the agreement of the defence is required for paper committals, this cannot be relied upon to guarantee a non-partisan assessment.

27 See the *Guardian*, 21 May, 1983, reporting a speech by Lord Lane at the annual conference of magistrates' clerks in Torquay, 20 May, 1983. Subsequently, an independent committee, chaired by Lord Roskill, was appointed in 1983 by the Home Secretary and the Lord Chancellor to look at the way courts conduct fraud cases. Their brief included establishing whether changes are needed in law or procedure to secure 'just, expeditious and economical disposal of such proceedings'. See also the James Report (1975).

28 Indeed in Parliamentary discussion on the Court of Criminal Appeal Bill in 1907 the then Attorney General had argued, in response to an amendment which sought to restrict appeals to questions of law and exclude questions of fact, that 'the effort to discriminate between questions of fact and questions of law was legally, if not intellectually, impossible' (Hansard Vol. 179, col 587, 29 July, 1907).

29 It may be noted that, in much the same way, the prosecutor justifies his decisions on the basis that he is not acting as a one-man jury, but represents an assessment of what twelve reasonable men *might* decide in the case.

30 There is ancient authority that 'no person is to be required to explain or contradict, until enough has been proved to warrant a reasonable and just conclusion against him in the absence of explanation or contradiction' (Abbott, CJ, in *Burdett*, 1820, quoted by Glanville Williams 1963).

31 Glanville Williams argued pragmatically that Wood's proposition was unworkable in practice since the trial judge would be embarrassed if the defence offered no evidence immediately following an unsuccessful half-time submission. 'It would be absurd if the trial judge now had to confess that the case for the prosecution was so weak that no reasonable jury could find that the charge had been proved beyond reasonable doubt, and that accordingly, he proposed to accede to the second submission when he had just rejected the first submission worded in identical terms' (1965: 346).

32 Even before *Galbraith*, it might be argued that the DPP went a step further than the judge when exercising his prosecutorial discretion. The trial judge could protect the accused from a perverse jury verdict through a directed acquittal at half-time. However, the DPP ostensibly went further than this simple pre-emption since he took into account predictions of the outcome of the jury's verdict. Thus, like the judge, the DPP was taking into consideration questions of sufficiency and credibility; unlike the judge he was additionally taking into account considerations of persuasiveness.

33 The Court of Appeal also frequently reviews fresh evidence.

34 Speculation over whether juries would acquit a case if the facts were to prove insufficient may incorporate thinking on whether they *should* have acquitted, i.e. an assumption that they may reach an inadequate view of the facts (see public interest discussion pp. 32–3, 99).

35 The following discussion draws heavily on Edwards (1984: 453–66).

36 Although overturned on appeal, this was on the grounds principally of a defective summing up. Unreported case No. 3172/C/83 Court of Appeal Criminal Division, 4 November, 1983. See also *Lawn* [1984] Criminal Law Review 114.

37 It is ironic that whereas the Attorney General's criteria for prosecution provide for *private* resolution of conflicts between police and prosecution – through

'arbitration' by the DPP – no discussion is offered of how *public* resolution might be achieved once cases reach the court. The White Paper on prosecution arrangements (Home Office 1983) similarly failed to address such conflicts.

38 Section 23 of the Prosecution of Offences Act 1985 enables prosecutors within the new Crown Prosecution Service to discontinue proceedings in the Magistrates' Court *without* the leave of the magistrates.

39 There are two definitions of *'prima facie'* included within the Royal Commission's report (see p. 12). The version offered at para. 6.10 is strikingly similar to the first school of thought *censured* by Lord Lane. The definition of a *prima facie* case implicitly approved by Lord Lane is given at para 8.8. Why the Royal Commission included two versions is open to speculation.

40 For a more detailed discussion, see Ashworth (1984).

41 As detailed in Regulation 3 of the Prosecution of Offences Regulations 1978: 'It shall be the duty of the Director of Public Prosecutions to institute, undertake or carry on criminal proceedings in any case which for any other reason requires his intervention.'

42 The *reductio ad absurdum* is that the jury has to decide culpability on the basis of expert advice that incalculable harm may have been caused by the defendant. Yet one of the foundations of criminal law is that it primarily punishes calculable harm (exceptions are inchoate offences, e.g. criminal attempts or reckless driving where no accident takes place). The justification for the special processing of Official Secrets Act cases must lie in society's 'net interest' in preserving a form of security which it knows little or nothing about.

43 'Why does democracy care about the rational application of legal principles? The answer must lie in the belief that the legal fabric, and the principles which form it, are good approximations of one aspect of the popular will, of what the majority in some sense desires. . . . Then it follows that those who by training and selection are relatively good at exploring and mapping the legal landscape can appropriately be given the task of evolving the law.' See generally Calabresi (1982).

44 Cohen (1962: 155) criticizes the lawyers' use of public interest as a mere repository for *ad hoc* pragmatic arguments: 'what lawyers use when positive legal anchorage is lacking'.

45 Leys (1962) states (quoting from Schubert), 'there is only one construct of public interest theory which promises to be useful either as a guide to responsible decision-making or behavioural research . . . [it] defines the public interest not as a substance but rather in terms of the structuring of the decision-making process.'

46 In this sense, the prosecutor's decision parallels that of the sentencer who also has to weigh individualized sentence options against those reflecting society's interests in deterrence, retribution, and incapacitation.

47 *Hansard*, Vol. 483, Col 681, 29 January, 1951. Lord Shawcross's reference to calling upon the defendant for an explanation is redolent of 'getting a case beyond half-time'. But, it should be noted that in 1951 the evidence required to achieve this was greater than that now required following *Galbraith*. He may thus have had in mind an evidential standard pitched at some point between *prima facie* and that required by the reasonable prospects test.

48 See Edwards (1984: 466) for a fuller discussion.

49 The DPP is, of course, subject to criticism from the courts in cases where proceedings are improperly brought. Similarly, an action for judicial review could be available. See de Smith (1980).

50 There is a residual jurisdiction of the court to dismiss a case for abuse of the

process of the court. The grounds for so doing are: (i) delay in proceedings causing prejudice to the defendant; or (ii) unconscionable conduct on the part of the prosecutor. See *R.* v. *Derby Magistrates' Court ex parte Brooks* (1984) 148 JP 609.

51 Some judicial support for the notion of 'perverse jury' acquittals 'in the public interest' derives from Lord Devlin, commenting that the jury in the *Ponting* case fulfilled a constitutional function (common in the eighteenth century but rare now). When asked to enforce a law which is against its conscience, the jury has 'a right to be perverse in the exercise of its legal and constitutional duty' (Interview on BBC Radio 4, 25 November, 1985).

52 The defendant similarly has a right of appeal against sentence; this procedure has more clearly resulted in a body of principle and precedent to assist sentencers in their sentencing decisions, as, for example, in *R.* v. *Aramah* (1982) 4 Cr. App. R. (S).

53 Indeed, if the judge shares their view that the prosecution should not have been brought in the first place, despite evidential sufficiency, he is prevented by the acquittal from giving expression to his view of what action the offence required by awarding a nominal penalty.

54 For example in the case of *Gibson*, which concerned the prosecution of a police officer for the murder of an alleged terrorist, in the Diplock Courts MacDermott J noted that the victim had been brought to the 'final court of justice' and that while policemen have to act within the law they are not expected to be supermen; shooting may thus be justified as a method of arrest. The defendant was acquitted. It was further implied in the press that such prosecutions were of dubious merit since they might result in police officers 'thinking twice' in what might be life-threatening situations.

55 The DPP has stated: 'The more serious the offence the more improbable it is that we would withhold from prosecution on the grounds of public interest. In murder, for example, if the evidence is good enough we always prosecute' (*Daily Mail*, 6 November, 1981). Similarly, the more minor the offence the more attention is paid to mitigating or exculpatory circumstances.

56 The police, in their role as 'definers of crime', enjoy a wide discretion to apply public-interest criteria in not reporting trivial incidents. However, since this discretion is not formalized, being subject to little control or scrutiny, it does not provide much scope for formulating a model of the role of public-interest criteria in decisions about prosecution.

57 Thus, in terms of the public interest, this may be viewed as a reversal of the general argument that people should not be put on trial unless convictions are more likely than not. Hence, the right to a public acquittal.

58 The present Director, however, denied that prosecutions are ever launched to 'clear the air'.

59 Such tactical undercharging has occurred: see *R.* v. *Canterbury and St. Augustine Justices, ex parte Klisiak* (1981) Crim. L. R. 253 and *R.* v. *Ramsgate Justices, ex parte Warren and others* (1981) Crim. L. R. 281.

60 When asked by the Home Affairs Select Committee on Police Complaints whether the tests of evidential sufficiency and public interest mesh, the Director said that they did not, but that 'some circumstances might be taken into account in both of them' (14 February, 1980).

61 In practice, the realistic course may be to fudge the issue by giving the offender an informal caution.

62 Ashworth (1984) similarly advances the argument that one disadvantage of full enforcement of the law is that there might be loss of public respect for law if it

were thought to be administered harshly or unsympathetically, as by prosecuting the old, the infirm, or the afflicted.

63 It has been asserted, by the former Crown Agent for Scotland, that prosecution policy in Scotland has undergone a dramatic change since the publication of Moody and Tombs's work. The movement is reputed to be towards fewer prosecutions, and this has had the effect of making it less likely that the police will refer cases which they anticipate will be marked 'No Proceedings'.

64 This may be partly a facet of the speedy 'marking' process by which cases are assessed by Procurator Fiscals: see Sheehan (1975).

65 Van Dijk stated: 'At this time less than half of the cases presented to the prosecutor by the police are brought to trial.'

66 As McBarnet (1981) has noted, such protection may be enshrined in the rhetoric of the English trial process, but is not necessarily guaranteed in practice. See also discussion of *Galbraith*, pp. 18–21; 152–55.

67 In law, Magistrates' Courts must accede to the prosecution's request to hold old-style committal proceedings.

68 For example, in written submissions by the Metropolitan Commissioner and the Association of Chief Police Officers to the Royal Commission on Criminal Procedure.

69 In considering consistency and fairness, much may also depend upon pragmatic considerations, for example, local resources. If there are special facilities available for dealing with, say, alcoholics, they may be diverted from the prosecution system. If not, they are prosecuted. This would no doubt be described as unfair. Sheer pressure of work may also cause the busy prosecutor to weed out more cases from the prosecution process.

70 Victims may, of course, complain direct to the prosecutor about lack of police action. This may result in a request by the prosecutor to the police for a report, and an ensuing prosecution if the report justifies this. The victim may also bring a private prosecution.

71 The new 'early cautioning schemes' in use by some police forces and the guidance issued by the Home Office (draft guidelines, HO, June 1984) as advocated by the Working Group on Cautioning may assist in circumventing this tendency for decisions not to proceed to rise to a more senior level in the police hierarchy (if cautioning is equated with not proceeding).

72 This drawback may be reduced by the process of internal rotation of staff employed at the prosecuting solicitors' department in question.

73 It also permits 'high fliers' to gain experience in prosecuting and 'dead ducks' to be kept out of harm's way.

74 For example, from the judge (see Chapter 2, Case 85).

75 Chapters 2 and 3 demonstrate the complex of shifting factors affecting a case's outcome. This suggests that the typical snap assessment at the end of a case is too simplistic.

76 The front page of *The Mail on Sunday*, 9 September, 1984, ran a story headlined 'Old Bailey Top Lawyers Sacked' inferring that four Treasury Counsel were to be removed from their posts following unsuccessful prosecutions conducted by them. The allegations were subsequently withdrawn by *The Mail on Sunday*, with the payment of substantial libel damages, but revision of the Treasury Counsel list none the less subsequently took place.

77 See also Butler (1983).

78 Acquittals ordered by the judge usually result from the prosecutor wishing not to offer any evidence against the defendant on a particular charge or charges.

CHAPTER 2
PRE-TRIAL DECISION-MAKING

THE RESEARCH APPROACH: QUESTIONS AND CONTEXT

The research aims

The aims of the empirical research were threefold: to detail the methods of working and the prosecution standards employed at the DPP; to articulate both constituents of the reasonable prospects approach – evidential sufficiency and what is meant by a prosecution being 'in the public interest'; and, through a description of the prosecution process, to contribute to the development of a code of 'good practice' for prosecutors.

The research started from the premise that prosecution is a *process*, not a single event or decision. The empirical inquiry aimed to explain the process and hence to provide a fuller understanding of the practice of the reasonable prospects approach – a somewhat delicate, if not elusive, concept. The Royal Commission firmly endorsed the 'reasonable prospects' test for meeting its criteria for prosecution policy and practice, yet did not elucidate it, beyond the useful but limited account of the Director's view of how 'reasonable prospects' work. It is easy to see why both the Royal Commission and the Director stopped short of fleshing out the bare bones of the skeleton. 'Reasonable prospects' characterize an approach to prosecutions: expressed as a 'form of words test' its potential may fall far short of its real value. In order to appreciate its actual value it was necessary for the researchers to immerse themselves fully in the process of the prosecution. The technical legal requirements and the ethical issues which arise are not amenable to any rigidly structured method; for example, written questionnaires or standardized questions would have failed to meet the research aims. Those who work within the DPP would have been likely to reiterate the approach to prosecutions given as a matter of public record. Although critical aspects of decision-making are minuted within the DPP, these records cannot be more than a first step towards an understanding of how prosecution decisions are taken:

they represent the indices of DPP reasoning, not a definitive account of it. Furthermore, as a case progresses, especially after it leaves the DPP for counsel and the court, the written record on it progressively diminishes so that oral question and observation become essential tools of research. 'Outsiders' such as counsel were even less likely to be amenable to any formal, routinized mode of research inquiry. Indeed, the very real concept of an autonomous Bar might have presented considerable problems for the trial stages of the research. Thus the research methodology was dependent upon the access and co-operation gained. This was outstandingly good, both within the DPP and from counsel.

The willingness of the Director's staff to discuss their approach to individual cases and their resultant decisions confirmed that the methodology was much more appropriate than standard questions could ever have been. Furthermore, the continuity of interest generated by following cases through to trial enabled rapport to be developed with counsel, and ensured that subsequent discussions took place in a highly focused way, avoiding the usual tendency towards generalities.

This privileged position helped to afford the researchers credibility with all prosecution representatives and engendered a relatively uninhibited reaction from others, such as the police officers. Finally, the research approach afforded some opportunity to outflank the practical impediments presented to any jury research following Section 8 of the Contempt of Court Act 1981: without any attempt to invade the 'privacy of the jury room', the constant presence of a researcher throughout the trial facilitates some informed observations and speculations about jury decisions.

So much for the advantages of the research method chosen; what were the disadvantages? First, the research findings on the particular cases studied are hard to verify and impossible to replicate. Neither problem can be fully overcome. None the less some verification could be obtained since the excellent access enjoyed at the DPP matured into a 'dialogue' between the researchers and members of the DPP's staff. This afforded some opportunity for limited assessment of the research analysis of cases. Beyond this, since an underlying aim was to generalize on the basis of the particular, it is for other practitioners as well as academics to judge whether or not the findings ring true. The general findings, though not the researchers' particular experiences, may be replicable.

Secondly, a potential source of objection to the study stems from its very emphasis on in-depth immersion in the details of the cases selected. Involvement may become too close; there are moot trading points between 'objectivity' at a distance, which impairs understanding, and closeness, which enhances understanding but jeopardizes objectivity. The research was (almost) exclusively drawn from the prosecution side of cases, and there can be little doubt that a 'sister study' on the defence side by the same researchers would have afforded some variations in perspective. Yet the recognition of such bias merely places a qualification upon the findings; and the scope for spelling out bias is probably greater in qualitative work of this kind than in quantitative work, where assumptions are more readily concealed.

Thirdly, the practical disadvantages of the research method adopted are not inconsiderable, in the fieldwork and consequently in its written presentation. In the field, resource constraints not only imposed limitations on the number of cases to be studied but also, to a lesser extent, on the type of cases followed. The interesting research possibilities of fraud cases had to be jettisoned at a very early stage owing to the length, complexity, and detail of most frauds handled by the DPP. Less predictably (to the researchers anyway), difficulties with the listing of cases and frequent delays meant that it was impossible to follow some cases which had been earmarked – sometimes after a significant amount of time had been spent on the case, for example, in attendance at a preceding 'old-style' committal. More generally, the logistical juggling demanded by last-minute adjournments would have merited the addition of an experienced barristers' clerk to the research team! In the event, the researchers were fortunate to receive much assistance along these lines from the DPP's court clerks stationed at the Central Criminal Court; although this also contributed to an underlying tendency to select cases where difficulties were likely to arise – since these were deemed 'interesting'. Another logistical problem, and one which seemed insoluble, was that the in-depth approach meant sitting through virtually the whole of each trial. It proved impracticable to follow more than one case at once, since it was unsatisfactory not to know what had been missed in one trial while the defendant was giving evidence in another trial. But sustained presence at individual trials was rewarded, because when legal submissions came up one of the researchers was present.

Thus, the research focused on the process of prosecution in order to chart its subtleties, rather than attempting to evaluate the reasonable prospects test in terms of conviction rates. Cases were followed through the various stages of the prosecution process, up to and including the trial stages, in order to highlight the way in which the prosecutor, applying the reasonable prospects approach, interacts with the working practices of other groups in the criminal justice process: the police and magistrates (Chapter 2); the Bar, the judges, and juries (Chapter 3). Before discussing which categories of cases were selected, a brief description will be given of what work the DPP undertakes and how this is done.

Departmental organization

Edwards (1984) implies that, with the restriction of the actual decision-making to the small coterie of senior staff of Assistant Directors and above,[1] vagaries of subjectivity are probably kept to a minimum. But there are several reasons why this is an oversimplification. First, while it is clear that the Assistant Directors form an important tier in the decision-making hierarchy, particularly since they share the Director's statutory powers,[2] Edwards probably underestimates the influence of the recommendations of the professional officers (themselves all barristers or solicitors). Second, since the involvement of the Director in individual decisions does not extend beyond a handful of exceptionally sensitive cases each year, he is not likely to have much opportunity to ensure that there is a consistent approach. Nevertheless, the Deputy Director may play an important role in this respect, since he is automatically involved in certain types of cases and frequently consulted in all types of cases where opinions diverge. Third, apart from some trials and committals in the Magistrates' Courts, the DPP has recourse to outside counsel for the presentation of cases. This creates some scope for counsel to influence the course of prosecution, certainly at the trial and often at pre-trial stages, where his advice is sought. Although the DPP retains a small number of Treasury Counsel[3] who are more likely to become *ad idem* with the reasonable prospects approach, this is not necessarily the case; and the volume of DPP cases requires recourse to other leading counsel and members of the provincial Bar – with whom working relationships are less close. Fourth, the work of the divisions at the DPP now extends across two buildings, with all professional officers having their own rooms, and an 'outpost' preparing cases for trial at the Central Criminal Court. The coterie of decision-makers is thus less tightly knit than Edwards implies.

The DPP's workload includes both consent cases and those

specified under the Prosecution of Offences Regulations 1978 which have to be referred to the DPP because of their serious, complex, or sensitive nature. Seven divisions handled the cases: two dealt with those emanating from the Metropolitan Police, three covered the rest of England and Wales, and one division specialized in fraud and bankruptcy proceedings. A further two divisions dealt with cases that came into the DPP under Section 49 of the Police Act 1964, involving allegations of criminal conduct *by* police officers; these represented approximately 60 per cent of the incoming caseload, but only a small proportion of them are prosecuted, and an even smaller proportion are actually undertaken by the Director's staff.[4] The remaining division, the Research Division, handled a 'rag-bag' of cases, including Public Order Act offences, contempt cases, and Representation of the People Act offences. It also gave advice where requested, both servicing the other divisions and advising law reform bodies. The Research Division also responded to government initiatives, for example becoming involved in the progress of legislation such as the Prosecution of Offences Bill.[5]

Files are allocated by the Assistant Director for each division to the professional officers, who prepare for each case a detailed minute which includes a recommendation on whether a prosecution should be brought in each case and on what charges. The files are returned to the Assistant Director, who routinely makes – or ratifies – the final decision as to whether and how a case should proceed. In some evidentially complex categories of case, such as attempted murder where intent is difficult to prove, the file is also sent to the responsible Principal Assistant Director for an opinion. Similarly, when the Assistant Director and the professional officer disagree, the case is referred 'upwards'. In some of the straightforward consent cases, where the evidence may not amount to more than a few pages of statements, a decision may be taken by the Assistant Director without the case being referred to any other member of the DPP. Although for some of the cases the general policy of 'double checking' decisions may seem unnecessary since many of the professional officers' recommendations are adopted by the Assistant Director, the research indicates that such file circulation ensures that, on the odd occasions where dubious recommendations do occur, they are largely not pursued. In this respect, the decision-making model has much to recommend it: the pursuit of weak charges can be avoided at a comparatively early stage in the prosecution process.

RESEARCH METHODS AND CASE SELECTION

Four research methods were employed: attachments to the Assistant Directors of four divisions; analysis of DPP files; following cases through to trial; analysis of the outcome of cases on a retrospective statistical basis.

In view of the wide range of cases coming into the DPP, it was necessary to focus the study on certain categories of case. For each method employed, the case selection was determined by a combination of pragmatic considerations and an assessment of the contribution which each category of case could make to the research aims. It should be stressed that since the research intended to describe 'best practice', a bias developed in the selection of cases towards those that were considered likely to raise problems for the reasonable prospects approach. Any criticisms of 'reasonable prospects' which emerge from this study must be assessed in this context.

1. Attachments to Assistant Directors

The initial phase of the study involved attachments to each of four Assistant Directors within the DPP (Metropolitan Division, South Division, and the two Police Divisions).[6] This resulted not only in an appreciation of the day-to-day work of the DPP, on matters such as file allocation and the passing of professional officers' minutes back to the Assistant Director; but also permitted some insight into the decisions made by some Assistant Directors in those comparatively straightforward cases where the file is not allocated to a professional officer for a detailed minute.

2. File analysis

Files were not analysed according to a rigid format. Although certain basic information was recorded for each file, the principal aim was to acquire a close familiarity with the facts of the case and applicable law. This enabled detailed discussions to be held with the professional officers and/or Assistant Directors responsible for the cases, in order to explore their reasoning and decision-making strategies. Furthermore, different categories of case raised different issues at different stages in their progress. The research effort was therefore focused on such crucial stages as decisions about charging (whether, whom, and what to charge), and the committal stages of a case, rather than on amassing standardized information inappropriate to the research aims. Two samples of cases were derived in this manner: the 'consent' sample of 157 cases, and the sample which comprised 85 non-consent cases.

(i) *The consent cases* In consent cases the police have to obtain the consent of the DPP before proceedings can be commenced. After that, it is usually left to the police to prosecute. The rationale which determines the categories of cases where either the DPP's consent or that of the Attorney General or the Solicitor General is required was discussed in Chapter 1 (pp. 8–9).

A total of 157 consent cases were examined; this represented virtually the entire consent workload for these categories in two divisions (South Division and Metropolitan Division) for the six-month period, January–June, 1983. These cases are accordingly numbered 1 to 157 and are discussed on pp. 70–83.

From the 100 or so statutes which require the Attorney General's fiat, or the consent of the Attorney General or the DPP before proceedings may be brought, the following offences were selected for inclusion in the study:

a) Section 5(2), Criminal Law Act 1967 (wasting police time).
b) Section 30, Theft Act 1968 (theft or criminal damage of a spouse's property by either the wife or the husband).
c) Sexual Offences Act 1967 (buggery, or gross indecency, where one man was under 21 at the time of the offence).
d) Sexual Offences Act 1956 (incest and attempted incest).

(ii) *The '85' sample* The categories of case included in this sample were designed to reflect the DPP's activities in non-consent cases. These cases are numbered 1 to 85 and are discussed on pp. 83–108. Cases in the '85' sample were selected for their possible bearing upon the following general issues: the need to approach cases 'in the round' and consider defence strategies; the assessment of the quality as well as the quantity of evidence; difficulties of matching the alleged behaviour with a provable offence (the 'moral/legal fit'); charging strategies where multiple defendants or multiple offences are involved. The cases selected comprised:

a) Murder – especially those where the issues of self-defence, provocation, or diminished responsibility were likely to be raised, since these alter the nature of prosecutorial responsibility.

b) Manslaughter, and its interaction with murder on the issue of intent.

c) Attempted murder – these cases are considered to be among the hardest to prove since the prosecutor has to establish an intent to kill, which he does not have to do in case of murder where lesser forms of *mens rea* are sufficient. Proceedings can only be pursued with the approval of a member of the DPP with at least the status of a Principal Assistant Director.

d) Offences covered by Section 18, Offences Against the Person Act 1861 – in essence serious assaults. Section 18 (as amended by the Criminal Law Act 1967 section 10(2), Sched. 3) states:

> 'Whosoever shall unlawfully and maliciously by any means whatsoever wound or cause any grievous bodily harm to any person, . . . *with intent* . . . to do some grievous bodily harm to any person, or with intent to resist or prevent the lawful apprehension or detainer of any person . . . shall be liable . . . to imprisonment for life.' (emphasis added)

e) Offences covered by Section 20, Offences Against the Person Act 1861 – still serious assaults but without the intent element. Section 20 states: 'Whosoever shall unlawfully and maliciously wound or inflict any grievous bodily harm upon any other person, either with or without any weapon or instrument . . . shall be liable . . . to imprisonment'.

f) Offences covered by Section 47, Offences Against the Person Act 1861. An assault is any act which intentionally – or recklessly – causes another to apprehend immediate and unlawful violence (*R. v. Venna* [1975] 3 All ER 788, 794, CA). Section 47 states: 'Whosoever shall be convicted upon an indictment of any assault *occasioning actual bodily harm* shall be liable . . . to imprisonment' (emphasis added).

'Actual bodily harm' means exactly what the words state – some actual bodily injury. It need not be an injury of a permanent character, nor need it amount to what would be considered grievous bodily harm. Although not necessarily less serious than Section 20 offences, charges under Section 47 of the Act are frequently brought if there is an insufficient break in the skin of the victim to constitute a 'wound', or the *mens rea* of intention to injure cannot be established. Except in the Police Complaints' Division the latter two categories do not normally come into the DPP in the first instance but represent reduced or additional charges in other cases. Taken together categories (a) to (f) may be termed the 'murder–assault continuum'. These cases were selected to enable study of the way in which prosecutors use the flexibility between charges brought within the continuum, dependent both upon the provable facts and the perceived seriousness of an incident.

g) Offences under the Prevention of Corruption Act 1909 and

1916.[7] These offence categories include cases where bribes are offered to police officers. They are of particular interest since, in some cases of corruption, the legal burden of proof shifts. Thus, once the prosecution have established the *actus reus* of the offence, the defendant has to establish that a bribe was *not* corruptly offered and/or received (see Section 2, Prevention of Corruption Act 1916).

h) Offences under Section 5A, Public Order Act 1936 (incitement to racial hatred).

i) Rape. Rape cases are only referred to the DPP where one woman is raped by more than one man on the same occasion or where one man rapes several women. Rape was considered likely to raise interesting questions of witness credibility, especially on the issue of consent.

j) A sample of cases, not confined to offence categories (a) to (i), being committed under Section 6(1) of the Magistrates' Courts Act 1980. These cases involved 'old-style' committals. 'New-style' committals do not entail calling live evidence at the Magistrates' Court, as used to happen in all cases. This now occurs only occasionally in 'borderline' cases; old-style committals permit some early assessment of witnesses and of likely lines of defence, and provide an opportunity for changes in the prosecution's strategy – indeed, the outcome of the committal may necessitate changes. Furthermore, and in contrast with decisions later handed down by juries, it is sometimes clear why the prosecution has failed since magistrates can give reasons for their decisions. Finally, there is the additional advantage that magistrates in discharging cases work to a legally more precise standard than that of 'beyond reasonable doubt'.

3. *Cases followed through to trial*

A small sample of eighteen cases initially included within the 'file analysis' segment of the research were followed closely through their trial stages, from the decision to proceed to the outcome at trial. The sample included offences of murder, attempted murder, manslaughter, rape, and Section 18, Section 20, and Section 47 assaults. These cases – numbered 1 to 18 – are discussed in detail in Chapter 3.

4. *The Old Bailey sample*

As a background to the 'qualitative' approach adopted for all the above cases, a quantitative analysis was also undertaken involving cases of murder, manslaughter, attempted murder, and rape tried at the Central Criminal Court. The analysis was retrospective, involving cases tried over approximately a one-year period prior to those cases observed 'live' at the Old Bailey (May 1982–July 1983). Information as to charge, plea, verdict, and sentence was collected for 258 defendants. These data are also referred to in the next chapter.

CASE FINDINGS AND ANALYSIS

The first and second research methods, attachments to Assistant Directors and the analysis of files, were used in relation to both the consent cases and the '85' sample. The empirical findings in respect of pre-trial decision-making are presented separately for the 157 consent cases and the sample of 85 non-consent cases. This is because, to a significant extent, 'consents' may properly be regarded as set apart from the remainder of the DPP's routine caseload.

Consents

As discussed in Chapter 1 (pp. 8–9, 28), 'consents' come to the DPP primarily because of the policy issues raised by those categories of case, rather than the factual complexity of particular cases. Although the prosecutor takes the opportunity to vet the police assessment of evidential sufficiency, this role may in practice be regarded as secondary to his consideration of whether a prosecution is merited.[8] Of course, the facts and the merits of a case are not strictly separable: the prosecutor is reliant upon the police for the evidence, and his view of the merit of a case will turn heavily upon this. Yet consent files are relatively slim, more like the 'short files' supplied by the police to their local prosecuting solicitors' departments than the typically fuller files prepared by the police for non-consent cases handled by the DPP. Thus the information base upon which the DPP decides consent cases is often a restricted one. In this sense an analysis of the consent sample can contribute relatively little to a discussion of how evidential sufficiency is weighed at the DPP, a topic upon which more light is thrown by the non-consent cases. On the other hand, the consent sample offers an important source of discussion of the public-interest element of the reasonable prospects approach to prosecutions.

A basic justification for including in a statute a restriction on the bringing of prosecutions is that, in its absence, there would be a risk of prosecutions being brought in inappropriate circumstances (Home Office 1972). As already referred to in Chapter 1, the factors which may contribute to such a risk include:

(i) an inability to define certain offences precisely, which leaves an ambiguity in the law;
(ii) the tendency of some offence categories, such as trivial offences, to encourage vexatious prosecutions;
(iii) the special relevance of some mitigating factors;
(iv) the desirability of maintaining central control in sensitive areas, such as race relations or censorship; and
(v) the need to take account of important public policy considerations.

All these factors bear on considerations of the 'public interest', both as defined in narrow terms (for example in the Attorney General's *Criteria*) and in a wider context in regulating prosecutorial discretion.

SECTION 5(2) (WASTING POLICE TIME)

The consent sample included 59 cases of 'wasting police time'. In 18 cases the decision was not to proceed, decisions to prosecute being made in the remaining 41 cases. During the period of the research proceedings were brought in relation to 34 of these cases, resulting in 33 convictions and one case being dismissed.

In general, wasting the time of the police is treated analogously to hoax calls to other emergency 999 services: public resources are being abused and genuine demands upon them may suffer as a result. The DPP operates an informal 'rule of thumb', with a rebuttable presumption of prosecution if more than five hours of police time were wasted and non-prosecution if less than five hours were wasted, but this may be varied widely in either direction. There were three prosecutions for under five hours and another for 'not much' time wasted. There were eleven non-prosecutions for over five hours, ranging from 6½ hours to 161½ hours.

There is another possible consequence of Section 5(2) offences: an innocent third party may come under suspicion and become subject to police questioning. One case produced two false arrests. Where this occurs the police file places emphasis upon it, often with less attention to how much police time was wasted (to this extent, the offence title is something of a misnomer for these cases). The consequence of false arrest is likely to be regarded less flexibly than the amount of police time wasted, with proceedings being almost inevitable. Indeed, serious consideration might be given, in some circumstances, to preferring a charge of attempting to pervert the course of justice.

Clearly there is an elaborate public-interest argument underlying all Section 5(2) cases: the balance lies between prosecuting malicious, reckless, or grossly negligent reports to the police which turn out to be false; and refraining from prosecuting ill-advised, stupid, or petty false reports to the police so that complainants should not be deterred (individually and generally) from future recourse to the criminal justice system. The argument emerges explicitly for some cases, such as allegations of rape, where the facts are especially hard to establish and the 'policy issues' are highly developed. Thus, in Case 20 there were no proceedings in respect of thirty-three hours wasted on a false complaint of rape. There is a tendency to afford rape complainants the benefit of any doubt unless there is, for example, malice. This raises the general point of motivation. Most of the false reports to the police arose following some misfortune, not of itself criminal, such as a motor accident where the driver seeks to avoid either insurance liability for negligence, or towing charges or, possibly, breath-testing for drink-driving, by abandoning the vehicle and reporting it as stolen. A serious view is taken of this type of action, unless an immediate 'panic' reaction to an accident is very quickly rectified. It becomes more serious if the deceit which it sets in train is allowed to progress. Another type of misadventure concerns incidents of rape where neither consent nor coercion is clearly made out. The complainant may seek to represent herself as entirely non-consenting or the man as entirely coercive, either through vindictiveness towards him or in an attempt to exonerate herself in the eyes of particular third parties, usually males such as husbands, boyfriends, or fathers.

A much smaller number of false complaints represent a secondary criminal action taken to cover up a primary action which was criminal *ab initio*. Examples would be employees' reports of theft made to conceal their own pilfering or till thefts from their employers, or a vehicle being set on fire in order to claim its insurance value.

As the title of the offence implies, the actions of the police as well as those of the offender need to be taken into account by the prosecutor. Consideration of the offence of wasting police time necessarily involves some consideration of the way in which police legitimately spend their time. Police forces do not generally divulge logistical returns showing how their time is allocated. Section 5(2) cases provide some exception to this general rule. The formal requirement to log the amount of time spent on a false complaint, and to show how it was spent, provides some insight into how time allocations are built up on particular cases. A cautionary note should first be entered: the amount of time actually wasted in respect of a small number of cases is not disclosed at all, or only hinted at through adjectives such as 'considerable' or 'not much'; and sometimes the figures put forward are clearly 'guesstimates' of the number of hours involved, as in Case 53: 100–200 hours. For most cases, however, a figure is stated by the police – indeed, usually it is extremely precise and detailed, with each separate operation logged in minutes. These figures reveal four points.

First, the police sometimes appear slack in treating seriously what are ostensibly dubious complaints. They are under some obligation to treat all reports they receive seriously and to attempt to respond to them (see the Police Act 1964). But investigations sometimes appear to proceed as carelessly at the early stages as they are conducted carefully later, once the complainant comes under suspicion. In Case 97 some 214 hours were wasted, yet the decision to invest this considerable amount of public resources apparently rested at constable level. Although this may represent an extreme case, clearly in some areas the police bureaucracy devours a not inconsequential amount of time almost automatically.

The inevitable use of police time is the second point. In Case 13 the defendant concocted a story about the theft of his car whilst he was out drinking, and its subsequent return to his home address in a damaged state. At a rural police station he would probably have been 'voluntarily detained' until sober, in order to get to the bottom of his preposterous account of what happened. Yet his call to New Scotland Yard was relayed to his home area (where the car was 'found'), then to the area in which he had spent the evening drinking (where the car was 'stolen'). This process of telephone and personal calls by the police automatically clocked up five and a half hours of their time (for which the defendant paid a £50 fine on conviction). A more extreme illustration of how expensive 'technological policing' becomes arose in Case 144. The defendant got drunk, telephoned his local police station, and informed the police that his premises were 'being broken into', in a spurious attempt to get a dumped car moved from outside his home. This call was relayed to a police traffic car and on to the Metropolitan Police helicopter, which flew 13 nautical miles, taking 32 minutes, to engage in six minutes' 'observation' of the defendant's premises. The time wasted was held by the police to be 'trivial' – although the financial cost must have been considerable – and no action was taken. The case was not recommended for prosecution.

Third, it is not always clear what proportion of police time has been wasted on the false complaint, and what proportion has been spent in establishing the falsity of the complaint. In Case 1, the five hours overall time claimed to be wasted included the time spent on the defendant's arrest. Sometimes the latter part of the investigation far exceeds the time spent on the original complaint – perhaps rightly, where wasting police time is a potentially serious matter – but some cases with extravagantly high numbers of hours claimed as wasted but not strictly categorized may excite some suspicion of a 'band-wagon effect' once a complaint is perceived as false. Putting these cases up to the DPP may provide a convenient way for police officers to get their time-sheets written up.

Fourth, the police may strongly influence the prosecutor's decision with regard to proceedings. This may be best illustrated by the correlation between whether defendants' previous convictions are included in the police report and whether or not the police urge a prosecution. Although not necessarily a determining factor in prosecution decisions of themselves, the presence or absence of previous convictions provides a fairly sound indicator of the general tenor of the police report and the outcome which the investigating officer wants. In the cases-prosecuted sample, eighteen defendants had previous convictions, six were shown as having none, and nine were undisclosed. In the no-prosecution sample, only two defendants were shown to have previous convictions, two had none, and thirteen were undisclosed. Another focus of police influence arises in respect of what may be termed 'therapeutic' decisions. In Case 119, a 17-year-old woman made a series of complaints about assaults and burglary, then confessed that they were false. There was a history of action on her part – such as false threatening letters to herself and her boyfriend, 'minor' arson, and self-mutilation – and it was suggested that they were 'cries for help' deriving from mental stress; however, there was no supporting medical evidence.[9] Similarly, there was no summary of the police time wasted, although it appeared to be considerable. No proceedings were taken. The perspective of the police had been marked and influential. How is the DPP to quarrel with them? By replacing a first-hand lay psychological assessment with a second-hand one?

It is suggested later that the DPP may not operate 'reasonable prospects' as stringently in relation to consents – which are routinely left to the police to prosecute – as in relation to those cases which it takes through to court. Against this, the uniquely high 'success' rate of 33 convictions in these 34 cases should be noted, although convictions are, of course, a very crude outcome measure of prosecution decisions.

Eighteen cases were not proceeded with, but the true proportion of cases in which the exercise of prosecutorial discretion led to an avoidance of proceedings was lower, for two reasons. First, in common with most types of case which constitute the DPP's overall caseload, four cases suffered from evidential insufficiency. This finding, out of a total of fifty-nine, represents an unusually low rate of filtering out on grounds of evidential insufficiency. Secondly, three otherwise sound cases were time-barred: the police had failed to present them to the DPP within the statutorily limited period of six months for prosecution. This finding appears somewhat surprising in view of the very nature of Section 5(2) offences!

SECTION 30(4) THEFT ACT 1968 (HUSBAND/WIFE THEFTS OR CRIMINAL DAMAGE)

The sample included nineteen cases of theft or criminal damage between spouses. Proceedings were brought in ten cases, resulting in eight convictions. A DPP memorandum offers the rationale for the consent provision in these cases, albeit somewhat obliquely: 'Whilst we are not in the marriage guidance business, we must have regard in appropriate cases to the prospects of reconciliation being damaged by the institution of proceedings.'[10] Such consideration quickly shades into discussion of the public interest. What interest does the public have in 'offending' which occurs in an essentially private context? The answer seems to be that the law will be allowed to intrude into domestic disputes if it appears that one spouse is systematically or repeatedly abusing the other's property: 'one would be less disposed to consent to [prosecution of] a minor matter unless it was the culmination of a history of incidents'.[10] The DPP observes the lawyer's customary caution with regard to use of the criminal law to pursue private disputes at state expense, and tries to avoid becoming a 'debt collection agency': 'One might bear in mind the relevance of the criminal proceedings to possible divorce proceedings. But one has to be on the look-out for vitriolic complaints deliberately made as a tactic in battles (legal or otherwise) between the spouses'.[10]

The motivation in Section 30(4) cases is usually obvious: matrimonial discord leading one spouse to appropriate or damage the other's property. Understandably, little attempt is made to inquire into the minutiae of the background of domestic strife. But if some other motivation, such as 'greed', is clearly displayed by the defendant this will act as an aggravating factor. The consequences of the offences were generally far from trivial in financial terms, ranging from £12 to £2,500 (or £500, depending on which party's valuation was accepted), with most of the prosecuted cases running into treble figures. The amounts in the 'no proceedings' cases were generally lower but still in double or sometimes treble figures. The non-material consequences were, of course, the effects which either spouse's offence had on the couple's relationship. The police rarely offer a view in relation to these delicate, and intricate, lines of argument. They remained enigmatic in all of the prosecuted cases. One case (118) came to the DPP already charged and this was allowed to stand. In two cases (83 and 71) the police began proceedings without obtaining the necessary consent. Whether this improper action implied a strong police opinion on the cases or simply procedural naïvety is difficult to tell. The 'no proceedings' were hardly more revealing of police opinion on the merits of the cases, although reservations were expressed in two cases (75 and 54), and disagreement between the investigating officer and the senior countersignatory was recorded in Case 75. That the police interest in the outcome of Section 30(4) cases was perhaps less keen than for Section 5(2) consents may be inferred from the generally scant information presented to the DPP. For example, in relation to offenders' previous convictions, in the 'no-prosecution' cases, eight were not given, compared with one case where the offender had several convictions for dishonesty (Case 137); in the sample prosecuted, three were shown to have convictions recorded against them, three were shown to be free from convictions, and four were not given.

The DPP minutes were generally more forthcoming than the police reports in giving some rationale for their decisions, at least in relation to the nine 'no prosecutions'. In three cases, and possibly a fourth, there was 'insufficient evidence'. In one of these cases, Case 84, the police claimed that there was a *prima facie* case; in two cases (54 and 69) civil proceedings were adjudged to be more appropriate; and in a third, Case 153, a reference to the 'interests of justice' probably amounted to much the same reasoning. There was one caution (137) and one enigmatic 'withdrawal' (10). On the point of evidential sufficiency there was, typically, little or no discussion of witnesses' credibility but, atypically, attention was paid to their *availability*: 'Obviously, we have to be satisfied about the adequacy of the evidence, and the fact that the spouse is willing to attend Court . . . it is prudent to check on the position before consent is granted, in case the spouses have become reconciled.'[10] Clearly this reasoning is particularly relevant to this category of cases, where spouses are, unusually, able to give evidence against each other.[11]

BUGGERY AND GROSS INDECENCY

The analysis in this section will not only draw on the sample of fifty-eight buggery/gross-indecency cases which came into the DPP under Section 8 of the Sexual Offences Act 1967 for consent to prosecute, but will also make comparisons with a statistical analysis compiled by a member of the Director's staff of every buggery/attempted buggery and gross-indecency case handled by the DPP in 1981.

The offences coming to the DPP's attention under these two consent provisions fall principally into two groups. First, offences occurring between consenting individuals in a 'convenient' place – often public toilets: these are primarily offences of gross indecency. Although they are 'victimless' in the traditional sense of the term, a wider definition of who suffers might include members of the public who either complain or who experience nuisance, or even fear, in silence.[12] A more controversial definition of the victim might also include the younger participant. In the majority of these offences both parties are prosecuted, where the DPP gives his consent, which suggests that this 'younger victim' definition is not influential in relation to the DPP's prosecution policy.[13] Indeed, where the younger participant is cautioned or no proceedings are brought, this is usually in order that he may be used as a witness against the older offender, as in Cases 145 and 148.

The second group of offences are principally of buggery between an adult and a young boy when the adult is in a position of authority, as in a family relationship, or in a schoolmaster–pupil relationship. These offences usually occur in private and are often reported at some considerable interval after the incident(s). A purely quantitative analysis of the 1981 cases would suggest that the reasonable prospects test effectively filters out those cases which are likely to result in acquittals. Convictions were obtained for 83 per cent of the buggery offences prosecuted and 90 per cent of the gross indecencies.

The detailed analysis of the fifty-eight cases indicates that these gross statistics are misleading. First, although in nine of the sample cases consent to prosecute both parties was refused, in eight of these the evidence was considered insufficient against one or both of the parties. Since these estimations of 'insufficiency' were based on the absence of admissions or corroboration, or on the dubious reliability of the complainants, it was clear that for some accused a *prima facie* case had not been established. Thus, the DPP was not necessarily exercising its discretion on the basis of its higher standard of evidence. The second misleading aspect of the quantitative analysis of the 1981 cases concerns the conviction rates. They may be abnormally high not solely because a stringent evidential filter has been applied by the DPP, but rather because of the large proportion of offenders who plead guilty.[14] Many offenders accused of gross indecency indicate that they will plead guilty; when they are 'caught in the act', there are usually both admissions and corroborations. Furthermore, in those cases where there are victims it is not uncommon for older offenders to indicate that they will plead guilty as a demonstration of remorse to prevent younger boys having to give evidence against them, as in Cases 50 and 94 which involved a teacher and a grandfather respectively. Alternatively, offenders may plead guilt in acknowledgement of their need for help, as in Cases 55, 65, 67, and 146; in the last case the offender, not atypically, asked for help for his 'uncontrollable urges'. There is considerably more than a 'reasonable' prospect of obtaining a conviction (through a guilty plea) in such cases.

The DPP, through its selection of charges, may further contribute to this tendency to plead guilty. Various illustrations of this exist: for example, incidents where lesser charges were brought to encourage a defendant to plead guilty and thereby prevent unwilling children from having to give evidence (Case 114); to ensure that a prosecution for buggery was not launched solely on the basis of an admission (Case 101, where gross indecency charges were brought instead); or where a charge of indecent assault was brought as well, against the contingency that the attempted buggery charge might fail (in a case viewed particularly seriously within the DPP).

Whether the evidence would have been sufficient had a larger proportion of these cases been contested is unclear. In Case 103, which was contested, the accused, a vicar, was found not guilty of gross indecency on the direction of the judge. Despite some forensic evidence, it seems possible that the case foundered when the dubious evidence of several young complainants was tested. If so, this is an indication that 'not guilty' pleas in other cases might have led to acquittals.

What might cause the DPP to proceed when the evidence is less strong than might be expected? Some cases are launched where the DPP believes that the public interest merits a prosecution and this may influence their view of the strength of the evidence. In Case 96, despite the Assistant Director's refusal to proceed on the grounds of insufficient evidence, the professional officer's minute was telling, in that he recommended a prosecution in the belief that the accused was 'a menace' and that the jury was sure to convict. A belief in the deterrent effects of prosecutions was also in evidence. Concern was expressed about areas where homosexual behaviour was blatant (Case 33) and about a notorious meeting point (Case 136). In the latter case a Principal Assistant Director advised proceedings where there were no admissions and no corroboration. Proceedings were brought, despite the professional officer's view that the case should not proceed. He explained that the requirement for corroboration was only 'discretionary'.[15] The decision to prosecute apparently showed an attempt to 'stamp out' the behaviour, in that public-interest considerations had encouraged the DPP to proceed despite weak evidence. But, if deterrence was the object of the prosecution, why not wait for another case to come forward with stronger evidence? If the rendezvous was notorious the delay should not be long. At trial, the case was dismissed. It is clear that at least some of these cases betray a violation of the reasonable prospects of conviction test: cases are prosecuted where there is technical doubt about the sufficiency of evidence – a course which is justified by the DPP's officers as being 'in the public interest'.[16] In marked contrast, in only one case (122) did the Assistant Director note that, despite admissions, the 'public interest did not require a prosecution', and cautions were advised.[17] However, it should be noted that where the evidence was sufficient against one party but not the other it was generally considered unsatisfactory to proceed, particularly where the individual admitting the offence was clearly less culpable, on the grounds of equity or 'fair play' between the parties.

The infrequency with which cautions were used may also have contributed to the high conviction rate. The DPP may be reluctant to advise a caution where an offender has been previously cautioned for a similar offence (as in Cases 24 and 26).[18] The use of the caution may be further curtailed where certain outcomes are considered desirable by the DPP which cannot be achieved without a prosecution: for example Case 5 where the offender was prosecuted for buggery (despite the police view that a caution would normally suffice in these circumstances – the act occurred in private with a willing 18-year-old) to ensure that he would be de-registered under Section 2 of the Residential Homes Act 1980 as a person suitable to provide accommodation for mentally disordered persons. Similarly, in Case 123, since the youth involved was considered to be in need of 'restraint',[19] the older man (no previous convictions, married, one son, architect, apparently eligible for a caution) was prosecuted along with him. If therapy, not punishment, was the rationale for the prosecution of the younger man, was it necessary to prosecute the elder? In Cases 145 and 148 young offenders were cautioned prior to being used as witnesses against older offenders. Cannot younger homosexuals corrupt older first-timers? It appears that either way the older man effectively forfeits the possibility of non-prosecution if he embarks on a homosexual act with someone under the age of consent. If the younger man has no previous convictions the elder man will be 'corruptive'; if the younger man has a history he will be deemed in 'need' of a prosecution, so the elder man is also prosecuted on grounds of fairness.

INCEST

The sample included ten cases of incest: seven father/daughter, two brother/sister, and one grandfather/granddaughter. Proceedings were advised in all of the cases, but only eight were dealt with during the research period, resulting in five convictions.

Questions of motivation by defendants – or victims – were occasionally considered, but there was scant overt discussion of the public interest since there is a strong presumption in favour of prosecution, not rebutted in any of the cases sampled. The strength of the public interest in prosecuting meant that evidential sufficiency was treated as secondary in some cases. Case 36 and Case 7 were respectively described by the professional officers as 'weak or borderline' and 'problematic'. Both were prosecuted and resulted in verdicts of acquittal. The facts of Case 110 were referred to the DPP by the trial judge following proceedings for indecent assault. The police view was that there was insufficient evidence for an incest charge. That view was not canvassed in the DPP minutes but a prosecution was brought, resulting in a directed acquittal. In general, the police did not appear to be influential with regard to the strength of the evidence, or in expressing an opinion as to whether a prosecution was merited.

These cases provide perhaps the clearest category of offences in which the public interest may 'drag up' the evidential-sufficiency limb of the reasonable prospects approach. It is not that evidential sufficiency goes undiscussed. Problems of witnesses' availability and credibility were canvassed at some length; these were generally that the daughters' intelligence ranged from 'backward' to severely subnormal (Cases 63, 124, 4, and 7), or that they had poor recall of 'stale' offences (Case 110). Yet prosecutions ensued despite these difficulties, which sometimes also involved questionable corroboration of the daughters' account of events or intimidation of wives by their defendant husbands (Case 110).

In general, the *moral* well-being of the victim appeared to be of paramount importance. 'Positive' public interest criteria involved the need to protect not only the victim but also any other younger daughters 'at risk'; instances where pregnancy resulted – signalling complete recklessness by the defendant; and instances where there was corruption, exploitation, or intimidation of family members. The last factor may also be seen in the context of matrimonial proceedings leading to disputes over custody of children. The strength of the public interest in a prosecution which intrudes into domestic family affairs contrasts sharply with the prosecutor's attitude in Section 30(4) cases. It makes little difference whether a prosecution might precipitate or compound a family breakup; or proceed in spite of the family staying together. Although the minutes do not reveal much explicit discussion of the 'dark side' of incestuous offences it seems likely that some general deterrent aims may underlie prosecutions in this area. There is no apparent shying away from 'the process as penal' philosophy – the belief that the process of prosecution in itself has penal consequences. Prosecutions are brought despite the emotional traumas likely to be felt not only by the defendant but throughout the family, since even acquittals are felt likely to deter other possible offenders from forming incestuous relationships.

SUMMARY

What general conclusions can be drawn from this discussion of consent cases? First, there is the suggestion that they receive less detailed consideration than do those non-consent cases where the DPP will handle the prosecution. Most consent files are far slimmer and less complex than those which constitute the DPP's own prosecution caseload. The influence of the police, and the DPP's dependence upon them for the raw material of decisions, is accordingly heightened. In the truncated process for consents it is comparatively rare for the prosecutor to request further information or verification from the police. The content of the police report, including such matters as whether defendants have previous convictions, is likely to be influential. This reliance upon the police may be defended on the ground that, with only rare exceptions, it is the police or their local prosecuting solicitors who will have to present cases at court. However, this has little weight in relation to non-prosecution decisions. Chapter 3 will show that such dependence on the police in consent cases is inevitable – yet not fundamentally different from the position in non-consent cases.

Secondly, the apparently high conviction rates for consent cases, despite a relatively low input of independent prosecutorial discretion, does not necessarily show that the police can manage very well without recourse to the prosecutor, given that cases attract pleas of guilty and/or are dealt with summarily. The buggery and gross indecency sample illustrates that conviction statistics do not constitute a useful form of feedback, nor indeed a helpful 'performance measure', for the prosecutor. Third, the DPP's professional staff get very little feedback on the outcome of those cases where consent is given. Once again, this represents an exaggeration of – rather than a departure from – the general difficulty which the professional officers may have in learning about how their cases turn out at court.[20] Fourth, the variation between different categories of consent cases further serves to confirm that the public interest is not a constant factor. The influence of public interest criteria is generally low for Section 30(4) cases and higher for Section 5(2) cases; for buggery and gross indecency it may fluctuate in either direction; for incest it is generally high (which may again draw attention to the paucity of feedback which the prosecutor gets about the outcome of cases). Fifth, the DPP's recourse to alternatives to prosecution, such as recommendation of cautions, may be seen to be somewhat sparse. Finally, these consent cases demonstrate that the rhetoric of the reasonable prospects of conviction test does not accord well with the practice of reasonable prospects; cases do proceed where the evidence is either insufficient or weak. Although this may be partially attributable to the format of the police reports in these cases, it is also clearly attributable to public interest considerations.

The '85' sample

WHO DECIDES WHAT, AND WHEN?

I contrast to the consent cases, the decision-making process in respect of cases in the '85' sample was typically a protracted one. The cases show that the series of questions – who decides, what and when – is deceptively simple. Because of the interdependence of the prosecutor with the police, counsel, and the courts, it is often extremely difficult to isolate and pinpoint crucial prosecution decisions. The 'bare bones' of the formal organizational arrangements within the DPP's office have already been outlined: this discussion fleshes them out, illustrating how the system functions in practice.

Prosecutorial decisions may be divided into three parts: those concerning the evidence, the law, and questions of policy. The professional officer, who looks at the case in the greatest detail after the police, is typically the next best placed to decide about the sufficiency of evidence – and perhaps also to assess its cogency. Assistant Directors and/or their seniors may be better placed to ensure consistency of prosecutorial policy owing to their larger caseload and their more extensive experience. This may also equip them to reassess the cogency of evidence. Counsel are in a more advantageous position when it comes to advising not only on the current state of the law but also the prospects of conviction – the 'law in action' as well as 'law in the books' – through up-to-date experience of judges and juries. Overall this line of demarcation follows the internal logic of how prosecutions are organized at the DPP, meeting obvious logistical assumptions arising out of the sequential involvement of the police, junior and senior DPP officers, and counsel.

The hierarchical nature of the internal mechanism is resented by some professional officers at the DPP, all of whom are either solicitors or barristers, especially those who previously enjoyed greater autonomy when employed in other prosecutorial agencies, since in theory it divests them of power to make prosecution decisions. In practice the process works in this way only some of the time. Professional officers' assessments are rarely overturned, although this happens more often to some professional officers than to others. If disagreement within the DPP persists, for example between the professional officer and the Assistant Director, and the Principal Assistant Director is equivocal as to which view should prevail, counsel's opinion may be sought. This occasional recourse to counsel serves to exaggerate the strength of pre-trial influence by the Bar; although, as Chapter 3 shows, counsel is extremely influential later, at the trial stage.

The greatest source of disagreement does not arise out of lawyers making technical errors about which laws apply or interpreting the same law differently; it arises from divergent moral or social views about whether and how the law should be applied. This is not meant to imply that a broad spectrum of political attitudes leads lawyers to adopt widely divergent approaches to the use of the criminal law, but rather that the application of the law cannot be characterized as simply a technical matter. There are two main reasons for this. First, alleged criminals do not use statutes as blueprints for their activities: even if 'the punishment fits the crime', the crime charged must first fit the action. This often turns upon how much law should be applied, rather than which particular part of it. 'Fine tuning' is required between one prosecutorial maxim, 'to charge at the highest level the evidence will stand', and another: 'being careful not to overload the indictment' (*Ambrose* (1973) 57 Cr. App. R. 538; *Beresford* (1952) 36 Cr. App. R. 1). Secondly, alleged criminals do not always act alone: where two or more potential defendants are involved, difficult and important choices have to be made about whom to charge, and with what, and whom to use instead as witnesses. Even operating a *prima facie* test, lawyers had to exercise some judgment in respect of these difficult questions. Using a reasonable prospects approach those difficulties are writ larger: lawyers are not confined to narrow questions of law, but must weigh estimations of relative moral or social culpability.

The conundrum may be illustrated by reference to three cases. The first suggests that, in such circumstances, the prosecution may be justified in putting the joint defendants 'in the frame together' despite variations in the strength of the cases against them, so as to see whether they trip each other up at trial. The *reductio ad absurdum* of doing otherwise, and assessing each defendant alone, would frequently lead to no prosecution at all. In this case, Case 74, a murder by a brother and sister of his lover, the evidence was stronger against him largely because of an admission to stabbing, albeit in self-defence. She admitted her presence at the incident and also attributed the stabbing to him. In addition, there was some circumstantial evidence against her. The DPP speculated that the oral admissions resulted from the police introducing her into his interview to put her story, which he then adopted in his admission – indeed the police were criticized for this action. In addition, there was medical evidence that he was too drunk to manage the physical circumstances of the murder alone, and she was physically stronger than him anyway. A rigorous application of 'reasonable prospects' would have precluded her prosecution; but he might then have plausibly altered his story to shift the blame on to her. Proceedings for murder were taken against both of them, with a charge of attempting to pervert the course of justice under Section 4(1), Criminal Law Act 1967, as 'insurance' against her complete acquittal. Subject to the questions raised in later discussion, it is difficult to quarrel with this 'all or nothing' type of reasoning even though strictly it departs from reasonable prospects. Both were acquitted of murder, although he was convicted of manslaughter on the grounds of provocation. She was acquitted of manslaughter but pleaded guilty to the lesser charge. Yet the other two cases suggest that an 'all in the frame together' approach is open to abuse.

In the second case, Case 49, the rationale for prosecution was not quite so clear. Of four potential defendants to a charge of murder, two blamed each other – with assistance from their respective girlfriends – and two denied any involvement. Following some internal disagreement within the DPP, it was decided that proceedings for murder should go ahead against all four (conditional upon an identification parade in respect of one of them). In the absence of informed or detailed discussion of where guilt had lain, the decision smacked somewhat of just putting all the participants before the court. Such an approach is redolent of the traditional police philosophy of putting cases to the court; this philosophy is formally rejected by the DPP, since it abrogates responsibility for prosecution and engenders a 'conveyor-belt' system.

In the third case, Case 61, a 'gang-bang' rape where, even if the victim had initially consented, it appeared that this consent was withdrawn when the defendants abused her, a 'put it before the court' approach was challenged by the defence at an 'old-style' committal. The Assistant Director had agreed to the prosecution, despite noting that the evidence was not strong in respect of all defendants – but had argued that the initiative to test it should be left to the defence. Such reliance on 'good' defence solicitors seems ethically doubtful but in this case they were alert and the evidence was tested at an old-style committal. One of the co-defendants was discharged: no identification evidence was brought against him, the prosecution resting only upon his co-defendants' evidence of his involvement. It was successfully submitted that this was not admissible. Only one defendant was later convicted of indecent assault; there were judge-directed acquittals on the rape and buggery charges.

Thus, the interdependence of prosecutions of joint defendants demands a careful exercise of the prosecutor's ethics. Yet this responsibility is not necessarily discharged by the prosecutor alone. The police may also have to engage in similar 'extra-legal' assessments of where the gravamen and primary responsibility lie in a complex case. The police do not enjoy the prosecutor's benefit of hindsight over how the case has turned out on paper. Sometimes the case may be neatly tailored to the evidence as it emerges, but often an erroneous start cannot readily be corrected. Strategic decisions about treating some of those present at the scene of the crime as defendants and others as witnesses during the investigation stage will not necessarily enhance court-room strategies at the prosecution stage. This discrepancy can manifest itself in a variety of ways: the police may defer to the prosecutor's decision-making through early consultation with him; if not, and he is unable subsequently to redress the balance of a case, he will be bound to continue along lines determined by the police. Hence the inextricable links between who decides what, and when, in the prosecution process.

There are a number of reasons why the line, drawn by the Royal Commission between investigation and prosecution, was somewhat artificial and optimistic. Two questions posed here embrace the practical problems faced by the prosecutor in applying reasonable prospects in conjunction with other participants in the criminal justice process. First, what constraints are placed upon decision-making where the prosecutor may be characterized as just one 'cog' in the prosecution machine? Secondly, if these constraints present difficulties for his decision-making, how are they dealt with? The final section of the discussion addresses the endemic problems associated with applying reasonable prospects.

SYSTEMIC PROBLEMS WITH REASONABLE PROSPECTS

The prosecutor as a 'cog'; does this matter?

This section sets out to show the vulnerability of 'reasonable prospects' in practice by placing the prosecutor in the context of the criminal justice system. The actions of others may 'tie his hands' so that he must proceed in a particular way – even when there is a poor chance of conviction. The DPP is constrained by what the police do with a case before it comes in; and he has little control over what happens to it in the courts after it leaves.[21] The course taken by a case will also be affected by the witnesses – including defendants – whose role the DPP needs to take into account both retrospectively (what they said in their statements) and prospectively (what they are likely to say, and how they say it, in court). This the DPP patently does, although police assessments of witnesses' past involvement in a case and possible future performance in court are not always discussed explicitly. The role of the police and courts – through the prosecutor's interdependency with them – receives even less attention.

The DPP is dependent on the police for the raw material upon which it takes its decisions. How 'raw' should these materials be? The more refined the form in which the police present them, the greater their influence is likely to be. A recurrent theme in the professional officers' minutes runs along lines such as: 'since murder is already charged, this should be allowed to stand' or 'the present charges can be sustained'. Yet such phrases often appear in a professional officer's minute immediately after a discussion of difficulties in proving these charges. This is not to suggest that where the police have already charged the defendant this is regarded as sacrosanct. There are occasional illustrations in extreme cases of quite the reverse position, where the police charges are clearly unjustified. What is suggested is that the phraseology, at least, leaves the reader with the uncomfortable question: yes, but if the police had not already brought this particular charge, would the advice still be the same? Although the 'prosecutorial juggernaut' may not yet have gathered speed at this stage, the professional officer is only human if he needs to be more confident when he recommends a charge which differs from one already brought than in those cases where no charges have yet been preferred and he has a 'free choice'. If this is so, influence through their 'first bite at the cherry' has a much firmer foundation than mere awkward phraseology in the prosecution minutes.

A striking example of the DPP following the lead – albeit a dubious one – offered by the police, arose in Case 51. The defendant had, during the night, taken her boyfriend's keys to his other lover's flat, gone there, entered her rival's bedroom, and made a 'frenzied attack' on her with a pair of scissors as she lay in bed. The stabbing was aimed at the victim's stomach, or at least this was inferred: injuries were confined to her legs only, it was thought, because she had awoken and retreated up the bed. The police had charged Section 18 of the Offences against the Person Act, 'wounding with intent'. The DPP endorsed this course. An intention to kill the victim could possibly have been inferred, if her stomach had been the actual focus of the attack. Her leg injuries required extensive surgery: in the region of the stomach they could readily have been fatal, but this line of thought was apparently stopped prematurely. It is more usual for the police to suggest an attempted murder charge and for the DPP to turn this down. Ironically, in this case, the facts might have supported an attempted murder charge had the police questioned the defendant as to her intent. Their omission to do so was not brought into a reasonable prospects assessment, of how damaging to the prosecution this was likely to be. It was simply accepted. Failure to articulate a particular line of reasoning does not necessarily mean that a 'reasonable prospects' rationale was never invoked. But, to say the least, it appeared to have been submerged beneath the DPP's acceptance of the investigatorial mistake – which might have been overcome at trial, notwithstanding the difficulty of proof with regard to attempted murder charges.

The police may also constrain the DPP's handling of the difficult and sensitive 'dock/box' division of defendants/witnesses. Where several persons are implicated in an offence, the police may take the view that their culpability is different and that without the evidence of the 'less guilty' there will be insufficient evidence against the 'more guilty'. Once they interview and charge persons on this basis, it may be impracticable for the DPP to adopt a different approach. Thus in Case 52, there were six potential defendants in a shooting incident. Three were charged with murder, Section 18, Offences against the Person Act, and conspiracy to cause grievous bodily harm. The remaining three were not charged at all but used as witnesses against the others. The facts of the case were so involved as to make it difficult to demonstrate whether the balance struck was right or wrong without going into immense detail. However, some questions may be raised. How can we be so sure that the three witnesses would refuse to give evidence against the others even if they were charged with some lesser offence – to reflect their lesser culpability – as the DPP recommended in this case? Is it too readily assumed that *any* prosecution will 'sour' potential witnesses against giving evidence? Might they not demonstrate sufficient 'gratitude' in return for comparatively light charges, which also leave less room for the defence to make capital out of their 'escape from prosecution'? Just how reluctant to testify does a witness have to be before he is 'written off'? Are the alternatives, of trying to compel witnesses to give their testimony through use of witness summonses, too rarely invoked? There were acquittals of all three defendants on all counts. The DPP also concurred with the police charges on Case 78, another murder, where the professional officer was explicitly critical of the 'dock/box' balance yet still accepted it. The Principal Assistant Director was only implicitly critical, although in this case the DPP 'stopped the rot' in that the police had wanted to use two further potential defendants as witnesses. Rather than challenge whether the police view on the participants' willingness to give evidence was pessimistic, the professional officer relied on the logical force of the existing evidence. Any evidence that these last two participants might give was already adequately covered by other witnesses. This graphically illustrates that the prosecutor must argue as best he can with 'the bird' in his hands, rather than about what remains in 'the bush'; the police generally determine both parts of this metaphor relating to evidence.

Case 83 was an exception. The police wanted to refrain from prosecuting a husband for drug importation for fear that his wife would not then give evidence against defendants charged with kidnapping, Section 18, Offences against the Person Act, and aggravated burglary, arising out of reprisals following her and her husband's default in a drugs deal. No grounds for these police fears were canvassed, yet the professional officer agreed that the husband should not be prosecuted. So did the Assistant Director, albeit reluctantly under a public interest 'greater good' rationale. The Principal Assistant Director was not happy at this and ultimately the decision was reversed. The husband was prosecuted. The wife still gave evidence against her kidnappers. All defendants were convicted on all charges. Case 15, dealt with in Chapter 3, points the other way: the DPP insisted on treating potential witnesses to a murder as defendants on drug charges and subsequently lost their possible co-operation; the case was also lost in respect of the murder charge. So the outcome of Case 83 should be interpreted with caution, to suggest no more than that the prosecutor should rigorously examine the views of the police about the willingness of participants in an incident resulting in a crime to give evidence, irrespective of whether they are charged with some offence themselves.

An allied problem arises even if all parties are subject to charges. It turns upon the 'pecking order' for separate trials arising out of some common series of offences, where defendants in one trial are needed as witnesses in another trial. The working assumption of the prosecutor is that the less serious cases should be disposed of first, so that the less serious defendants may then be used as witnesses in the ensuing trials of the more serious offenders. Indeed, the general policy adopted by the DPP is to ensure that, wherever possible, potential witnesses are 'weighed off' prior to giving evidence, so that imputations about their motivation may not so readily be made by the defence. This leaves some intractable questions outstanding. Relative seriousness between offences is not always easy to determine. For example, is it considered to be more serious for a defendant to shoot at policemen or for an innocent victim to be shot at by policemen? Even if apparently open questions like these can be answered, is the evidence of witnesses whose own criminality has already been dealt with necessarily more persuasive than the evidence of those still awaiting trial? It is interesting to combine both sets of questions, to speculate on whether the prosecutorial working assumption might be reversible according to the relative seriousness of the offences: is an untried thief likely to be a more persuasive witness against a murderer than vice versa? (In practice, this example is unlikely to arise since cases involving theft charges would routinely come to trial more quickly than those involving murder. But, the dilemma remains for offences of more nearly comparable seriousness.) The order in which the trials take place may be important for the purposes of the prosecution, and yet the courts may frustrate the prosecutor's strategy by hearing them in a different order to that envisaged by the DPP. In Case 71, a 46-year-old man was charged with indecency offences involving two 14-year-old boys, who were also charged with blackmailing him. The DPP reached these prosecutorial decisions on the assumption that the boys would be dealt with first, in the juvenile court. When that court exercised its prerogative of committing the boys for trial the DPP became anxious that the consequent delay would bar them from being used as witnesses in relation to the indecency charges. The resultant embarrassment led the DPP to hope for a guilty plea from the man. In the event the defendant pleaded guilty to indecent assault, and a gross indecency charge was withdrawn against him though not against the boys. One pleaded guilty and the other was convicted.

Finally, there is a more extreme form of constraint on the prosecutor. A small number of cases come into the DPP already committed for trial. In these circumstances the prosecutor's hands are virtually tied to proceed with the prosecution. They have often been put into the courts' purview by the police or their 'dependent' prosecuting solicitors. In Case 59, the DPP was consulted because the police sought the extradition of a rapist from Germany. He had absconded five years previously, after committal and before trial. His co-accused, who was more clearly culpable, had been convicted. The case against him was assessed as 'thin'. Yet the DPP, who had not conducted the committal, felt obliged to proceed since he had already been committed. A conviction resulted, with the defendant receiving four years' imprisonment. Similarly, in Case 60, the DPP felt bound to endorse a sensitive theft case referred by the Metropolitan Police solicitors 'for confirmation', despite its weakness, since a magistrate had already issued a warrant. There was a consciously ambiguous suggestion that counsel might try offering no evidence at trial. Lastly, in Case 67, a theft which jeopardized industrial relations in Fleet Street, the DPP felt compelled to proceed with a prosecution begun privately (in concert with the police) in spite of the 'slight' prospects of conviction, which were borne out by subsequent acquittals.

Coping with disputes: the incremental approach

Some disagreements within the DPP are not resolved, or not fully resolved, before cases leave it: cases are launched tentatively, for example via the 'old-style' committal route, in order to obtain access to greater information before a final decision is made about the charges to be placed on the indictment. This is termed proceeding on a 'reserved' basis. But it means that the DPP effectively concedes some influence over its cases to other actors: counsel, the defence, the magistrates, and the courts. Although such a symbiotic relationship may appear unobjectionable in theory, it is problematic in practice where 'reasonable prospects' is not a universal standard.

(i) *Counsel* The prosecutorial discretion allowed to counsel by the DPP varies greatly between cases. One possible explanation might be that counsel has greater latitude where the DPP is uncertain about the basis on which to proceed, whereas he is subject to greater constraint if the DPP has developed a firm position on a case. Some difficult technical decisions which are usually and properly taken before committal may be reserved for counsel on the basis that evidence may be clarified at the committal. In Case 36, an arguable charge of attempted murder was allowed to stand with the intention of 'leaving it to counsel to draw up the indictment' as he saw fit. Such an approach, as will be discussed later, may have unintended consequences, in that the charges on which the magistrates commit may not always easily be reversed.

(ii) *The Magistrates' Court* Disagreement within the DPP about the strength of the evidence may be resolved through recourse to the Magistrates' Court. Case 80 illustrates how this 'incremental' approach may backfire. The prosecution intended to seek committal on a murder charge, primarily on the strength of the opinion of the prosecution pathologist. However, on the day prior to committal the pathologist 'retreated' from his opinion after learning of the contrary opinion of the defence pathologist. The prosecution withdrew the murder charge and proceeded, albeit unhappily, with a manslaughter charge. The prosecution had by that stage lost confidence in its pathologist and recognized that the evidence on the manslaughter charge was significantly weaker than had been thought. Yet the lay bench committed on the manslaughter charge. Although the DPP subsequently proceeded only on lesser charges, some prosecution momentum ensued. There was recognition of just this difficulty in that it had been argued in respect of this case that there was a 'greater responsibility to get it right in the Department' for a lay bench of examining justices than for a Stipendiary Magistrate. But this cautious approach was not applied until after the committal. Following the dubious committal on manslaughter, the DPP proceeded with an indictment only on the lesser charges of maltreatment, illegal burial, and fraud: convictions ensued. Although the prosecutor's hands are tied as to whether to proceed after committal, the same is not necessarily true as to how he proceeds. None the less, the general problem arising out of the lack of clarity about the DPP's autonomy in relation to the courts clearly makes it uncomfortable for the prosecution to adopt a lofty 'reserved position' philosophy, and put marginal cases up for committal.

(iii) *The higher courts* The DPP does not defer to the jury as readily as other prosecutors because of his disdain for the 'put it up to the courts to decide' approach, associated with the *prima facie* test. However, as the Attorney General's *Criteria* state, if the decision-maker finds himself at a genuine 'point of balance' between proceedings and 'no action', proceedings should be begun. This 'failsafe' approach, intended to guard against the precipitative exercise of the discretion not to prosecute, only reduces the 'prosecutor's dilemma' in cases where he is left with a 'genuine balance' about the prospects of conviction. Can the 'point of balance' be determined with any greater precision than guilt or innocence? Might not this shift in the location of responsibility contribute to inconsistency in prosecutions? For the prosecutor, the sometimes difficult choice between bringing murder or manslaughter charges may be resolved by proceeding on a 'reserved' basis. It is necessary first to make a distinction between the three routes by which murder indictments may result in convictions for manslaughter: provocation, diminished responsibility, or the defendant's 'lesser intent' (i.e. neither an intention to kill nor to do really serious bodily harm) (*R. v. Moloney* [1985] 1 All ER 1025). Eighteen of the 38 accepted pleas (47 per cent) in a sub-sample of 149 murders drawn from the retrospective statistical analysis of 258 Central Criminal Court cases were on the grounds of diminished responsibility. In these cases the DPP has no alternative but to proceed on the grounds of murder, as diminished responsibility is only a defence and may not be charged initially. Yet at an early stage in the prosecution the DPP may become well placed to exercise discretion as to whether to accept a plea of manslaughter, on the basis of its own expert evidence in conjunction with that supplied by the defence. In turn, acceptable pleas of diminished responsibility, as opposed to a jury finding of diminished responsibility, are more frequently associated with hospital rather than penal disposals (Dell 1983).

The defence of diminished responsibility was initially viewed as one appropriate to be put to the jury and not one where the judge should accept a plea (*Matheson* (1958) 42 Cr. App. R. 145). This situation has changed so that where medical evidence is not challenged a plea of guilt is often accepted by the trial judge (*Vinagre* (1979) 69 Cr. App. R. 104), although there have been some notable refusals such as the Sutcliffe case. The overwhelming proportion of diminished responsibility convictions are obtained via guilty pleas; trials only occur where the prosecution adduces rebutting evidence or the defendant denies the offence. Dell asserts that 'juries seldom determine diminished responsibility cases, and it is the judges, by accepting pleas of guilty, who in the event decide whether the offender's mental responsibility was impaired'. Judges hardly ever refuse to accept a plea of diminished responsibility where the prosecution are content, but the prosecution may challenge both the findings of its own experts and those of the defence. It might therefore be argued that the DPP, who conducts all of these cases, is in the potentially influential position of being able to sustain murder charges rather than reduce them to manslaughter. For example, in Case 57, where the Assistant Director instructed the professional officer to 'proceed cautiously' with a murder charge, there was a conviction for manslaughter by reason of diminished responsibility, resulting in Section 60 and 65 orders under the Mental Health Act 1959.

Finally, it should be noted that the Crown Court may restrain the prosecutor's discretion even more markedly than does the earlier magistrates' committal. In Case 85, a Section 18, Offences against the Person Act assault, the trial judge placed very considerable pressure on the prosecution to accept a plea under Section 20 of the Act – on the grounds that it would not affect the sentence. This pressure was backed up with a threat to make the prosecution pay the costs which, though financially unimportant since the DPP meets all except witness expenses in any event, would have represented public censure. The DPP succumbed but the judge then gave a sentence more appropriate to a conviction on a Section 18 offence. The defence, in turn, lodged an appeal. The Principal Assistant Director argued that the DPP should wait until the 'right case comes along', then dig his toes in by refusing to bow to pressure from the judge to accept a plea which, in the prosecutor's view, did not adequately reflect the gravamen of the offender's actions. However, such disputes are difficult to anticipate.

Two conclusions may be drawn from consideration of what the DPP has to consider in reaching prosecution decisions and how he goes about it. First, there is an inherent tension in prosecutorial decision-making in that, although the prosecutor gains more information as the case proceeds – vital to his 'reasonable prospects' prediction – at the same time he also tends progressively to lose effective control over whether it may be halted. In its most extreme form, this characterization of the prosecution process may be stated thus: the DPP may either make effective decisions early in the prosecution process which are badly informed or make informed

Crown Prosecution Service

Northern Region

Suite 101
1st Floor
Sunlight House
Quay Street
Manchester M3 3JU

Telephone 061-835-2842
Ext.

Director of Public Prosecutions
Allan Green QC

Deputy Director and Chief Executive
D. S. Gandy OBE

Regional Director
B. H. Crebbin

With Compliments

decisions later which are not effective. Secondly, a decision strategy that entails avoiding early decisions as a means of attempting to satisfy 'reasonable prospects' may undermine the basic philosophy behind the DPP's approach. Although the DPP should not be blamed for past police errors which are beyond correction, it should bear greater responsibility for anticipating the courts' actions in those marginal cases where proceedings are begun somewhat speculatively. If cases are begun on a 'reserved position' basis it is not always clear where final responsibility for decision-making rests; if the DPP acts as a 'non-decision maker' in passing cases on, this may contribute to a 'prosecution momentum'.[22]

Endemic problems with reasonable prospects: the social context

A key distinction between reasonable prospects and the *prima facie* approach to prosecutions lies in the way in which social criteria for decision-making are woven into the legal ones. Although it is artificial to attempt fully to separate the social from the legal strands of 'reasonable prospects' – indeed this is the central difficulty in using this approach to prosecutions as well as in trying to describe and analyse it – the discussion which follows focuses on the 'social element' of prosecution decision-making.

What emerges from this section is that assumptions about 'juror sympathies' are legion, and that predictions about their behaviour differ between decision-makers. First, the need to predict jury behaviour infuses inconsistency into prosecution decisions through the way in which evidence is considered – the legal element. Secondly, the question of whether the evidence is likely to persuade a jury is posed – the social element. Third, there is a further social assessment of the case 'in the public interest' which places limits (on socio-political grounds) on the predictions about how the jury will behave. However, the presence of two social contexts in the decision to prosecute not only leads to the possibility of 'double-counting', that is the jury's view may be taken into account twice, and not necessarily with similar effect, but also causes practical interaction between the 'reasonable prospects test' and the public interest perspective. This constitutes a departure from the reasonable prospects approach 'as advertised', in that its two elements are not assessed sequentially.

In Case 9, a possible attempted murder which had been charged under Section 20 of the Offences against the Person Act by the police, a 'battered wife' shot her husband in the arm and chest with her son's shotgun. In a bout of marital violence the husband had brandished a machete at the daughter. The wife got hold of the gun and claimed she had fired without taking aim since she was scared stiff. Clearly there was some doubt about her intent. But prosecutions are frequently launched on the basis of inferred intent – from a combination of the weapon used and the injuries sustained. The difficulty was compounded in this case by the husband's refusal to give a statement. There was also the possibility that the wife might raise self-defence. The professional officer and the Assistant Director thought that even the charge under Section 20 of the Offences against the Person Act had a 'very slim' prospect of conviction, but advised proceedings none the less. The case was referred upwards and ultimately no prosecution was brought. This decision was based on two grounds: not only that the evidence was characterized as weak but also that there would be jury sympathy for the wife (and perhaps, by implication, antipathy for the husband). The first ground was largely legal but also partly social – how the jury would perceive the evidence. Then the second ground was entirely social – how the jury's perceptions were expected to be coloured.

Cases 2 and 3 both involved baby deaths and were evidentially quite similar; yet 'no action' was taken against the defendant in Case 2 whereas the defendant in Case 3 was prosecuted. In Case 2 the defendant's explanation of the death as an accident prevailed, because the Principal Assistant Director concluded that he could not see a jury deciding that death had resulted from a fit of temper, given a background of apparent parental love and care. In Case 3, the defendant's previous conviction for assault was explicitly influential and the case proceeded on a manslaughter charge. Can these divergent decisions be explained in terms of 'reasonable prospects'? Probably not: the criterion seems to be a broader social one.

This exposes reasonable prospects to further criticism: that its 'morality' limb allows room for valuations of the defendant's 'social worth'. Two types of jury acquittals commonly occur in these domestic tragedies. First there are acquittals on the evidence. One of the ways in which the prosecution case may be weakened is if at the trial the defendant challenges his admissions to the police. It would not be difficult for a father to assert that he was suffering considerable emotional stress when he made his statement to the police just after the death of a child and so dispute that statement. Defendant 2 might have done this, had he been prosecuted.

Defendant 3 was less likely to do so since that would expose him to the possibility of cross-examination on his previous conviction by the prosecution (Section 1(f)(ii), Criminal Evidence Act 1898). Similarly, defendant 2 might have been in a better position to advance an innocent explanation in court than defendant 3. Should prosecution decisions be based, even partially, on a moral assessment stemming from one related previous conviction which would be inadmissible in evidence? Again, following the Principal Assistant Director's reasoning, defendant 2 appeared more eligible for such an acquittal than defendant 3. But a prosecutor's decision which follows such reasoning guarantees defendant 2 a benefit which he might have anticipated. If the 'lion's den' is good enough for defendant 3, why should defendant 2 be protected from something which was more likely to favour him anyway?

Case 84 fell in an area where there has been legislative recognition of juror sympathies: 'motor manslaughter'. Despite some doubts over the defendant's precise mental attitude, the professional officer argued it as a clear case of 'motor manslaughter' – the car had been used as a weapon to frighten. The (lay) magistrates committed on this basis, but the indictment was none the less drawn up under Section 1 of the Road Traffic Act 1972, namely causing death by reckless driving. It had been suggested that a jury would be more readily persuaded of this offence. If the legislature has acted in recognition of this presumed tendency amongst juries, can the prosecution be criticized for following its lead? Case authority answers this in the negative (*Lawrence* (1981) 73 Cr. App. R. 1; *Seymour* (1983) 77 Cr. App. R. 215, H.L.). Ultimately, the DPP took the view that the case was one of those extreme examples for which manslaughter should be charged despite the availability of the alternative but, arguably in the eyes of the jury, more attractive offence of causing death by reckless driving. Thus divergent assumptions about jury sympathies were propounded. The outcome of the case was that the defendant was convicted of manslaughter, vindicating the DPP's ultimate approach, although the sentence, six months' youth custody, may indicate that the judge did not entirely share the jury's perspective.

Some further light may be cast upon how the prosecution takes jury reactions into account in reaching decisions by a comparison of cases where there will be a jury with those where there will not (summary cases) or, perhaps more telling, those where there may or may not be a jury ('either way' cases). The central question is: should the prosecutor take the level of tribunal into account when deciding whether to prosecute? Here it is vital to distinguish the prosecutor's assessment of the impact of the 'social context' of a case upon the tribunal from his wider assessment of how the social context meets 'public-interest' arguments for or against prosecution in spite of the likely outcome. Failure to achieve this distinction may underlie a divergence of views within the DPP over whether the level of tribunal should influence a reasonable prospects assessment. Since 'reasonable prospects' purports to be a jury-based approach to prosecutions *per se*, the level of tribunal ought not to influence the assessment under the *test*. Yet the public-interest limb of the wider *approach* will allow some scope for variation since it recognizes pragmatic factors, such as costs, in the prosecutorial decision.

In Case 18, a trivial shoplifting of goods worth 51p, the defendant elected for trial whereupon the police prosecuting solicitor sought to withdraw the case. Although the magistrates reluctantly agreed, their clerk wrote a complaint to the DPP. The DPP took the matter up with the chief constable, who defended the decision by reference to judicial censure of prosecutions of 'trivia' in the Crown Courts. The DPP conveyed this argument back to the clerk, together with some pragmatic advice that he should try to avoid local 'exploitation' of the policy (presumably by keeping it quiet from defence solicitors!). It is notable that this case was, of course, referred to the DPP for a retrospective view. Another case of trivial shoplifting which arose in the same county was referred for a prospective opinion. In this case (17) another senior member of the DPP held firmly that such differentiation was wrong, and the case went for jury trial. This latter stance was reaffirmed in another sensitive theft case, Case 67.

A further troublesome difficulty with the prosecutor anticipating 'sympathy votes' is that the jury may engage in 'moral accounting' (Walker 1980: 124–25). This is most plainly seen where the defendants are policemen and the victims have criminal records. The 'social worth' of the respective parties may induce a 'greater good' approach which sets the morale of a generally applauded police force against a villain 'schooled in hard knocks'. If the prosecutor engages in 'second-guessing' the jury and wants to do so accurately, this encourages him to make social-worth assessments too. The DPP patently avoids the pitfall to which this avenue of possible social bias may lead. Reasoning with the police/villain example, he refrains from second-guessing (or at least disregards it) and prosecutes in the face of juror sympathies – often unsuccessfully.

Case 16 illustrates this side of the coin. It involved an assault by an off-duty woman police constable at a takeaway restaurant. At the end of a five-day trial there was an acquittal. What was remarkable, in view of the length of the trial, is that the jury took just one minute to reach its verdict. This phenomenon is also referred to in Chapter 3, where a jury scarcely concealed its yawns in respect of a similar case. Hence, 'the police do a difficult job well, so what if one of them occasionally oversteps the mark?'[23] The DPP is well aware of this line of thinking, yet often proceeds none the less. What this tends to show is that the 'impartial jury' referred to in the Attorney General's guidelines on prosecution may be a fragile legal construct, and therefore certain limitations need to be placed upon prosecution assumptions about jury sympathies. If these sympathies are judged to be too unreasonable – or 'illegitimate' – proceedings are taken in spite of the possible or likely outcome. But where should the line be drawn between acceptance of 'decent' jury sympathies and their rejection as untenable? Lay jurors may take a different view of what is termed reasonable from that of the professional lawyers – who may label juries as 'perverse' by adopting the narrow lawyer's views: namely that the evidence justified a conviction, and mitigation was for the judge, not the jury, to assess. The converse wider view accepts the validity of juries assessing mitigation: as a 'microcosm of society' they determine whether society has an interest in convicting and punishing defendants. The difficult choice between these viewpoints cannot be properly made, or even spelt out, unless they are considered separately: is a jury *likely* to convict on the basis of this evidence? and *should* a conviction be returned in the interests of society? The second question could more properly and effectively be discussed, it is submitted, within the public interest element of the decision whether to prosecute. This would accord with the DPP's theoretical model of decision-making. In practice these processes, which should ideally be kept distinct, are collapsed into one another.[24] 'Reasonable prospects' assessments are boosted in the early stage of the prosecution decision by covert anticipation of the influence of public interest considerations. These considerations are supposed to be contingent: if there is no 'reasonable prospect', the concept of public interest need not be invoked. Yet the evidence above shows that the social context of cases is considered in the decision on whether or not to prosecute. Some consideration of the social context is to be welcomed, but the present mix of legal, social, then more social considerations tends to fuse the different elements in prosecution decisions, so making them both impenetrable and, consequently, not exportable to the Crown Prosecutor.

An empirical critique of the Attorney General's *Criteria*

This section will provide a critique of the concept of public interest employed in the Attorney General's *Criteria*. The discussion will show, on the basis of the difficulties arising in the '85' sample, that the criteria are deficient when it comes to practical guidance for the prosecutor. The DPP attempts to meet this deficiency by extending the use of the concept of public interest. This extension of the Attorney General's criteria will also be discussed. The analysis will be divided into five sections:

(i) the impact of actual (objective) and attributed (perceived) case seriousness;
(ii) 'fair play' between defendants within a case;
(iii) achieving a balance of charges within a case (the need to bring the highest charge which the evidence will sustain, as against overloading the indictment);
(iv) the climate of public opinion; and
(v) means and ends – can prosecution decisions be justified in terms of outcome measures (the 'greater good'; the individual's 'needs') which result in the inconsistent handling of cases as between individuals or groups?)

ACTUAL AND ATTRIBUTED CASE SERIOUSNESS

Over 30 per cent of the prosecutions brought and conducted by the DPP are for murder. At first glance, these cases might readily be described as serious in terms of their intrinsic gravity. However, this is too simple, for it ignores the distinction between actual and attributed seriousness. Murders may be subdivided into two major groups: intentional and other 'professional' homicides committed in the pursuit of crime; and 'murders' among family members, friends, and acquaintances, which might more properly be characterized as 'domestic tragedies'. For the decision-maker, the cases in the first group are primarily straightforward, since there can be no dispute about their actual seriousness; to pursue them as murder requires little soul-searching. In contrast, the second group provides many examples of cases where the DPP is impelled in law to proceed on a murder charge even though it is recognized that a jury *may* regard the defendant sympathetically (even where there is no justification on the evidence) and convict only of manslaughter, if at all. Some of these are prosecutions launched despite a recognition that 'the environment is wrong' for a conviction on the charge preferred. The question arises: if there had not been a corpse to 'account' for, would a prosecution have been launched? Case 9 (see pp. 95–6) – the battered wife who was not prosecuted for shooting her husband – is one such example.

For the purposes of discussion it is necessary to distinguish between cases where seriousness cannot be disputed and those where it may be. The general principle that actual case seriousness outweighs the impact of the general public interest criteria (principally individual mitigation) is hard to fault. There surely must be an overriding public interest in ensuring that serious offenders are brought to justice. As the Attorney General's *Criteria* states, 'the graver the offence the less likelihood there will be that the public interest will allow of a disposal less than a prosecution'. In practice, how are cases resolved that are objectively serious when general public interest criteria suggest that there should be no proceedings? The DPP seems to exercise the discretion not to proceed in some such cases. For example, in Case 12, a 'glassing' in which the victim required eighteen stitches in his face, an expediency/public-cost decision was made not to proceed since it would have been necessary to extradite the defendant and bring back the witness from the other countries to which they had gone.

What is the situation in those cases where attributed seriousness may be subject to dispute, so that not everyone would agree with the public interest in prosecuting? Case 64, an infanticide, was a good example of such a situation although, as ultimately the accused pleaded guilty, there is no means of knowing whether a jury would have shared the DPP's view of seriousness or regarded her sympathetically. The accused was already receiving psychiatric treatment and the prosecution could not, therefore, readily be categorized as 'therapeutic' in the sense that the ends – compulsory treatment – would justify the means. Instead, the DPP took the view that unless the defence specified that her condition would worsen as a result of proceedings, the existence of her condition was not a sufficient mitigating factor to outweigh the public interest in proceeding in such a serious case. However, the case shows that individual outcome measures – in her case that a prosecution would have been personally damaging – are weighed in the decision to prosecute and may, although they did not in this particular case, override the general public interest.

Many of the 'police cases', that is offences allegedly committed by policemen, might readily be described as trivial at first sight, since the alleged behaviour often amounts to no more than common assault. However, against the background of a large number of cases where no proceedings are brought (either because of insufficient evidence or where the DPP takes the view that the case would be better dealt with by internal disciplinary action), some of this 'trivial' behaviour is prosecuted. This is partly because it is the *office* held by the suspects which constitutes the gravamen of the charge, and partly because where police officers are willing to give evidence against colleagues, the general interest in maintaining public confidence in the police means that their behaviour is regarded more seriously, even if juries do not always share such views.

Perceived case seriousness may also outweigh individually based mitigating factors, such as the presumption that very elderly offenders will not be prosecuted. In Case 26, a 76-year-old offender of previous good character was prosecuted under Section 1 of the Prevention of Corruption Act because his offence, allowing spectators into a sports stadium for cash without issuing tickets, was felt to have potentially serious consequences (i.e. dangerous overcrowding). Prosecuted along with him were three younger offenders. Two questions arise: had one of the offenders had special mitigating characteristics, rather than membership of a general category of offenders (i.e. elderly offenders), would this have outweighed the attributed seriousness of the behaviour? Secondly, would this in turn have resulted in the remaining three offenders escaping prosecution to ensure fair play between defendants? The questions are 'chicken and egg': was the elderly offender prosecuted solely in order to ensure an equitable approach with his co-defendants, or because attributed seriousness outweighed his age-based 'mitigation'?

In previous discussion it has been suggested that the interaction between 'reasonable prospects' and public interest occurs because the first tends also to constitute a part of the second. Do any other bases for such an interaction exist? A number of factors may contribute to the interaction. Thus, in Case 6, a man who stabbed and strangled his wife (non-fatally) whilst apparently suffering a temporary psychotic breakdown of a religious nature was deemed to be in need of treatment. Ironically, his mental illness contributed to the DPP's difficulty in establishing the necessary intent for attempted murder. Despite this a prosecution did take place in an attempt to ensure compulsory treatment for him although he had seemingly recovered.[25] The defendant pleaded guilty and received a hospital order under Section 60 of the Mental Health Act 1959. Can decision-makers really distinguish between the influences that a factor may have at the various stages of the sequential model of decision-making? Even if they can, those influences, although from a common source, may not all point in the same direction. The decision-perspective shifts and this may introduce dilemmas. How are such dilemmas resolved? Similarly, which perspective takes precedence? If the reasonable prospects assessment is positive, 'negative public interest criteria' may legitimately outweigh this. However, if the reasonable prospects assessment is negative should the public interest receive consideration? The discussion on 'fair play' in the next section supports the earlier conclusion that a public interest in proceedings can, in practice, outweigh a negative reasonable prospects assessment.

'FAIR PLAY' BETWEEN DEFENDANTS WITHIN A CASE

The presumption that individuals who have committed similar kinds of offences, with similar degrees of culpability, should be treated in similar ways is a strong one. In Case 67, a number of defendants were accused of trivial theft from their employer. When the case arrived at the DPP for advice about continuing proceedings, seven defendants had already pleaded guilty and been sentenced. Despite the trivial nature of the offences the DPP felt obliged to advise the continuation of the proceedings, partly because of the 'hands tied' argument where the process had been commenced, and partly because non-continuation would be unfair to those already prosecuted. Hence, the DPP's concept of fair play may outweigh the presumption that proceedings are not merited in the public interest where the offences are very trivial and likely to attract minimal sentences, as expounded in paragraph 9(2)(i) of the Attorney General's *Criteria*. In Case 15 the DPP withdrew proceedings against a police officer for corruption, following his serious suicide attempt, on the grounds that the interests of justice do not require that a man be 'hounded to his death' for this offence. It was canvassed within the DPP that since his co-defendant was less culpable, proceedings against him might be dropped as well, but ultimately the prosecution continued. It might be suggested that although it is fair to prosecute an individual to maintain consistency of proceedings between co-defendants despite individual mitigating factors (an intra-case basis), it is not 'fair' not to prosecute co-defendants where others have received the full benefit of an individually based mitigating factor (an inter-case basis). Alternatively, should the distinction more appropriately be drawn in terms of 'not straining the quality of mitigation'? Fair play concerns treating like with like: distinctions may legitimately be drawn between defendants where one represents a real suicide risk – a special mitigating factor – but not drawn on the basis of a general mitigating factor like age. It should also be noted that mitigating factors which, under the 'official DPP model' of public interest consideration, may permit proceedings not to be taken even where there is evidential sufficiency, do not all carry the same weight.

The remaining questions parallel some of the difficulties faced later in the criminal justice process: at appellate review of sentences. The Court of Appeal outwardly strives for parity of sentencing as between co-defendants. If the concept of fair play outweighs general mitigating factors, is the result that cases concerning a single defendant enable mitigating factors to have full effect, whereas in cases involving multiple defendants mitigating factors have limited applicability? This would result in more individuals being prosecuted than might have been, had their cases all been treated separately. Does the notion of 'fair play' between individuals involved in the same case lead to the prosecution of individuals with strong mitigating factors, even if the offence may be characterised as trivial and the evidence as weak, compared with individual defendants involved in separate cases where invoking fair play does not lead to such close scrutiny? Case 65, a comparatively 'non-serious' corruption case, involving three police officers and two civilians, suggests that this is so. The evidence was less than sound against some of the defendants, but the option of pursuing disciplinary proceedings against the police officers and not prosecuting the civilians was rejected on several grounds including the premise that this would be unfair to the police officers, who were in any case to be prosecuted because of the public interest in ensuring an 'honest police force'. Finally, if 'fair play' between co-defendants can outweigh individual mitigation and evidential shortcomings, why does the concept of fairness between defendants in separate cases (i.e. a consistent approach) not similarly outweigh those evidential and public interest factors that are invoked to justify not proceeding?

ACHIEVING A BALANCE OF CHARGES WITHIN THE CASE

Questions of balance in the charges brought are not confined to cases involving joint defendants. Even for single defendants, the question of what charges to place on the indictment may be problematic. The DPP takes the view that it is unfair to 'throw the book' at the defendant. This may be justified since, in the context of serious criminal activity, there is insufficient public interest in pursuing that offender for a less serious offence. There is authority to support this position (*Ambrose* (1973) 57 Cr. App. R. 538).

The DPP also takes the view that it is unfair to achieve by the 'back door' what cannot be achieved through the 'front door'. Thus, in Case 20, the DPP decided against prosecuting a man for indecently assaulting his daughter, despite evidential sufficiency, where the more serious and completely separate offence of incest (the reason why the case had been referred by the police) could not be pursued because of lack of evidence. This case also illustrates how fairness to the offender might produce a decision which the victim or the victim's family regard as unfair. Perhaps for this reason, the 'no back door' approach does not necessarily amount to a cardinal rule. In Case 21, where there was no 'reasonable prospect' of a conviction under the Public Order Act in respect of racist slogans, proceedings were taken for criminal damage in respect of the property on which they were daubed in paint.

Finally, seriousness may outweigh the concept of balance. In Case 82, involving a series of armed robberies, a charge with weak evidence was kept in the indictment in the hope that the co-accused might ultimately provide evidence against each other. The evidentially weak charge was considered too serious to drop. Thus, the evidentially more sound charge, which did reflect the gravamen of the offence, served to shift an additional charge into the prosecution bracket. Hence, the context of an offence can have a determining effect on whether proceedings are brought in relation to any specific charge.

THE CLIMATE OF PUBLIC OPINION

The DPP takes into account changes in public opinion when assessing the likelihood of a conviction. However, is this an assessment that a jury would not be prepared to convict because they would not accept that the behaviour amounted to a criminal offence (failure to meet the reasonable prospects test); or because the jury felt that the prosecution should not have been brought (that there was no public interest in proceeding)? In other words, what forms the basis for the DPP's attention to juries to assist his decision-making in future similar cases?

Raising this question serves to illustrate how the very vagueness of the concept 'public interest' permits latitude for justifying decisions that may not meet harder criteria, and creates a distraction from such shortcomings. Thus, in Case 19, a prosecution under the Public Order Act, it was suggested that 'the county of Clwyd is as good a venue as one might find... [there is] no colour problem and a tradition of racial tolerance'; such an environment was felt likely to affect the prospects of conviction since the defence line was anticipated to be whether racial hatred was stirred up in the minds of those reasonable jurors. The defendant was convicted. Similarly, in Case 23, which came into the DPP for advice as to whether certain election leaflets contravened the Public Order Act, it was suggested that 'the composition of the jury and atmosphere for *this* offence is vital... a Hampstead jury would probably convict; a Whitechapel jury would almost certainly acquit'. Another argument raised in support of a decision not to prosecute concerned the prediction that, at the time of an election, a jury would allow a Parliamentary candidate 'a little extra latitude in putting forward his views'.

Such arguments about the climate of public opinion, and the bases on which juries might or might not convict, not only provide a basis for considerable variation between individuals' assessments of the 'prospects' of a case but also help to 'confuse' or integrate 'reasonable prospects' assessments with the 'public interest' in proceedings. In relation to the reasonable prospects test the concept of the impartial jury is invoked; whereas in relation to the wider reasonable prospects approach, partial or impartial juror behaviour is used as a microcosm of wider public opinion, to test whether a jury would deem there to be 'merit' in proceedings. In the discussion of public interest in Chapter 1 an attempt was made to distinguish public opinion from public interest, a wider concept in which public opinion plays only a part. However, in practice, the terms seem to be used interchangeably.

MEANS AND ENDS

Whether the effects of a prosecution can be used to justify inconsistency in the process of prosecution is a question relevant to the assessment of both 'reasonable prospects' and 'public interest', since both concepts include outcome measures as relevant criteria. It should also be noted that these outcome measures are couched in terms of the consequences for the individual and for the wider public, in terms of the likelihood of further similar offending by other individuals.

The Attorney General's criteria acknowledge that the evidential standard may be raised where the cost of a prosecution may not merit proceedings, as in Case 69 where extradition would have been necessary before proceedings could be brought, or where the impact of an acquittal would be particularly unfortunate. The sample of 85 cases has illustrated how, in practice, the evidential standard may also be lowered where the consequences of failure to prosecute would be unfortunate (as in serious cases) or 'unfair'.

Arguments couched in terms of the general deterrent impact of prosecutions do not frequently appear in professional officers' minutes – perhaps wisely so when the paucity of research literature in this field is acknowledged! Yet, once such issues are raised, the argument can be invoked to support more than one course of action. Thus in Case 23 (the potentially racist election leaflets) it had been suggested that proceedings should not be taken because the 'risk of failure is too high' and there would be 'damage to the public interest by acquittal' (i.e. publicity for the organization). However, the counter-argument was that this risk of failure had to be weighed against the certainty that the impact of failing to proceed would have, namely, encouragement to the organization in question to repeat its behaviour, and a disincentive to future complainants. Where general deterrent arguments are invoked and hold sway, they can result in quite similar cases being treated differently. In Case 53, both the corruptor and the corruptee were to be prosecuted, with deterrence firmly in mind, and despite very weak evidence against the corruptor; the rationale involved a public interest argument that without 'corruptors' there would be no 'corruptees'. In Case 54, only the police corruptee was to be pursued (to conviction), with the corruptors – middle-class motorists – apparently receiving the benefit of their previous good characters.

Arguments couched in terms of the individual impact of proceedings may be seemingly more clear-cut; the 'therapeutic' nature of the prosecution in Cases 58 and 4, where the offenders were both experiencing psychiatric difficulties, was persuasive despite substantial individual mitigation. In Case 10, the defendant had murdered his grandmother on whom he doted. He had attempted suicide both before and after the murder. The prosecution was anxious to get him quickly into a special hospital for supervision and treatment, and the case proceeded apace.

The impact of a prosecution on an individual may be considered disproportionate even in comparatively serious cases where there may be strong general deterrent arguments for proceeding, as in Case 70, a concealment of birth by a Muslim girl. One of the views put forward by the police was that such offences were becoming more prevalent, and that the publicity resulting from a prosecution would have a general deterrent impact. The case was somewhat confused, in that it was not certain whether the baby had been born alive, but the Assistant Director nevertheless disagreed with the police view, noting that even the anticipated nominal sentence would be disproportionate, bearing in mind the suffering the girl had already endured. The minute read: 'the interests of justice do not require proceedings against her'. Thus, individual mitigation may occasionally outweigh both individual and general deterrence arguments.

Since both individual and general outcome measures seem to be invoked in discussions of both 'reasonable prospects' and public interest criteria, they provide a platform for considerable elasticity in decision-making. Earlier the dilemma was posed as to how professional officers cope with features of a case that may impel them in opposite directions at different stages of the prosecution process. The discussion of means and ends provides further support for the suggestion that public interest considerations will shift the case into the prosecution bracket, to allow it to become one where 'the court shall decide', so helping to avoid some of the 'unrealistic' decisions that would otherwise result from a rigorous application of 'reasonable prospects'.

CONCLUSIONS

The findings in this chapter illustrate two main points. First, that the prosecutor's 'reasonable prospects of conviction' assessments are vulnerable in that he is dependent upon the police for the quality of the information with which he assesses the case. He may also be constrained as to how the case proceeds where he does not enjoy a completely free hand: the police, counsel,[26] then later the courts, may also give effect to their views. These findings may be characterized as showing that 'reasonable prospects' are subject to situational variations. Secondly, even if these practical difficulties could be overcome, the reasonable prospects approach to prosecutions is theoretically flawed. There is insufficient separation of the social and legal elements which inform both the prosecutor's assessment of whether proceedings are likely to result in conviction (the reasonable prospects test) and whether this would be socially or morally desirable (the wider reasonable prospects approach). The elasticity in decision-making, which the legal and social interchange in both of these elements in the prosecution process allows, seems to produce endemic variations in the use of 'reasonable prospects' as articulated by the DPP.

Situational variations

There has been no specific discussion of 'no-prosecution' decisions. Such decisions are reached for some cases handled by the DPP – notably in the 'consents' category – but generally the nature of its caseload channels prosecutorial discretion into more detailed decisions about levels of charges; about determining a 'core/peripheral' balance between potential defendants and witnesses in cases involving numerous participants; and about decisions to ratify or repudiate charges already brought by the police or, more rarely, to bring charges for the first time. In all these respects, the influence of the police is, and will probably remain, extremely important and sometimes crucial. Once it is recognized that the prosecutor is most often confined to such relatively detailed decision-making, rather than straight yes/no questions on whether any proceedings should ensue, it can no longer be assumed that his scope for autonomy is unbridled. How could it be, given that he shares responsibility for prosecutions with the police, counsel, and the courts? This makes the prosecutor's 'reasonable prospects' assessments of charges and case-strategies vulnerable to their influences. But the way in which responsibility is shared is not the same for all cases and this can lead to situational variations in how reasonable prospects may be applied by the prosecutor.

This critique, that the prosecutor is constrained to depart from reasonable prospects 'in the real world', is borne out in its most accentuated form in consent cases, where the DPP exerts least influence. The prosecutor has only a brief period of control over those cases; he is always heavily reliant on the police for his information, and usually he relinquishes control of the case after endorsing or varying the police view. Yet consents should not be regarded as freakish or completely atypical of cases within the DPP's remit, but rather as an extreme example of the vulnerability of his exercise of prosecutorial discretion to the actions of others. In a similar vein, prosecutors may feel less constrained to adopt the course recommended by the police or counsel in those cases where they can draw on the views of experts to support alternative courses of action; and more constrained where they can only counter the views of the police with what are clearly their own personal value judgments. The demarcation between 'expertise' and 'value judgments' represents a rational refinement of the reasonable prospects approach, in that it attempts to achieve a balance between exercise of the lawyers' technical expertise in respect of the law and deference to the jury in respect of morals. The difficulty with such a neat analysis is that objective/technical is too simplistic a category: for example, legality and morality are typically fused in the cases of diminished responsibility. It is suggested that, to the extent that legality and morality overlap, such decisions should more properly lie under the heading of 'public interest'; and this points up the principal source of endemic variation in the reasonable prospects approach.

Endemic variations

There is insufficient separation between the social and legal factors which comprise the prosecution decision. This is not to argue that social factors should be ignored by the prosecutor, but that they should be clearly categorized – and kept apart from the legal factors – so that the two may be sequentially applied to avoid 'social reinterpretation' of legal issues (the textbooks suggest X, but any jury would incline to Y). This problematic tendency is compounded by a free-ranging use of public-interest arguments. Not only may public interest criteria be concealed within consideration of the evidential limb of reasonable prospects (a jury would, or should, infer an intent to kill in this case, but not that one . . .) but they may then act as 'trumps' to upset that socio-legal assessment. Although this may be 'fair', in that the concept of public interest may be invoked to counter an uncomfortable socio-legal assessment of jurors' views, it is confusing. Public interest may get two or even three 'bites at the cherry' of prosecution decisions – once, quite legitimately, after the evidential limb of reasonable prospects has been satisfied. Yet this may have been preceded by the prosecutor 'second-guessing' the jury's perception of the evidence. This is arguably legitimate but is confusing and runs the risk of 'double-counting'. Furthermore, the prosecutor may have anticipated this 'second-guess' even earlier, by reaching a pessimistic view of the evidence himself. Such an early pre-emption of what constitutes the public interest is not legitimate but may be difficult to discern. The revised prosecution test proposed in Chapter 1, which clearly separates the legal from the social aspects of prosecution decision-making, might be characterized as a step-by-step approach as against the present 'hop, skip, and a jump'.

NOTES

1 For a description of the organization of the Department, see p. 7, and pp. 64–5.

2 Section 1(5) of the Prosecution of Offences Act 1908: 'An Assistant Director of Public Prosecutions may do any act or thing which the Director of Public Prosecutions is required or authorised to do by or in pursuance of any Act of Parliament or otherwise.'

3 At the time of writing the Treasury Counsel system was being reorganized with a significant reduction of personnel.

4 Approximately 12 per cent of the incoming caseload is prosecuted (only 4 per cent if road traffic offences are excluded) with only 5 per cent of these being undertaken by the Director's staff.

5 At the time of publication, the Research Division had been renamed the Special Casework Division and a new division created, the Crown Prosecution Service Planning Division. This enabled the Department to cope with its new responsibilities for training and policy initiatives.

6 These divisions were selected by the Director and a Principal Assistant Director in consultation with all the Assistant Directors. The selection was not a random one: the researchers had a minimal part in the decision.

7 Cases under Section (g) and (h) require the Attorney General's consent to prosecution.

8 In theory, the reverse should be true; at least one prosecutor staunchly maintained that this was the approach he adopted.

9 Glanville Williams (1985: 120) similarly argues that there may be a justification for proceeding in cases where doubt exists about the accused's intent but where psychiatric treatment may be desirable.

10 Memo prepared for Director, for Criminal Law Revision Committee, November, 1982.

11 This is because Section 30(2) of the 1968 Act provided an exception to the normal rules on competence and compellability of spouses. Section 80 of the Police and Criminal Evidence Act 1984 has changed the position in respect of these 'normal rules'.

12 There were a number of cases in the sample (for example Cases 48 and 35) where members of the public using the toilets at the time of the offence had been motivated to contact the police.

13 In 90 per cent of the 1981 sample, both parties were prosecuted where consent was given and one was a party under 21.

14 This is not to imply that the evidence is in any sense insufficient, for it is logical that in guilty pleas there is likely to be at least *prima facie* evidence, merely that it is not tested.

15 The DPP action here might be contrasted with Case 20 in the '85' sample where incest proceedings were not brought because there was no corroboration.

16 See also Williams 1985.

17 Even in this case only one of the accused had made a statement under caution and that did not amount to an admission of the offence but an apology; thus, the evidence might have been successfully contested had proceedings been brought.

18 In keeping with the judicial approach to sentencing: once an option has been tried and failed it may be considered inappropriate for that offender (Ashworth *et al.* 1984).

19 The police report asserted, 'W is a potentially dangerous person, both to himself and young children ... well on the way to becoming homosexually promiscuous ... desperately in need of medical treatment to curb his homosexual tendencies.'

20 Section 30(4) Criminal Law Revision Committee memo: 'Normally these cases are LTP [left to the police], and we do not get much feedback on the outcome.'

21 The DPP can, of course, suggest different charges: they can ask for more evidence and in some cases, notably frauds, cases will reach the DPP long before the investigations are complete. None the less, in some cases prosecutors may lack the imagination or confidence to seek such alternative routes; in others there may be no other way to handle the case.

22 The observation of Judge Ruben in Case 63 was: 'The Juggernaut got under way and nobody was prepared to stop it.'

23 See also Williams (1985: 116–17) on police cases.

24 See the exposition of the prosecution decision in the public interest given by the former Attorney General, Sam Silkin, in Chapter 5.

25 In cases of real difficulty arising from the defendant's mental state, Section 1 of the Criminal Procedure (Insanity) Act 1964 is available. This enables a verdict of not guilty by reason of insanity to be returned. The defendant is then liable to be detained in hospital during Her Majesty's pleasure.

26 The potentially influential role of counsel is only touched on in this chapter: Chapter 3 demonstrates that it is of considerable importance.

CHAPTER 3
THE PROCESS OF PROSECUTION

INTRODUCTION

This chapter is based on eighteen cases, which were followed up in-depth from the DPP's decision to bring a prosecution, right through to trial on indictment. It aims to demonstrate how the initial assessment that a case had a 'reasonable prospect of conviction' was or was not borne out by the facts. It thus provides a basis for evaluating the predictions of experienced prosecutors at the DPP who adopt the reasonable-prospects test.

Assessing the 'correctness' of the prosecutor's reasonable prospects predictions solely in terms of the *outcome* of this sample of eighteen cases would produce a somewhat bleak picture of his abilities. Of the twenty-six defendants involved,[1] ten were found guilty as charged – a 38 per cent 'success' rate; nine were completely acquitted – a 35 per cent 'failure' rate. Of the remaining seven, four were convicted of lesser charges, and three convicted of only very minor offences.

How might this unexpectedly low 'success' rate be explained? A partial answer may lie in the fact that the eighteen cases might generally be characterized as 'high class', in that they principally concerned either serious crimes, professional offenders, or the peculiar category of prosecutions of police officers.[2] In these serious cases there may be a tendency for the prosecutor to proceed 'in the public interest' even when the sufficiency of the evidence does not meet the high standard required by the reasonable prospects test.[3] An additional explanation is that the cases chosen were selected because they were problematic – some involved old-style committals (which are likely to be the more 'marginal' cases) and others had inherent evidential difficulties. It is thus not surprising that the retrospective analysis of comparable DPP cases involving 235 defendants tried at the Central Criminal Court (see Chapter 2) found 'better' success rates; 140 defendants were found guilty as charged (60 per cent) with a further 48 guilty of lesser offences (making 80 per cent overall).[4]

However, it will be maintained in this chapter that the

effectiveness of the reasonable prospects test cannot and should not be assessed in terms of the outcome of cases. It is therefore inappropriate to refer crudely to 'success rates': for to use outcome as the criterion of success implies that prosecutors can predict the nature and shape of the case as it will appear to the jury and thus its verdict. This is totally unrealistic. Furthermore, rates of conviction and acquittals by a jury are in themselves so difficult to interpret that they cannot be taken as an index of prosecutorial efficiency. Cases which ought to succeed may fail and vice versa, so that just looking at the result of a case is too crude a way of determining whether it was placed on a sound footing at the beginning. For this reason the method of detailed examination of a small number of cases was preferred, both to a major statistical study of case outcomes and to a numerically larger, but arguably more superficial observational study. By this means, it was possible to study the *process* of prosecution, to chart how and why cases change between the decision to prosecute and the decision to convict or acquit. Although aspects of each case are considered in this chapter in isolation at the various stages of their progress, it should be stressed that there can be no certainty that the relevant decision-makers similarly viewed the cases in this way. In this light, the chapter should be regarded as primarily descriptive, and not as the authoritative account of why cases turned out as they did.

Several grounds for this stance emerge from the in-depth study. Although the DPP is an 'independent' prosecutor, he has, like other prosecutors, only limited opportunities to exercise discretion, both before and after the decision to proceed is made. The prosecutor applies the reasonable prospects test to information provided by the police; it is they who determine the quality of the initial script on which the DPP goes to work. The nature of the investigatorial processes the police adopt, the decisions they make about whom to charge and whether to take witness statements, and the manner of their statement-taking can all significantly tie the prosecutor's hands.

The exercise of discretion within the DPP as to whether to proceed and on what basis also emerges as a role constrained by the evidence of victims, witnesses, and experts. On paper witnesses may provide a seemingly firm foundation for a prosecution. At court and under cross-examination they may fail to 'come up to proof' or have their credibility seriously impugned. The need to satisfy the multiple criteria of 'legal, decent, honest, and truthful' makes witnesses extremely vulnerable. Thus, an apparently straightforward case on paper may become significantly less convincing as the evidence emerges in court.

Furthermore, as the case proceeds through to trial and its conduct becomes a matter for counsel and the court, the effect of the 'independent' prosecutor's decisions may be further undermined. The delicate balance which the DPP has struck between charges and defendants may be disturbed by the decisions of magistrates at committal, counsel in framing the indictment, and the judge in severing indictments, so that a case adjudged by the prosecutor to pass the reasonable prospects test may lose a vital element at any of the subsequent decision-making stages.

The in-depth study also illustrates the inherent imbalance in the criminal justice process. During the early stages – investigation and pre-trial procedures – the prosecution enjoys some advantage over the defence both in terms of resources and the psychological advantages inherent in the interrogation of suspects. But this situation is reversed in the later trial stages of the adversary process – a process not necessarily designed to establish the truth, but more to ensure 'fair play'. The implications of this for the 'reasonable prospects' assessment are that the DPP may be seen as taking its decisions on the case at its strongest, 'on the papers'. From that point onwards the case may be gradually eroded as evidence and witnesses are challenged by the defence. The prosecution's advantages at the early stages of the criminal process may help it to satisfy the high standard of evidence demanded by the reasonable prospects test, but the defence rightly has the advantage in attempting to satisfy the comparatively low standard of proof (creating, for most cases, a 'reasonable doubt') necessary to achieve an acquittal.

In addition to this potential for erosion, there is little that a prosecutor can do to rectify damage done to the case or to put it back on course when his strategy proves unsuccessful in the early stages. Compared with the defence, prosecutors are but eunuchs in the ensuing trial process. Not only are the hurdles of committal and directed acquittals the finishing point for some defendants, but even where only certain charges fall, their overall impact on the case may be damaging. If the prosecutor changes strategy in mid-stream, he risks ridicule from the defence and appears confused in the eyes of the jury. Thus, the prosecution has to pitch the case correctly from the outset.

Finally, the in-depth approach is used to examine the relationship of the prosecutor to the jury: when and why should juries be permitted to consider cases where the prosecution may no longer believe that the case has 'a reasonable prospect of conviction'? How and why do juries return convictions in these cases? The sample of cases suggests that the answer may lie in the mismatch between the way juries interpret and apply the 'beyond reasonable doubt' standard, and formal legal assumptions about what it should amount to. Objectively the prosecution may not have eliminated all doubt, but subjectively the jury may for various reasons feel able to tolerate degrees of uncertainty.

The prosecutor faces multiple difficulties in making accurate 'reasonable prospects' predictions. He is faced with a series of predictive variables which he should, could, might, may, could probably, could possibly, and couldn't possibly get right. His inability to identify which issues may crystallize at trial will only be compounded by his inability to predict whether and how juries will take account of these issues. What follows is a detailed scrutiny of the prosecutor's difficulties and of what happens to criminal cases between the initial decision to prosecute and their outcome at trial. Emphasis is placed on how cases may be subject to change, in what particular ways, who is influential with regard to alterations, and why. Thus, this chapter assesses the 'reasonable prospect of conviction' test not in terms of outcome measures, but in terms of the *process* of prosecution and the impact it has upon that process.

I PRE-TRIAL

The police

The investigation and interrogation techniques of the police play 'a vital part in the criminal detection process' (Irving 1980: 152). They also provide the basis of information on which the DPP's decisions as to whether and how to proceed with a case are made. Ultimately, the way in which the police fulfil their role as primary gatherers of evidence will affect the shape and outcome of the prosecution case. How this occurs, and the extent to which the interest of the police in the broader aims of criminal detection (Steer 1980) conflicts with the DPP's interest in successful prosecutions, will be explored in this section.

In illustrating how the approach of the police affects the prosecution's case some points of caution should be stressed. First, from the perspective of the police, it is debatable whether a group of selected contested cases should form the backdrop against which police procedures are evaluated; the police may prefer to draw attention to rates of guilty pleas and confessions.[5] Secondly, the discussion is limited to those cases in which it was decided to prosecute; Chapter 2 touches on the implications of policing procedures for decisions not to prosecute. Third, this section on policing techniques is based on retrospective knowledge, since the earliest the cases were drawn into the sample was the stage at which they arrived at the DPP; the findings are therefore necessarily tentative. Fourth, the assumption is made that the resources the police have, and the considerable psychological advantages they enjoy in comparison with suspects (Irving and Hilgendorf 1980), make it likely that at the early stages the prosecution net will be cast too widely rather than too narrowly; individuals may risk being wrongly suspected. Thus any criticism of the police would tend to be in terms of their being too assiduous. Finally, although the *Judges' Rules* (Home Office 1964)[6] make it clear that interrogations should be managed in such a way that resulting statements are voluntary, in practice there is considerable divergence between these rules and, first, the conditions the courts are prepared to tolerate before statements become inadmissible, and, secondly, the degrees of coercion actually experienced by suspects (Irving and Hilgendorf 1980: 11–12).

INVESTIGATING CRIMES

The main finding in respect of investigations is the great difficulty experienced by the police in penetrating the social milieux in which some of the alleged offences took place. In 10 of the 18 cases the characteristics of the witnesses or the circumstances in which the alleged offences took place were not conducive to establishing clearly what happened. Of the alleged offences some occurred among vagrants, some among heroin users, some in a West Indian shebeen, and some in an illegal gambling den frequented by Chinese and Vietnamese. The associated aura of illegality not only hindered the investigations, but also made it difficult for the prosecutor at the trial effectively to convey the 'flavour' of the circumstances in which the offence took place to predominantly white jurors of good character. This added to the sense of unreality which frequently pervades criminal trials.

A similar problem can also arise in the investigation of offences allegedly committed by police officers – four in this sample. There is a greater preparedness to prosecute where other officers are willing to make full statements for the prosecution. However, in those circumstances where officers disapprove of the behaviour of colleagues, but not to the extent of labelling it 'criminal', it may be extremely difficult for sufficient evidence to be collected to justify a prosecution, let alone to enable one to succeed. In this respect, the police are clearly responsible for 'policing' their colleagues; the standards they apply do not necessarily match those with which the public are expected to comply (Ericson 1985). Moreover, as suspects police officers may be in the advantageous position of being able to hamper the progress of an investigation (Case 6). Very few of the cases, from the investigatorial perspective, could thus be described as unproblematic. Problems at the investigation stage will be writ large at trial, where difficulties of establishing the 'truth' beyond reasonable doubt may be insuperable if the investigation has been less than perfect.

INTERROGATION AND STATEMENT-TAKING

These eighteen cases illustrated how the success of the prosecution can be influenced by three interrelated aspects of police practice and decision-making: (i) how much evidence and of what type to gather; (ii) how to gather the evidence; and (iii) whom to charge and with what offence(s).

In relation to the quantity and type of evidence to be gathered, a tendency on the part of the police to collect as much evidence as possible, so as to 'make absolutely sure', may handicap the prosecutor in certain circumstances. In Case 14, the police questioned the accused so persistently that he gave three versions of the events surrounding the fatal injection of heroin into the victim. At trial, all three versions emerged, enabling the defence to exploit the differences by adopting the 'tactics of confusion'.[7] If the questioning had stopped after the accused had given the second version and before he confessed to injecting the victim, there would have been more scope for the prosecution to charge him jointly with another person. In the event, the other party was used as a prosecution witness, but proved unhelpful to the prosecution case. This illustrates the interrelationship of the difficulties of collecting evidence with problems concerning whom to charge.

The irony was that the prosecution rested their case largely on the basis of the second interview with the accused; had the police been more aware of the technical legal niceties of the charges brought, they might well have avoided the pitfalls of persistent questioning. Similarly, in Cases 2 and 10 the police laid charges for which there was quantitatively and/or qualitatively insufficient evidence of the precise *mens rea* required for those charges;[8] failure to appreciate the subtleties of proving such charges may have caused them to overcharge – placing the DPP in a position that could not be rectified.

In respect of whom to charge, those cases which involve several persons who are more or less directly implicated in the alleged offence often require an important decision to be taken at a relatively early stage – namely, whom to charge, and whom to use as witnesses. It may prove tactically wiser to treat as a witness, rather than as a suspect, someone who was only peripherally involved. If he is cautioned, the possibility of prosecution is brought to his mind and he may not speak freely; whereas as a witness he may speak more fully and give assistance to the police.

Although there is a strong argument that the police should seek, and be provided with, early legal advice in such cases, it is also true that lawyers are not always able to judge the tactical situation as well as the police. In Case 15, a homicide, the police took the view that two of the persons involved should not be charged with the relatively minor offences they appeared to have committed. The DPP differed, and proceedings were brought on the basis of this advice against these two minor participants. When they were subsequently asked to give evidence for the prosecution against the major defendant who had been charged with the murder, they declined to co-operate. He was subsequently acquitted of the murder. The police believed that, had the two minor participants been called to give evidence, the principal defendant would have been in greater difficulty regarding his defence of self-defence. Thus the outcome might have been different if the two minor defendants had not been charged.

These tactical decisions are difficult. Neither the police nor the DPP will necessarily always be right. They are decisions which may determine whether a case will succeed. That the police's role comes before the prosecutor's in the sequence of decision-making means that their decisions can tie the prosecutor to proceed along a particular course. For example, the DPP's freedom to *drop* charges in serious cases is somewhat restricted (particularly where the *prima facie* standard is met, but there is not sufficient evidence to satisfy the reasonable prospects test).[9] Whether a case comes into the DPP ready charged, and if so at what level, may significantly influence decisions as to the future course of a prosecution. In this sense, the prosecutor applying the reasonable prospects test intervenes in a pre-existing context, the boundaries of which have been defined by the police. If the prosecutor is not to be handicapped in the subsequent prosecution, he needs to be brought in at the stage at which the police make these crucial decisions.

Methods of interrogation have been the subject of much academic discussion and public debate (Royal Commission on Criminal Procedure Report 1981: paras 4.68–4.135). Police representatives have often said that the existing judges' rules are unduly restrictive. Any departure by the police from the rules gives the defence the opportunity to challenge the admissibility of the evidence thereby obtained, on the grounds either that it was given involuntarily or simply that the judges' rules were breached. In the heroin case (14) discussed above, the police had obtained some of the defendant's admissions by the dubious means of placing the two suspects together in a cell in the hope that they would 'sort it out between them'; this only emerged at trial and was undoubtedly damaging to the prosecution. There was an acquittal. Although the prosecutor may be able to read between the lines and ascertain that confessions might be challenged at trial, greater willingness by the police to 'come clean', and highlight such potential areas of difficulty, would undoubtedly be helpful to the prosecutor.[10]

It is also the case that the judges' rules conflict with the demands implied by the reasonable prospects test. Where officers interpret the rules strictly they may actually hinder the prosecutor in his role, by failing to gather sufficient evidence. This is because Rule 3 in combination with principle (d) of the rules requires that the police should cease questioning when they believe they have sufficient evidence to bring a charge, i.e. when they have satisfied the *prima facie* standard. If, realizing this dilemma, the police press on with their questioning, in order to provide the prosecutor with sufficient information to exercise his 'reasonable prospects' discretion, answers thus obtained risk being excluded from the trial on the grounds that the rules have been breached. Thus, the efforts of the police to bring a defendant to court may jeopardize the prospects of a conviction. Furthermore, the requirements of the prosecutor may differ from the priorities of the police. The prosecutor may be said to require not merely reliable evidence on key elements of the case but also an absence of flaws which the defence might use as a basis for attack, such as departures from the law or the rules on the questioning of suspects, repeated questioning which creates a multiplicity of accounts of the alleged offence, and, of course, the charging of someone who would have been better regarded as a witness. In contrast, the police do not necessarily share the same priorities and are not entirely dependent on the prosecutor to determine whether they are policing effectively. 'Putting a defendant in court' may sometimes be regarded by the police as an independent and sufficient goal. For example, a police officer, having watched a co-defendant in Case 1 'get off' at committal, said that this amounted to 'a result', since that individual had been in custody for months awaiting committal. Similarly, the predominance of guilty pleas and the difficulty faced by a defendant with previous convictions who wishes to attack police evidence (Section 1(f) (ii), Criminal Evidence Act 1898: see *Mirfield* [1984], *Criminal Law Review*: 66–7) may be incentives for the police to 'cut corners': in the knowledge that the usual guilty plea will mean that the conduct of the interrogation is not closely scrutinized. If tape recording and the new code for the questioning of suspects[11] have a regulating effect on police interrogation practices, this in itself might improve the prospects of the prosecution in major trials of the kind studied here.[12]

Finally, the impact that police procedures can have on the course of a prosecution necessitates close collaboration between the police and the prosecutor. This should begin at the earliest stages and preferably before any charge is laid. Such collaboration is particularly important if the recommendation in the White Paper, *An Independent Prosecution Service for England and Wales*, that the police should retain the decision to charge, becomes law.

But the tensions between the police and the prosecutor described in this section may mean that such attempts to ensure closer and more effective collaboration between the prosecutor and the police will have unintended consequences.[13] Greater awareness of those factors that influence the prosecutor's decision, experience of the trial process with its *rare* exclusion of evidence following breaches of the judges' rules, and knowledge of the sometimes 'lottery-like' nature of jury decisions, may all contribute to scepticism by the police about the prosecutor's role under reasonable prospects.

Departmental decision-making

The discussion of decision-making within the DPP in relation to this sample of eighteen cases will illustrate that real constraints exist in respect of serious cases, both as to *whether* to prosecute and as to *how* to prosecute. The decision-making focused principally on *how* to prosecute, since public interest factors associated with the seriousness of these cases largely made prosecution inevitable. Thus, the sequential model (evidential sufficiency first, public interest second) was reversed.

Decisions not to prosecute in serious cases most commonly occur where the quantum of evidence is not sufficient to sustain a *prima facie* case. For example, in Case 17 one of the three potential defendants involved in an incident during which an unarmed civilian was shot had an irrebuttable justification of self-defence; no proceedings were taken against him. Similarly, early appraisals of insufficiency of evidence in Cases 3 and 15 would have resulted in decisions not to proceed had not the subsequent emergence of further evidence pushed the quantum of evidence beyond *prima facie*. Although decisions not to prosecute on grounds of public interest do occur in serious cases (see for example Case 9 in Chapter 2 – the husband/wife attempted murder) public interest factors may have a greater impact on the manner in which the quantum of evidence is assessed in serious cases than in less serious cases. As Chapter 2 showed, assessing evidential sufficiency under the reasonable prospects test is an inherently subjective task. In marginal cases, namely those where evidence fulfils the *prima facie* test but falls short of the reasonable prospects test, there appears to be an interaction between public interest and evidential sufficiency, so that the former factor can serve to 'drag up' a case that evidentially may not satisfy a rigorous application of the reasonable prospects test. This may occur either consciously, so that the prosecutor gives greater weight to considerations of evidential sufficiency, or unconsciously, so that his subjective perception of the weight of the evidence is altered. Either way, cases that are weak in terms of reasonable prospects may none the less proceed to trial.

WHETHER TO PROSECUTE

Only one case in the sample could be categorized as trivial (Case 8) in respect of the charges brought (common assault); but the circumstances – a police officer allegedly assaulting a skinhead woman – significantly increased the seriousness with which the case was viewed. Although the professional officer at the DPP felt that the case should most realistically be dealt with through police discipline procedures, the view was ultimately taken that since two other police officers were prepared to give evidence against the accused (which is unusual in alleged police assault cases), it was arguably in the public interest to prosecute. The accused was subsequently acquitted. Two interpretations are offered. First, the public interest factor may have 'dragged up' what was recognized to be an evidentially problematic case, which failed when a more stringent criterion, beyond reasonable doubt, was applied. Alternatively, the jury took a different view of where the 'true' public interest lay. They may have reacted to the triviality of the case and acquitted on the grounds that policing is a difficult enough job, without such prosecutions being launched (see p. 99, pp. 179–80 on juries).

As has been made plain in Chapter 2, the public interest can also prevent a prosecution where the reasonable prospects test is satisfied. In Case 11 the DPP maintained, as a matter of principle, that where the more serious and more appropriate charge of unlawful sexual intercourse was time-barred by statute,[14] they would not agree to a charge on the lesser offence of indecent assault. Hence, there was to be no 'back-door' prosecution. This approach was, however, subsequently undermined when a further statement from the victim clearly alleged a series of rapes: the DPP then had little choice but to proceed on that basis. This provides an example of the 'facts' constraining the 'how' element of the prosecution: the DPP were not 100 per cent sure that the victim was telling the whole truth, but if they were to prosecute at all, it had to be on the basis of charges that could be substantiated by the evidence which they anticipated she would give. This may seem all too obvious. But it illustrates the point that it is the minutiae of evidence given by 'legally naïve' witnesses which shifts the grounds for a prosecution from one legal category to another. Witnesses are not necessarily to know the particular legal significance of what it is they assert (and may therefore subsequently fail to deliver that form of words in their evidence at trial), but the content of their statements may none the less tie the prosecutor's hands, and determine that a particular legal course be adopted. Similarly, where the police have obtained a confession that will not clearly be inadmissible, both the 'whether' and the 'how' elements of the prosecutorial decision may be constrained. Charges will need to reflect, as a minimum, that to which the defendant has confessed.

Since many of the cases involved difficult or marginal decisions it was not unusual for them to come under the purview of a range of decision-makers, from the most junior professional officer to the more senior members of the DPP, and often to be given early consideration by counsel too. For example, in Case 3, which concerned a man whose wife had apparently drowned in the bath, the case came into the DPP charged under Section 47 of the Offences against the Person Act of 1861 and under Section 2 of the Suicide Act. The possibility of changing the charges to either murder or manslaughter was raised and then rejected by the professional officer. Despite the Assistant Director's (AD) view that there was sufficient evidence to justify both the existing charges, the Principal Assistant Director (PAD) took the view that there was only enough to justify the assault charge; the case was committed on that basis. A third post-mortem then provided evidence more consistent with a homicidal drowning. According to the professional officer the evidence then reached 'the edge of a sound case'. He therefore advised a murder charge, supported by the AD, in the 'public interest'. Two PADs disagreed with this view but were prepared to send the case to counsel. He advised that there was 'at least a 50 per cent chance of conviction'; meanwhile, the pathologist's opinion that there was evidence of a homicidal drowning strengthened further. The use of the DPP's terminology by counsel seemed to add to the impact of his opinion, for the PAD decided that the case would have to go to court on the basis of a murder charge. The case was recommitted. A conviction on the charge of murder resulted. The case illustrates how a preliminary decision not to prosecute is rightly vulnerable to the emergence of further evidence, and highlights the subjectivity of the reasonable prospects of conviction test where different decision-makers weigh the same evidence. It also shows that such a test is vulnerable to influence by 'outsiders' (the opinion came from non-Treasury Counsel) who may assess the evidence in terms of *their* understanding of the DPP's test. The DPP may find counsel's conclusions difficult to resist, particularly in the light of counsel's greater experience of the trial process. Thus, if the reasonable prospects test is to be extended successfully, it is essential that both the police (see pp. 45–50, 116–21, and 50–2) and counsel should be informed of, and adhere to, its philosophy.

That the decisions in this sample of eighteen cases were all decisions in favour of prosecuting may be said to reflect three factors. The first two – the seriousness of the cases and the malleability of the reasonable prospects test – have already been discussed. The third factor is the Attorney General's *Criteria for Prosecution*. These recommend that where there is a 'genuine point of balance' a case should be put to the court. This point of balance (or 'uncertainty') seems to be reached at a lower standard of evidence in more serious cases. To resolve evidential doubts in serious cases by a decision not to proceed would be an onerous responsibility for the prosecutor because of the finality of the decision.[15] Yet the decision to 'put it to the court' is not necessarily an end to the prosecutor's responsibility, as Case 19 illustrates. The professional officer there remarked of witness G in his note: 'G will have to be treated with considerable caution.... It is a weak murder case, but G's evidence must be a matter for the jury.... I think it will end up as manslaughter, but I feel we should proceed on this basis for murder.' In making this assessment he reiterated the police officers' doubts about the credibility of the witness. At trial, counsel, having had the opportunity to assess the witness live, did not hold him out to the jury as a 'witness of truth'. Although the DPP had reserved its position (or alternatively failed to exercise a reasonable prospects judgment at an early stage) in relation to the application of the 'quality' element of its test, counsel more clearly pre-empted the jury by advancing his own conclusion about the witness's reliability. Thus where the DPP abides by the Attorney General's criteria, it does not necessarily mean that the court decides the case: it may be counsel who takes on the responsibility of the prosecutorial role. If the prosecutor believes that he can retain control over the case through counsel even once it gets to court, there may be less incentive for him to make an irrevocable decision not to prosecute at an early stage. Hence, a momentum towards prosecution in these serious cases may be more apparent than in less serious cases.

HOW TO PROSECUTE

In much the same way, the flexibility the prosecutor enjoys in serious cases as to *how* to proceed may be more apparent than real. First, the overall shape of the case as it appears to the prosecutor may affect its perceived viability. In Case 4, where there were several charges of rape and associated offences, speculation within the DPP concerned not the individual credibility of any specific witness, but concentrated on whether the jury would recognize that a series of victims making similar allegations could not all be telling lies. Although the assumption was made that the jury would share this quantitative assessment (and thus the reasonable prospects test would be satisfied), the basis for this assessment was undermined when the judge decided to sever the indictment. The cases had to be tried separately, and the result was that some of them were weakened below 'reasonable prospects' because there could no longer be any qualitative corroborative effect from the series of similar offences. Should the DPP have anticipated severance? Had they done so they might not have proceeded in some of the cases; as it was, the accused were convicted or pleaded guilty to the majority of the charges, despite the weakened evidence on some of them.

Secondly, the decision as to how to proceed may also be constrained by the views of the police or counsel. In Case 5, the investigating police officer's strongly expressed view (supported by the professional officer) that the case should proceed against five defendants, rather than two of them as advised by the AD and counsel, resulted in the case being taken at committal on this basis. Ultimately, at trial, the case was only placed on a murder footing against the two defendants; but it is still noteworthy that the police view held sway at the early stages. Similarly, the view of counsel in Case 6 led to the severance of charges by the prosecution. Although the DPP had believed that the stronger evidence on one charge would 'drag up' the weaker charge, counsel predicted that the opposite 'draw down' effect would occur. His view prevailed.

Not infrequently the DPP may be constrained within an approach with which it is not entirely happy. An example of this occurred in Case 10 – a fatal stabbing by a daughter of her father – where the AD noted: 'I do not envisage a conviction for murder but there is certainly an issue for the jury.' Similarly, in Case 2, which came into the DPP charged as attempted murder, the professional officer believed that 'ultimately the jury may only convict on the S.18'; that is Section 18 of the Offences against the Person Act 1861 – proof of which does not require the prosecution to establish an intent to kill (see Chapter 2, pp. 67–8). The AD also foresaw the possibility of an acquittal since 'a readiness to kill to effect his escape is not the same as an intent to kill'. Treasury Counsel subsequently agreed that the decision to charge attempted murder had been based on the public interest (the accused shot a police officer at close range), not on the prosecution's ability to substantiate the charge beyond reasonable doubt. There was a directed acquittal on the attempted murder charge.

This case may be used to illustrate a further proposition; namely, that although the 'how' of prosecutorial decision-making may be constrained, the impact of prosecutors' decisions extends considerably beyond their role of 'gatekeepers'. In Chapter 2 the prosecutor was identified as an influential decision-maker in resolving questions concerning the acceptability of pleas of diminished responsibility. Such pleas (rather than a jury verdict of diminished responsibility) are more likely to result in hospital disposals than imprisonment. Similarly, the prosecutor's decisions on whether to accept pleas inextricably link him with the sentencing process. In deciding what charges to pursue the prosecutor places the offender's behaviour within a particular context by labelling it, as in Case 2, 'attempted murder'. Even where legally the labels may be subsequently rejected, the colouring that the case receives may stick. In much the same way that directed acquittals may shake the jury's confidence in the overall case, can the construction of the prosecution's case influence the judge's view on sentencing?[16]

The facts in some cases may also create difficulties for the prosecution if there is no suitable charge to reflect the gravamen of the behaviour under consideration. Despite evidential sufficiency, there may be a problem of presenting the evidence to the jury in a form that fits a label and produces a good legal/moral fit. For example, Case 13 involved a bizarre series of events including, as alleged by the prosecution, an attempt by one of the defendants to make a serious assault on his friend during the course of an apparent robbery on him by a third party. The two accused, although jointly charged, had committed the offences with two different states of mind (A only to rob, B to commit assault and possibly murder). The charges brought by the police, aggravated burglary against both defendants, were regarded as 'ill-founded', but even within the DPP there was considerable debate as to what were the appropriate charges, particularly against defendant B. Ultimately, a charge was brought under Section 21 the Offences against the Person Act 1861 of attempting to choke, suffocate, or strangle with intent to cause grievous bodily harm. This little-used section did not meet with either the approval of the judge, who commented that the prosecution had misinterpreted the spirit of the Act, or the agreement of the jury, who acquitted on this charge and convicted on a charge of assault occasioning actual bodily harm. Since an attempted murder charge had been given serious consideration by the DPP, this outcome highlighted the technical difficulties of presenting a case where human behaviour – although undoubtedly evil in intent – does not neatly transgress a particular statutory provision.[17]

Finally, whether and how a prosecution is launched may be affected by the 'forward-looking' approach which the reasonable prospects test necessarily entails – attempting to anticipate likely lines of defence and rectifying any flaws.[18] For example, in Case 15, the AD and the professional officer both originally took the view that the case should not proceed on the existing murder charge, since the explanation of self-defence given by the accused was not capable of being rebutted by the prosecution beyond reasonable doubt.[19] This case also illustrates the use of a standard higher than reasonable prospects in specific cases.

In Case 1, which initially involved two defendants charged with murder, the DPP's view was that there was an arguable case for retaining the murder charge against both defendants (raising some doubt as to whether the DPP would have charged murder if the police had not already done so). Again, the DPP failed to achieve the committal of one of the co-accused. It was therefore impossible for the jury to share the prosecutor's initial understanding of the case since they were faced with not two defendants, but only one. The decision as to how to proceed may thus be upset between the decision to proceed and the case coming to trial. The result is that the case presented to the jury 'looks' quite different to that originally considered as meriting prosecution.

This small sample shows that, in serious cases, the DPP rarely exercises his power to drop charges altogether. More frequently, charges will be altered. But, even given this, it is unusual for the DPP in serious cases to adopt a prosecutorial course which is greatly at variance with that preferred by the police. This apparent reluctance of the DPP's officers to exercise their discretionary powers is attributed principally to the seriousness of these cases, in that public-interest considerations determined not only that a prosecution would ensue, but also the basis on which this would occur. Thus, cases proceed even when the evidence may not stand up to a rigorous application of the reasonable prospects test. This also helps to explain why there were so many acquittals in the sample; namely, that although public interest considerations may override evidential questions on the decision to prosecute, the persistence of any concomitant evidential inadequacies will not necessarily be overcome at trial.

Committals

Seven of the cases in the sample went to trial after full ('old-style') committals. The fact that this proportion is untypically high is due to the fact that 'difficult' cases were selected for study.[20] Three of the committals may be largely ignored.[21] The remaining committals arose out of two murder and two rape cases. In these four cases the common theme underlying the reason for committal was to enable the strength of the evidence to be tested. Since one of the central difficulties for the prosecutor arises out of his ignorance of how credible and persuasive his witnesses will be, some insight may be gained into this if they are called at committal. Where this causes the prosecutor to reappraise his case, persuading him that an acquittal is the likely outcome, a reapplication of the reasonable prospects test might mean withdrawing the case from the court. But, as shown in Chapter 1, magistrates work to a less exacting evidential standard and they may commit cases which the prosecutor decides are likely to fail at trial. As a result the committal may bind the prosecutor to go on with the prosecution. In this sense, there is little to be gained by the prosecution from full committal of cases where the decision to prosecute was marginal. Furthermore, the extra hurdle of committal rarely confers further opportunity for the prosecution to trip up defence witnesses since the defence case is typically reserved, to maintain its element of surprise or 'ambush' until trial. Thus there may be little adversarial advantage to the prosecution.

There may, in contrast, be both short- and long-term advantages for the defence. The immediate effect may be that the defendant is simply not committed for trial. In the long term, the sooner and more often Crown witnesses give evidence the greater the potential for the defence to capitalize on inconsistencies which almost inevitably arise on each occasion a story is related. This parallels the 'cuts over the eye' syndrome in a boxing match: once a cut has been opened up, subsequent blows may be aimed at it. Cross-examination of prosecution witnesses in these four committals by the defence varied according to the type of offence. In the murder cases it was aimed at dissuading the magistrates from committing for trial; and in the rape cases at attempting to open up weaknesses in the Crown's case, which could be exploited at the trial.

Of the two murder cases (1 and 15), one of the two original co-defendants in each case was not committed. In Case 1 the Stipendiary Magistrate found no case against defendant D because the key prosecution witness's version of D's involvement partly conflicted with that of two further Crown witnesses. The evidence of these witnesses was not treated as manifestly unreliable since, on their testimony, A was committed for trial. It should be noted that the magistrate had cast apsersions on all the witnesses, suggesting that some or even all of them might have been treated as co-defendants rather than witnesses. Even on a wide interpretation of *Galbraith*, is it dubious to allow depositions from doubtful witnesses effectively to negate the evidence of the key witness, also admittedly unreliable, and yet still rely upon it to commit defendant A?

In Case 15, defendant W was committed for trial for murder before defendant S was apprehended. The only non-circumstantial evidence against S arose out of W's statement under caution. This evidence could not be put before the court because S's committal proceedings took place *after* W had been committed. The Stipendiary Magistrate found the remaining evidence insufficient for a *prima facie* case against S. This case raises a moot general point: at trial, incrimination by one co-defendant of another does not become evidence against the second *unless* adopted by the first from the witness-box. Does this principle extend to committal, as logic would suggest, so that the principle would more properly read... unless *and until* adopted? If so, where the defence position is usually reserved at committal, it would have made no difference if the prosecution had attempted to have W and S committed together since W would not have been called to give his evidence. Therefore, the prosecution of S was ill-founded anyway. In this respect 'testing the evidence' at full committal may make a crucial difference for some defendants, who would otherwise be committed 'on the nod' through the paper committals route, only to become vulnerable to incrimination by their co-accused at trial.[22] It is worthy of note that in both Case 1 and Case 15, where the strength of the prosecution's case was eroded by the loss of co-defendants, defendants who were committed on murder charges were ultimately acquitted at trial.

In the rape Case 4 some 'cuts over the eye' were opened up, such as discrepancies between the depositions of the complainants I and T in respect of two of the defendants – C and H. At trial, defence counsel were able to compare and contrast their witness statements, depositions at committal, testimonies at the first (discontinued) trial, and testimonies at the second trial. In the rape Case 18 there was a similar pattern between committal and trial except that the defence was restricted to sequential inconsistencies arising from only one complainant. Both committals also provided some early indication of how the complainants' characters would be blackened by the defence. In Case 4 this placed in jeopardy their continued attendance throughout the trials. In spite of all these difficulties on the prosecution side, there were eventual convictions in both cases.

In the short term, the balance of advantage and disadvantage appears unevenly spread between the defence and the prosecution.

The defendant may avoid having to go for trial in circumstances where a paper committal would otherwise act simply as a conduit. In contrast, although the ethically minded prosecutor may welcome the chance to filter out cases where the committal suggests that later conviction is improbable, the process may bind the prosecution to continue, unless palpable weaknesses prevent the magistrates from committing a case. In the longer term, too, the balance of advantage in using old-style committals rests with the defence. Opportunities to trip up witnesses arising from the 'extra hurdle' are generally confined to the defence. Indeed, where the prosecution case suffers from presentation by a professional officer who is only an occasional advocate, subsequent employment of even the most experienced counsel at trial may not resuscitate it. This potential disadvantage is not usually shared by the defence. Defence counsel who start to 'get their teeth' into a case at committal are more likely to follow it through to trial. Any new information which emerges during the committal may be exploited by defence counsel, who enjoys continuity of responsibility, but may be lost or less adequately transmitted by the prosecution, in the process of handing the case over to counsel.

II THE TRIAL

Opening speeches

Once the jury has been sworn and the charge(s) put to the accused, prosecuting counsel begins the trial with an opening speech for the Crown. This is an address which reminds the jury of the charges, explains points of law if necessary, and clarifies the role and standard of proof demanded of jurors as arbiters of fact. Prosecuting counsel thus paves the way for what ensues in the course of the trial by presenting an overall view of the case – not just a general picture, but rather a jigsaw to illustrate how the testimonies of the *dramatis personae* of defendant, victim, and witnesses should fit together if the Crown's version is to be accepted. This opening speech may have considerable significance for the conduct and outcome of the trial. So much is simple, but what are the pitfalls? They may be said to lie along the continuum between saying too much or too little, both in technical and in strategic terms.

In technical terms the prosecution should be at pains to exclude any reference to material which may turn out to be inadmissible, for example, confessions to which the defence intend to object

(Archbold 1982: 4–177). On the other side of the coin, if additional evidence emerges during the trial which has not been mentioned in the opening speech, prosecuting counsel is not allowed a second address on such points. Thus it is a question of getting the balance right. How far points of reference for the jury should be developed, between the extremes of a bare skeleton or a fleshed-out version, is left to counsel's discretion. There is, however, one standardizing influence in this respect: the prosecutor should not become a persecutor. Observation of this maxim, and of another, that the prosecutor is not under a duty to 'struggle for a verdict', constitute a restraint as to 'form'. Counsel should avoid unnecessarily emotive language to excite sympathy for the victim or antipathy towards the defendant. This restraint partially extends into 'content' as opposed to 'form' in cases likely to arouse such jury reactions, in that here counsel has a duty to warn jurors to inhibit such feelings so as not to influence their verdict. In short, he should conduct himself as if he were a 'Minister of Justice'.[23]

The adversarial 'batting order', which allows the final say to the defence, arguably confers the early advantage on the prosecution to offer the jury a blueprint with which to assess the evidence.[24] In Case 5, prosecuting counsel justified his long and detailed opening on the grounds that the case was unusually complex. It involved charges of murder and arson against two foreign defendants who were found to have set fire to an illegal gaming den in which eight other foreigners died. The trial was lengthy and complicated by difficulties in interpreting language. The possibility of confusion in the evidence was immense. So, prosecuting counsel, by setting out clear guidelines in his opening speech which were largely followed in the trial, may have counteracted any tendency by the defence to exploit confusion in the evidence, in order to cast doubt on the guilt of the accused.

Another potential difficulty for the prosecution in providing a blueprint, where ethnic defendants and victims are concerned, arises from culture gaps when juries are largely composed of native Caucasian British citizens. In Case 4, three Rastafarians were charged with a series of rapes and indecent assaults on West Indian women. In an aborted first trial it became clear in evidence that the victims' sexual expectations were lower and their toleration of male violation higher, than that customarily displayed by white women victims. Since the trial turned largely upon the issue of consent, the absence of 'recent complaints' – that is, evidence that the victims complained of the rapes shortly after their alleged occurrence – and the victims' initially deferential testimony might be explained in terms of these cultural differences. When the re-trial began, prosecuting counsel – capitalizing on the 'rehearsal' of the first trial – was able to convey something of the cultural flavour of the victims' and defendants' milieu to the jury, composed of one black and eleven white citizens. This tactic also apparently achieved some pre-emptive effect upon defence cross-examination of the victims, since the line of questioning pursued by defence counsel displayed less incredulity of the victims' sexual expectations and tolerance than at the first trial.

The extent to which counsel in his opening address raises the jury's expectations as to the content of witnesses' evidence depends upon the measure of confidence the Crown has in its witnesses. In this, counsel suffers the same handicap as the DPP: he is reliant upon others for his information. The obvious way of prudently allowing for the unpredictability of testimony is, according to Emmins (1983), to 'open the case low' – slightly to underplay what a witness is expected to say. He argues that, in this way, if the evidence subsequently turns out to be weaker than it was on paper, the jury will not necessarily be aware of this apparent undermining of the prosecutor's case. Excessive claims by the prosecution may thus provide one explanation for acquittals. The opening speech may set the tone of the trial so as to allow the defence to capitalize upon some deficiency on a point which may not anyway have been essential to the prosecution case. Thus in Case 17, where prosecuting counsel specifically opened the case by presenting the victim as a 'defenceless man' attacked by the police, the prosecution was subsequently embarrassed by evidence that he was not wholly inert throughout the incident. When these minor, perhaps involuntary, movements (allegedly for a gun) were combined with 'heat of the moment' arguments, the officers' actions in shooting at and striking the victim seemed less unreasonable than in the initial version put forward in the prosecution opening. Although counsel had attempted to rebut self-defence in his opening, he was forced to shift his ground once the assertion that the victim was inert was challenged. Having opened on the basis that there could be no justification for any attack on a motionless man his argument altered along the lines that, even if the victim was moving a little, surely just sitting on him would afford the other police officers sufficient protection against a gun being drawn. Was it necessary for the first defendant allegedly to 'pistol-whip' the victim or the second defendant to shoot at him from a distance of 12 feet?

Where, having failed to 'open low', the prosecution revises its claims in the light of the testimony given, it may invite ridicule from the defence, who are typically intolerant of any such either/or ('two-horse') approaches by the prosecution. Maintaining a two-horse strategy throughout the case invites comments from defence counsel along the lines of 'the prosecution cannot even make up its own mind, members of the jury, yet it now asks you to do what it cannot'. This was seen in Case 14. The defendant was charged (among other things) with manslaughter and unlawfully administering a noxious substance with intent to endanger life. His girlfriend had died following an injection of heroin at her own request. Also present was another man, H, whom the prosecution used as a witness. The defendant had confessed to the police but now pleaded not guilty; H merely denied that he had injected the victim. The prosecution presented H's evidence in the light that either he was a witness of truth, so by elimination the defendant was the culprit, or, if H was lying, he was a guilty party but the defendant was still guilty since he had assisted. The defence heavily criticized the prosecution for this two-horse strategy. Furthermore, since H was not indicted, the alternative hypothesis was scarcely likely to be attractive to the jury anyway. The defendant was acquitted on both principal charges.

One case in the sample shows that in exceptional circumstances the prosecution may choose to 'open high'. In Case 8, where a police officer was charged with assaulting a suspect after she had already been subdued by two other officers, prosecuting counsel opened the case with a vivid description of the incident and implied that such conduct by a police officer might reflect discredit on the police generally. This opening clearly went beyond the 'Minister of Justice' approach, but might be justified on the facts. The woman assaulted, a young skinhead, had been a key figure in an outbreak of public disorder with racist overtones, and it was probably thought necessary to open the case strongly in order to counteract any sympathy for the defendant police officer and antipathy towards the victim in the circumstances in which the assault was allegedly made. None the less, the defendant was acquitted.

So a balance must be struck between pitching the opening too high or too low. Such a conclusion is easy to formulate but difficult to achieve in practice. Case 18 provides a good example of counsel achieving the 'true pitch'. It was a rape case: a 'gang-bang' involving three defendants. There were internal inconsistencies within the victim's testimony as to who did what to her and when. In addition she had convictions for brothel-keeping and had recently made similar allegations against other men which were false, or at least quickly withdrawn. The usual prosecution handicap of only second-hand knowledge of how the victim was likely to give evidence had been reduced by an 'old-style' committal. This revealed not only her inconsistencies, but also her 'warts and all' approach to giving evidence. She was shaky in detail but very certain of the fact that she had been raped and otherwise assaulted. The DPP took the view that the case should be opened on a 'full and frank' basis, which may subsequently have cut some of the ground from under the feet of the defence when they further blackened the victim's character. A majority finding of guilt was returned.

This approach in opening seems not only unobjectionable but also to represent a logical reconciliation of the countervailing influences upon prosecution counsel which have been discussed. If the jurors genuinely are arbiters of fact it ill behoves advocates to steer them in any direction by advance speculation about, or selective 'editing' of, the evidence before it has even been called.[25]

Witnesses

PROCEDURE

After the prosecution have opened, the evidence of the witnesses 'whose names appear on the back of the indictment' is produced in either written or oral form. According to Pattenden (1982a: 158) prosecution witnesses can be categorized into: those whom it is necessary for the Crown to call in order to prove guilt beyond reasonable doubt; and those necessary for it to call in order to discharge its duty to present fairly to the jury all relevant evidence capable of belief.[26]

After taking the oath, witnesses are examined in chief by prosecution counsel; with questions which are not leading, but are designed to elicit the relevant evidence the witness can give. Where this procedure is successful the witness will give oral evidence of those matters in his statement necessary to establish the factual basis of the prosecution case; this is called 'coming up to proof'. The witness will then be cross-examined by defence counsel in an attempt to cast doubt on evidence conflicting with the accused's case, or to reveal additional facts of assistance to the accused; this may be achieved either through factual questions or questions designed to undermine the witness's credibility. The prosecution then has the opportunity to re-examine the witness on any matters arising out of cross-examination (but not, unless the judge has given leave, to ask for fresh information which the defence would then have no opportunity to challenge). Finally the judge has the discretion to put questions to the witness. As Pattenden (1982a: 113) notes, counsel or an unrepresented accused may have overlooked, deliberately or inadvertently, some point – or the judge may be in some doubt as to the meaning of evidence. The judge has a duty to ensure that justice is done and 'if he thinks that justice requires him to put questions, then he had the right and the duty to intervene', and in extreme cases to call witnesses (per Scarman, LJ, R. v. *Evans*, CA, unreported 3255/C/73, 29 January, 1974).

Although it can be argued that the adversarial system, as opposed to an inquisitorial system, may not be the best way of establishing the truth, the procedures outlined above are supposed to ensure a thorough airing of the issues and the evidence. Pattenden (1982a: 113) considers that these procedures are based on the assumption of 'self-interest' by both sides. Here, the argument will be pursued that the witnesses for both sides are neither equally 'self-interested' nor equally capable of fulfilling that self-interest. Indeed, it is suggested that the role of the witness at trial cannot be separated from the process whereby individuals become witnesses; and that this process introduces an element of inherent bias, favouring the defence and disadvantaging the prosecution.

REASONABLE PROSPECTS AND THE WITNESS IN THE ADVERSARIAL SYSTEM

For the prosecutor applying the reasonable prospects test, predictions of witnesses' performance in court are central to the assessment of whether there is sufficient evidence to justify proceeding. However, these predictions, even where the prosecutor makes them conscientiously, are fraught with difficulties. First, the reasons why individuals become witnesses, for instance their proximity to the crime or their special expertise, may in turn make their testimony more (or less) vulnerable at trial. Secondly, the trial process places a premium on oral evidence; most prosecutors base their assessments of witnesses on written evidence, namely statements taken by the police shortly after the event.[27] These statement bundles are then sent to the DPP where various assessments are made about the evidence and the witnesses (see Royal Commission on Criminal Procedure 1981: 211). Although these assessments may be supplemented by the views of the police as to the witness's likely performance in court, decisions at the DPP are essentially based upon the quality and quantity of the evidence as it appears on paper. At trial, the need for witnesses both to remember events accurately and appear confident, can undermine evidence which was seemingly persuasive on paper. Third, the content of witnesses' oral evidence has to be just what it is in their written statements; saying less, or more, can provide grounds for the defence to attack. Finally, the evidence of witnesses remains vulnerable even after they have left court; the reliability of their evidence may be reassessed by either counsel or the judge when addressing the jury. Since the defence only have to establish a reasonable doubt in the jury's minds, the routes whereby this may be achieved are legion. Making accurate predictions about witnesses is, for the prosecutor, clearly a precarious task.

The prosecution are required by law to disclose to the defence the names and addresses of material witnesses whom they do not intend to call and the known previous convictions of the witnesses they do intend to call (Archbold 1982: 4–180). Whether the prosecution were under a further duty to disclose the statements of such witnesses was for some time unclear.[28] The Attorney General's guidelines on disclosure now go well beyond the minimum legal requirements.[29] As a general rule, all unused material (with some specific discretion to withhold) will be disclosed by the DPP to the defence before or soon after committal. This is not necessarily disadvantageous to the prosecution. It has been demonstrated for example that prosecution disclosure of material to be used may elicit pleas from defendants who might otherwise have been prepared to contest the case unsuccessfully (Feeney 1985).

By the time the accused comes to trial the defence may be in possession of various written versions of what the prosecution witnesses are likely to say.[30] But, with the exception of police officers and expert witnesses, most witnesses will have no record of what they initially said to the police – nor necessarily any appreciation of the factors that influenced the DPP's decision to call them. Although witnesses are allowed to refresh their memories from their statements before going into court (*R.* v. *Richardson* [1971] 2 All ER 773), when this does happen, it usually means the witness glancing over his statement immediately prior to being called. And when they make use of this facility it is desirable that the prosecution inform the defence (*Worley* v. *Bentley* [1976] 2 All ER 449). Thus, prosecution witnesses are one of the most disadvantaged groups at trial. The opportunities for the defence to undermine their credibility are considerable: departures from their initial statements will be immediately apparent to the defence but not necessarily to the witnesses whose recall of what they saw, what they said to the police, and what the police recorded, may be imperfect and internally contradictory.

Finally, it should be noted that many civilian prosecution witnesses are unfamiliar with the criminal process and, in contrast with the defendant, may have not been preoccupied with the nature of their evidence in the period between the event and the trial. Indeed, as the prosecution does not routinely rehearse its witnesses, in some cases the witnesses may inadvertently make reference to inadmissible or prejudicial material which can result in the jury being discharged. Hence, the 'non-professional' prosecution witnesses may be characterized as being comparatively unprepared for the demands which will be made upon them.

ASSESSING WITNESSES: THE INTERACTION BETWEEN PERSONAL AND EVIDENTIAL VARIABLES

Prosecution witnesses may be characterized by being placed along a continuum according to their degree of objectivity and involvement in relation to the incident (see *Table 1*). Thus, they range from (i) expert and technical witnesses providing evidence after an incident, through (ii) those non-involved, primarily civilian, witnesses who happen to be present at an event, but whose overall comprehension of it may be limited, to (iii) individuals directly involved in the incident. This last group may include the following: victims; individuals present throughout the incident who play a largely passive role; 'co-conspirators' against whom there may be some evidence of involvement in the incident, but evidence which is insufficient to establish either a *prima facie* case or a reasonable prospect of conviction; individuals who have been separately convicted.

At each point on the continuum, witnesses' credibility may be attacked on different grounds (see *Table 2*). Hence, that which makes observers and victims into witnesses, namely their proximity to events, will also make their versions of events fallible. Similarly, the objectivity which expert witnesses bring may lay them open to attack on other grounds, namely that the accuracy of their reconstruction of events depends upon their 'expertise'. This may be challenged by other, 'non-present at the event', experts. Finally, the police as investigators *and* witnesses may have their character and credibility challenged where a defendant wishes to contest the voluntary character of a confession.[31] Such challenges will initially be heard in the absence of the jury in a 'trial within a trial'. Of the four which took place in the sample of cases no police evidence was excluded by the judge following such challenges.[32] The allegations are then put again to the witnesses in the presence of the jury: their impact is hard to assess – but two of the four cases did result in acquittals – despite the judges' rulings that the confessions were admissible.

TABLE 1
The likely characters of prosecution witnesses listed in order of their probable increasing degree of involvement with the defendant and his subculture as emerging from the sample of eighteen cases

Nature of witness	Character in issue
experts/pathologists, etc.	good
police technical experts	good
police witnesses (observation/reports)	good
police witnesses (investigation/interrogation)	good but open to allegations
non-involved civilian witnesses who observed part of the incident or events prior to or preceding the incident: necessary to provide background information	principally good
passive observers	unknown
active observers	unknown
victims	unknown: good or bad depending on degree of prior involvement with criminal subcultures/defendant
non-prosecuted co-participants	possibly or probably bad
convicted co-participants giving evidence for the Crown	bad

Table 2

A check-list for prosecutors of the opportunities for attack on witnesses' character, their credibility, or the credibility of their evidence emerging from the sample of eighteen cases

Information content

1. quantity/nature of event – limited evidence
   spontaneous event
   continuing event
2. observed/interpreted event correctly
3. quality – professionalism in recording/observing
   access to independent recall
   contemporaneous notes
4. likelihood of proof – not up to proof
   – up to proof
   – beyond proof
5. opportunities for reinterpretation of evidence to jury by key participants
   before ⎱ evidence given
   after ⎰

Witness confidence

6. quality of articulation
7. self-perception/definition
8. experience of courts
9. ability to tell *whole* story, as eroded by the rules of evidence

Susceptibility to attack on memory fallibility

10. time delay
11. anticipation of event/preparedness
12. involvement/stress
13. drink/drugs
14. injury

Motivation to tell truth (and nothing but)

15. varnished/unvarnished/lies
16. assumed and actual motivation
17. partiality/likely bias/involvement with accused
18. force loyalty for police witnesses
19. likely gain from evidence – parole
    – financial
    – (lesser sentence)
20. likely self-incrimination
21. trials within trials

A. CIVILIAN WITNESSES

(i) *Inaccurate perception of the incident* When assessing witness testimony jurors have to consider not only the credibility of witnesses – whether or not they are telling the truth – but also the inherent credibility of their evidence. Witnesses may simply misunderstand or misperceive the events to which they are witnesses and although their recall at trial is faultless, they may be inaccurately reporting those events to the court. For example, in Case 9, where the victim fell from a fifth-floor balcony, the issue was whether the eyewitness saw the accused push the victim or whether he saw the accused attempting to prevent the victim deliberately throwing herself off the balcony.

The very nature of the events that witnesses are asked to recall may have contributed to their inability to perceive them accurately in the first place. Observers who witness crimes of violence may themselves experience stress; this factor, in combination with their lack of understanding of events that may have been totally unexpected, may jeopardize their accuracy (Yarmey and Tessillian-Jones 1983). Similarly, witnesses are often under the influence of drink or drugs (twelve of the eighteen cases involved these factors), or the physical condition of the victims may prevent them from accurately perceiving events (in Case 17 the victim suffered some lowering of consciousness resulting from blows to his head, and in both Case 13 and Case 18 the victims were blindfolded during the course of assaults).

(ii) *Inaccurate recall* The fallibility of human memory is notorious (Yarmey and Tessillian-Jones 1983). With the exception of those who make a note of events as they happen, witnesses may readily be accused of failing to remember them correctly. The delay before cases are brought to trial may exacerbate this factor to the extent that, in some cases, the 'truth' as remembered by the witnesses may simply not be possible to establish. Again, the nature of the events can be crucial. Often witnesses find it difficult to recall in the correct chronological sequence an incident which may have built up over the course of some hours. For example, in Case 1, a fatal stabbing in a shebeen, the disruption preceding and relevant to the victim's death had ebbed and flowed over some hours. Yet it may be vital to the prosecution's case to establish the precise chronology of events.

(iii) *Witness confidence* Research has suggested that the confidence with which a witness gives evidence correlates with the degree of accuracy and credibility that assessors attribute to the evidence. But a witness's *actual* accuracy does not correlate with his perceived confidence (Wells and Lindsay 1983). Witnesses who assume they are remembering events accurately may appear more confident and thus more credible. Similarly, witnesses who assume no one will believe them, for example the victims of attempted murder in Case 16, may lack confidence and therefore credibility. It is a comparatively easy task for counsel to shake a witness's confidence by highlighting inconsistencies between his evidence in court and that given to the police. Whether those inconsistencies are peripheral or relevant to the major body of his evidence may be immaterial when compared with the overall effect on the witness's confidence; hence, an attack along the lines of 'if you can't get this minor detail right, why should we believe you about the important issues?'

(iv) *The 'victim-witness-defendant' subculture* The close involvement and partiality of some witnesses in relation to the accused may make them either reluctant to give their evidence (for example, in Case 14 one of the principal prosecution witnesses shared a flat with and was a good friend of the accused); or faltering in relation to detail (for example, in Case 11 the victim, the foster daughter of the accused had to give evidence of his sexual abuse of her over a lengthy period); or simply comparatively inarticulate in contrast with counsel (for example, in Case 7 – a 'wino' accused of attempting to murder another vagrant by pushing him in front of an underground train – both the defendant and the victim were alcoholic vagrants whose manner of giving evidence became the subject of not inconsequential mirth at trial). All of these factors which affect the manner in which evidence is given may interact with the perceived confidence of the witness and hence his attributed credibility (see (iii) above).

Furthermore, the general difficulty of requiring witnesses to recreate an event at trial verbally which may have been for them an essentially visual experience, may highlight any inadequacies in their evidence. For example, where witnesses are asked to speculate about distance, their initial guess of, say, 20 feet, may not correlate well with their ultimate agreement that it was 'about the length of the courtroom' – say, 45 feet. The undermining effect of this process may be exacerbated if the evidence of the witness in the box is contrasted with their statements, which will normally have been recorded by comparatively articulate police officers.

(v) *Witness motivation* The shared subculture of many of the participants at some trials may also contribute to a perception of the victim/witness as being less than wholly credible, particularly where they have an apparent motive for telling less than the unvarnished truth. Previously convicted co-defendants are especially vulnerable. In Case 13, the witness, Mr X, was attacked by the defence on the grounds that giving evidence for the prosecution not only resulted in his receiving a comparatively light sentence for his part in the incident, but would also increase the prospect of his receiving earlier parole. Other witnesses' alleged motivations for appearing at court included intimations of financial gain from the publicity (witnesses in Case 17) and revenge (the principal prosecution witness in Case 9 was the victim's ex-husband). In addition, actual motives may be misperceived. The rape victims in Case 4 made no early complaint, because, according to them, they were frightened of the defendants. Yet the defence was able to insinuate that the victims subsequently concocted their stories solely in order to recover property misappropriated at the time of the rapes. Similarly, witnesses who appear to be (or who have been) rehearsed are open to challenge. In Case 18 the defence tried to make some capital out of the fact that the victim had attended a Rape Crisis Centre and was supported at court by one of its representatives.

(vi) *Evidence content* Where witnesses fail either to come to court – there were many examples of them going missing or becoming unavailable before trial – or to 'come up to proof', the work of the defence has been done for it. Where witnesses do 'come up to proof' their evidence or their credibility may of course be challenged. However, there are further difficulties where witnesses go 'beyond proof' – adding detail to their evidence not present in their statements. This provides the defence with the grounds for suggesting exaggeration or fabrication on the witness's part. Why was this detail not mentioned to the police at the time when it was presumably fresh in their memories? The defence asks the jury to accept that recall is *most* accurate immediately after an event – which is an assumption of questionable validity. But the fact of the matter is that many details do not assume any importance until the trial stage, and therefore may not have been the subject of police inquiries, nor have been explored in the witness's statement; these gaps can prove extremely damaging to the prosecution's case. Thus, in Case 17 the evidence of an eyewitness that defendant A had fired wilfully into the tyre of a car was, in combination with defendant A's lack of clarity on this point, very influential in the decision as to the nature of the charges preferred. At trial, another witness stated that he saw defendant A shoot downwards 'at the tyre'. This witness's evidence was attacked by defence counsel because it had not been in his original statement to the police. When asked during cross-examination whether it was a 'recollection or deduction', the witness retorted, 'I *saw* it.' But this was effectively devalued, through juxtaposition with an occasion when the witness's credibility was successfully undermined, and he had resorted to saying that he 'couldn't remember/couldn't say'. The witness was subsequently described by defence counsel as 'utterly unreliable'. The subtle erosion of this witness's testimony was confirmed when the judge, in his summing up, inferred that the bullets went into the tyre by accident, since to shoot into the tyre was incomprehensible, and 'wholly out of character' for defendant A.

Sometimes juries may assume that witnesses have gone 'beyond proof' when, in fact, they have not. This is because the prosecution's case is not necessarily based on everything that witnesses allege they saw; where allegations cannot be corroborated they may be excluded from the prosecution's case – as being likely to damage the witnesses' credibility. However, witnesses will not necessarily know this. They are often 'in the dark' about the prosecution's strategy. Hence, in Case 8 the victim complained at trial that she had been kicked during the course of the assault by the accused. This allegation had been excluded from the charges brought; the prosecution's case was founded on only a punch in the stomach, which was all that was corroborated by police evidence. When the victim complained of the kick at the trial, she may have appeared, to the jury at least, to be exaggerating. The prosecution's construction of the case and selection of the evidence to support it may have had the result of undermining the victim's credibility. The defendant was acquitted.

Another problem facing the prosecutor attempting to assess eyewitness testimony, when it is in the form of a written statement, is to identify gaps in the chronology of a witnesses' potential evidence. Although the DPP's criteria for prosecution (Barnes 1975; Royal Commission on Criminal Procedure 1981: Appendix 25; Attorney General 1983) do not draw specific attention to the need to identify gaps – namely, the failure of witnesses to observe and detail events which they logically should have seen if their version of the chronology of events is to be believed – the failure to do this can have serious repercussions at trial. Although several eyewitnesses in Case 17 claimed to have watched the victim from the moment he emerged from the car to the point of his being handcuffed, no witness observed defendant B shooting the victim during this period, an action admitted by the defence. Their failure to do this gave considerable scope for defence counsel to undermine other more pertinent aspects of the witnesses' evidence. For example, their assertion that the victim's body did not move after it fell out of the car was challenged on the basis that if the witnesses had failed to see one important event, namely the shooting, they might equally well have failed to see another. Defence counsel was able to describe the civilian witnesses as doing their 'honest, but muddled best'.

The fallibility of eyewitnesses at court need not, however, prove fatal to the prosecution's case. In Case 5 the prosecution and the resultant conviction were almost entirely reliant on the testimony of one eyewitness. Yet this witness had partly confused the two defendants' identity. Similarly, in Case 18, the rape victim, the only 'eyewitness' to the event, altered her account of the chronology of events on no fewer than four separate occasions (three of them whilst in the witness-box) and was repeatedly confused about which defendant (of three) she was alleging was involved in which form of abuse. Her direct appeals to the jury when she was challenged about these contradictions – a good example of 'victim brinkmanship' – went as follows:

WITNESS.	All of this is irrelevant – all I care about is that they raped me.
DEFENCE COUNSEL.	Which of the two versions are correct?
WITNESS.	*Both* are true.
DEFENCE COUNSEL.	You can't tell a consistent story can you? . . .
WITNESS.	All I want is for them to be *done*. I'm not on trial.

All three were subsequently convicted.

B. PROFESSIONAL WITNESSES

Witnesses who are experienced at giving testimony, for example, police officers and expert witnesses, do not share the gamut of disadvantages experienced by civilian witnesses, and may not as easily have their evidence challenged by the defence. Professional witnesses have often compiled their own statements and thus retain control over the expression and content of their observations. They often have a record of events made at the time that they happened, which they are normally given leave to produce at court; this makes them less vulnerable to allegations of inaccurate recall. It may also make them appear more confident, and hence more credible as witnesses. Finally, these professional observers may be characterized by others in more flattering terms than civilian witnesses. For example, in Case 17, a police officer was described as 'more skilled in observation and memory' than civilian witnesses,[33] although he had failed to see an incident which logically he should have seen if the totality of his evidence was to be accepted (see p. 145). In his summing up, the judge made explicit reference to that which the officer claimed to have seen, despite his failure to see that which he should have seen. Professional witnesses may therefore be able to retain their credibility *despite* their mistakes whereas civilian witnesses may lose it *because* of their mistakes.

Expert witnesses (pathologists, doctors, forensic scientists, etc.) are in the privileged position at trial of being able to give 'opinion evidence' to prove matters requiring specialized knowledge, on which the court would be unable properly to reach a conclusion unaided. Unlike other witnesses, they may, by virtue of their expertise, be assumed by the jury to be both objective and independent. However, like other witnesses, expert witnesses are open to cross-examination (and their credentials and competence can be challenged). Although experts come to court to give their opinions (i.e. their conclusions) the factual basis of these can, of course, be challenged.

The content of an expert's evidence may be of fundamental importance both in the decision to launch a prosecution and in securing a successful outcome. But prosecution decisions launched on the basis of a misunderstanding of expert evidence can as easily collapse at court, once the route by which those conclusions were reached is explored. The potential for misunderstanding between the prosecutor and his expert witnesses – particularly where those experts do not fully explain their 'findings' in terms comprehensible to the prosecutor – is considerable. Of the eighteen cases studied in depth, nine substantially depended on expert evidence. In Case 17 both the attempted murder charges and the charges under Section 18 of the Offences against the Person Act 1861 against defendant A were probably influenced by the evidence in the statements of two doctors that the victim had suffered a fractured skull. To the layman, a fractured skull sounds serious; to a lawyer it can, under certain circumstances, sustain a Section 18 charge. Yet at trial, it emerged in examination in chief that the surgeon considered the injury 'trivial'. The prosecution were clearly surprised by that evidence. How might this have come about? Was the nature and seriousness of the fracture to the skull explored with the experts before the trial? Were the prosecution inhibited about testing their own evidence prior to trial to a point equivalent to cross-examination? Were the medical experts unaware of the specific legal niceties of the charges, and did they therefore not volunteer further details of the nature of the fracture? As a result of this evidence the nature of one of the Section 18 charges against defendant A was amended at the request of prosecution counsel: from that of causing grievous bodily harm with intent so to do, to 'wounding with intent to do grievous bodily harm'. Similarly, once the less serious nature of the fracture emerged, the prosecution's suggestion that, 'taken as a whole', defendant A's actions could substantiate the charge of attempted murder became less compelling. There was subsequently a successful submission of no case by the defence on this charge.

The failure of experts fully to explain their reasoning in writing at an early stage can also have a reverse effect: namely, the case can strengthen at trial once those reasons are given in detail. In Case 18, the doctor who examined the rape victim noted in his statement findings consistent with 'intercourse, sexual abuse, and actual bodily harm from assault'. At trial, he declined to say whether the intercourse was consensual or not. Yet, when describing the discoid bruises on the victim's body, he stated that this was a classic sign of fingertip injuries produced when the victim is held or restrained. Their appearance on her inner thighs 'suggested her legs had been held apart'; the influence of this deduction on the court and on the jury is hard to assess, but in the context of the oft-repeated dictum that 'all a woman has to do to prevent herself being raped is to keep her legs together', the evidence was undoubtedly powerful. The defendants were all convicted.

It is suggested then that expert evidence, at least in terms of its content, builds a somewhat unpredictable element into the prosecutor's case. In terms of its form, experts' evidence may be relied upon with greater confidence by the prosecutor. As has already been outlined, their evidence benefits from attributions of expertise made by judges, and may arguably be more persuasive to jurors.

Although experts are generally regarded as impartial witnesses, it is also apparent that, unless an expert were likely to venture an opinion favourable to the side calling him, he would be unlikely to be used. But, since experts are often called to rebut one another, it is evident that even among the experts there may be no certainty about the interpretation of findings and the drawing of conclusions. So, under certain circumstances expert evidence can be as fragile as that of civilian witnesses; the problem for the prosecution is that its fragility, and the preference of experts to give opinions in terms of probabilities rather than certainties, can be considerably more damaging to the prosecution case.

But can form and content be so easily divided in respect of their effect on a jury? Case 12 highlighted the failure of expert evidence to be persuasive where there is contradictory expert opinion. In this case the prosecution's expert was at a disadvantage in that he based his conclusions merely on photographic evidence; the defence pathologist had examined the body before cremation and concluded that the cause of death (the victim's throat was slit) was suicide. The disadvantaged prosecution expert requested a second opinion (also based solely on photographic evidence) which served to confirm his own conclusions that the wound was the result of homicide. In attempting to strengthen the evidence in this manner the prosecution then felt obliged to call both experts at trial (to prevent defence allegations of 'shopping around' for a convenient opinion). The potential for expert disagreement on fine points of detail was thus considerable. At trial, the prosecution's case was further weakened by a shift in the *opinion* of one of the experts and a shift in the *factual* basis of this opinion. This contradiction in his written and oral evidence was put to him by defence counsel and acknowledged.

Further damage in the jury's eyes may have been done when it emerged that the two prosecution experts had discussed the case together long before the committal. Thus, what might have been seen as supporting/corroborating evidence became capable of being seen as collaboration between the witnesses. Finally, it emerged that a third doctor who had examined the body *in situ* and was also acting as a prosecution witness, had amended his statement to concur with the other two prosecution experts' findings. The prosecution's expert evidence was in tatters; the defence received the full benefit of their pathologist who had carried out the post-mortem and could therefore rely on his first-hand observation of the body. The defendant was acquitted. Clearly, the prosecutor is mistaken if he assumes that because the evidence is to be given by an 'expert' it requires less detailed scrutiny than that of a civilian witness.

As an aside, it is perhaps worth noting that although experts may be motivated to ensure that the court fully comprehends their findings, it may also be true that experts 'desire' a verdict that validates their findings. That some experts willingly defer to those more experienced within their own profession suggests that even expert evidence may not be wholly objective; experts may simply be motivated by different factors (such as the desire to appear professionally competent and credible) from those motivating civilian witnesses.[34]

Finally, control of the evidence offered by experts generally rests with the advocates who call or cross-examine them. If experts volunteer gratuitous evidence, not requested by counsel, they may risk characterization as 'bad witnesses' and jeopardize their future forensic employment. Thus, the expert may acquiesce in the lawyers' selectivity regarding the evidence.[35]

If expert evidence is to form a major plank in the prosecution case it has to acquire a degree of predictability. This in turn requires the prosecutor not only to understand the expert's opinion, but to have explored thoroughly the factual basis for that opinion. Ideally this 'exploration' needs to be pursued almost to the point of cross-examination. The situation noted by Nash (1982) that 'Some of us don't even know what our doctor is saying when he comes to court. But as long as the conclusions are right that's OK, and with a bit of luck nobody's going to question him too much' is a recipe for prosecutorial disaster.

WITNESS CREDIBILITY – VULNERABILITY TO REINTERPRETATION

In theory, the assessment and evaluation of witnesses' credibility is a matter for the jury. In practice, the jury's view may be influenced by what counsel or the judge says about the witnesses. Even where witnesses 'come up to proof' and do not substantially contradict themselves under cross-examination, their credibility may remain vulnerable to assertions made by the 'legal experts'. In Case 17 the judge in his summing up said of one witness – despite her coming up to proof – that 'the extent to which you can rely on her evidence is very doubtful' (a somewhat questionable remark – since the judge may have had knowledge about the witness not shared by the jury).

To take another example: the principal prosecution witness in Case 9 was an eyewitness to the victim falling from a fifth-floor balcony, yet he was 'reluctant' during examination-in-chief to implicate the accused. However, counsel skilfully elicited from him the remark that the accused had 'flipped her' over the balcony. Under cross-examination his evidence was strengthened by the retort 'have you ever seen someone thrown off a balcony?' and references to 'the night of the murder'. The witness may, of course, have been forced into a corner by counsel and responded by exaggerating his evidence but, none the less, he substantially came up to proof. Yet prosecution counsel, in his closing speech, devalued this evidence, by stating that he was an unsatisfactory witness whose testimony provided a 'brittle foundation' for a verdict of murder. The judge further undermined the witness's credibility by stating in his summing up that 'the Crown didn't hold him out to you as a witness of truth'.[36] The witness's credibility had thus been reinterpreted to the jury by the legal experts.[37]

SUMMARY

For the prosecutor applying the reasonable prospects test, predictions of witnesses' testimonies should be fundamental to the decision as to whether a prosecution is brought. However, the many sources of vulnerability of oral testimony mean that, as a general rule, witnesses are not likely to improve beyond the substance of their written statements. Furthermore, for the prosecutor making predictions on the basis of these 'black and white' statements, account should be taken of the subsequent 'in colour' malleability of witness testimony as given at trial. Hence, the case on paper is likely to represent the high-water mark of the prosecution's case.

The vulnerability of witnesses' testimony derives from the factors that makes them witnesses. They may be involved with the accused either directly or through a shared milieu; both may make their evidence subjective or partisan. Where an individual becomes a witness to an event because he happened casually to appear on the scene, his non-preparedness for the event may similarly provide only a partial appreciation.

The reliance of the trial process on oral evidence also makes witnesses' testimony vulnerable. Any slight variations in the witness's testimony or even additions to explain those variations can result in a witness's credibility being impugned. The prosecution's witnesses are differentially disadvantaged, both since the rules on disclosure may help to facilitate defence 'magnification' of any of these variations, and because civilian prosecution witnesses may be both unrehearsed and without motivation in contrast with defence witnesses. In the exchanges between an experienced defence counsel and the naïve prosecution witness, the latter usually 'comes off worse'.

Although the balance may be somewhat redressed by reducing the delays involved in bringing cases to trial and allowing witnesses some measure of rehearsal, the defence will continue to enjoy a considerably greater advantage at trial than the prosecution. Similarly, the primary importance of the role of the police in taking statements cannot be overemphasized; the need for cogency, coherence, and continuity is paramount. The fact that juries rise above some of the more spurious challenges to witnesses' credibility is a credit to their common sense. Juries apparently recognize that giving witness testimony is easier said than done. However, it would be preferable for the prosecution not to adopt a strategy that is reliant on the common sense of juries. Thus the prosecution should thoroughly explore the quality of its witnesses' evidence and not proceed if the witnesses are found wanting; if it does proceed it should present its case in a realistic manner.

Half-time submissions

The submission of no case to answer, usually termed the half-time submission, was dealt with in detail in Chapter 1. The defence is entitled to make the submission at the end of the prosecution case. If the Crown has failed to adduce sufficient evidence – all the necessary ingredients of the charge(s) alleged to have been committed by the accused – the judge should direct the jury to acquit. Indeed, the judge may take this initiative himself, in the absence of a defence submission. Apart from comparatively rare 'ordered acquittals' at full-time, the earlier half-time consideration of the case represents the last opportunity for a lawyer (the judge) to 'bypass the jury and determine whether they are allowed to decide upon the defendant's guilt or innocence (McCabe and Purves 1972). After this stage, judicial discretion is very largely limited to determination of what the jury may consider in order to reach its findings.

The criteria to be applied by the judge at half-time in deciding whether to withdraw the case from the jury were also dealt with in Chapter 1, by reference to the leading case of *Galbraith*. The assessment by the judge of whether there is a case to answer represents a significant hurdle for the prosecution to overcome. For the vast majority of cases which are committed via the paper committal route,[38] this examination of the evidence is the first independent check on the prosecutor's technical legal assessment that there is sufficient evidence for the defendant 'to be put to his proof', namely to respond to the prosecution's charges. For the minority of cases which come to trial via 'old-style committals' (usually restricted to examination of only part of the prosecution case), half-time submissions act as a check on whether prosecution witnesses have 'come up to proof' and whether their evidence is sufficient to allow the case to proceed. Within the sample of eighteen cases there was evidence that the examining magistrate(s) and the trial judges disagreed about the sufficiency of evidence under *Galbraith* submissions. This suggests that determining 'sufficiency' under *Galbraith* is no easy task. Emmins (1983) has plausibly argued that if prosecution evidence, when given in chief, turns out to be inherently weak or inconsistent with other evidence, the judge should allow the submission of no case, but that where these difficulties emerge in cross-examination by the defence, the case should more properly be left to the jury. The findings discussed in this section suggest that the position may, in practice, be less clear cut.

HOW *GALBRAITH* WORKS IN PRACTICE

Numerous unsuccessful defence submissions illustrate the considerable confusion as to the position following *Galbraith*. The judges appeared to approach the issue with great caution. There were directed acquittals on specific counts in just two cases (2 and 17), which both revealed questionable *prima facie* cases at earlier stages. In two further cases (9 and 11) 'directions' given at full-time could equally well have been given at half-time. In Case 11 the complainant failed to come up to proof with regard to penetration so that a rape charge was altered to one of attempted rape.[39] In Case 9 the judge acquiesced in the prosecution closing on a manslaughter basis in lieu of murder. The principal prosecution witness had been impugned; yet no half-time submission was made. And in a third, Case 10, the judge's ambivalence at half-time – where he 'would have acceded if sitting alone' (*sic*) – found practical expression later, when he summed up in terms tantamount to an ordered acquittal on the principal charge: 'dismiss any consideration of murder'. A manslaughter verdict was returned. The last illustration may lend some support to the argument in Chapter 1, that since *Galbraith*, judges, when acting as 'filters as to fact', might be relocating the exercise of their discretion to a point later in the trial. Because the position is unclear, judges may tend not to accede to a half-time submission but to strive to determine the outcome of the case through summing up in a particular way. In contrast with directions given by the judge to the jury, this influence is not amenable to appeal by the defence.

Official concern has been expressed at the amount of court time devoted to trials within trials, although Vennard (1984) suggests that such concern may be exaggerated. In contrast to this, it seems from this sample that, because the post-*Galbraith* position is unclear, considerable time may be wasted on half-time submissions with legal argument often extending over several hours.[40] Seven unsuccessful submissions were made. In one further instance – Case 18 – defence counsel intimated that he was minded to make a submission but was swiftly disabused of the idea by the judge. Only two of the seven rejected submissions attracted any judicial censure. In Case 15, where the prosecution had inferred intent from evidence that the defendant armed himself in advance of his attack on the victim, the judge described a submission based on self-defence as 'ill-founded'. In Case 1, where defence counsel sought to cast doubt on the motivation of prosecution witnesses who inculpated the defendant, the submission was disparagingly dismissed as consisting of 'jury points', with only lip-service paid to *Galbraith*.

In Case 17 there was a successful submission in respect of the attempted murder charge against the first defendant. This is relevant to two points made earlier: that paper committals do not represent a filtering mechanism, and that unpredictable difficulties may arise at trial where the prosecution treats expert medical witnesses 'at arm's length'. In respect of this second point, even before the expert gave medical evidence that the fracture to the victim's skull was not a serious injury, proof of the necessary intent to kill was problematic. It rested on the interpretation placed upon the action of the first defendant – opening fire into a confined space and in close proximity to his target – *together* with the inference that could be drawn from the severity of the victim's head injury which had resulted from this same defendant 'pistol-whipping' him. In his opening address, counsel used the euphemistic expression 'taken as a whole' to indicate the bases on which he believed intent to kill could be inferred from these actions. Even the combined inferences were tenuous in respect of the necessary *mens rea*, and once the inference from firing in a confined space had to be taken in isolation, it was palpably weak.

In Case 2 there had been an old-style committal specifically on the charge of attempted murder. The *mens rea* on this charge was arguably even weaker than in Case 17, yet the charge went for trial. (Interestingly, the examining Stipendiary also had recourse to the phrase 'taken as a whole' in finding a *prima facie* case.) The defendant had fired two 'loose' shots, together with a warning, at about which time the victim pulled the defendant's shooting hand against himself and the defendant discharged a third shot which struck the victim in the groin. As soon as the victim was disabled, but still vulnerable, the defendant fled. The Assistant Director's response to the minute prepared by the professional officer at the DPP was that a willingness to kill – in order to avoid arrest – is not equivalent to an intent to kill, necessary for an attempted murder charge to succeed. Why was the defendant charged and committed in this way? The argument put by Treasury Counsel was that people who go around shooting at policemen should expect to be so charged. When directing the acquittal on grounds of evidential insufficiency the judge apparently reaffirmed this view by remarking that the defendant 'had no right to complain'. Clearly, evidential insufficiency, in respect of the necessary intent, was 'dragged up' by public interest considerations when the prosecution decided on the charge: but when the judge had to decide upon the submission of no case, evidential sufficiency became the primary or sole issue, and the inevitable result was prosecutorial 'failure'.

PROSECUTORIAL PRACTICE AND HALF-TIME SUBMISSIONS

What is suggested here, in contrast to other stages of the trial, is that the DPP usually *is* in a position to make a reasonably accurate prediction with regard to half-time submissions. When a submission of no case in a prosecution by the DPP succeeds, the reason is less likely to lie in technical incompetence in assessing the strength of the evidence, than in either an 'arm's length' approach to expert evidence, as in Case 17, or 'public interest' reasons for pursuing a particular charge. It would be unwise to extrapolate too widely from two cases which both turned on the notoriously difficult question of intent in attempted murder, but it remains true that no submissions, or no successful submissions, were made in the remaining sixteen cases. This comparison may be contrasted with the case outcomes, findings of guilt in 12 of the 18 cases (7 of the 12 on lesser charges or on only some charges).

Although the main burden of the argument in this chapter is that such outcome measures are too crude, the contrast – albeit artificial – is pertinent in respect of the alternative test put forward in Chapter 1, namely, 'no reasonable expectation of a directed acquittal'. Apart from the dubious inclusion of attempted murder charges in Cases 2 and 17 all the cases sent for trial by the DPP passed the half-way stage at trial. If this were regarded as the test of the DPP's prosecution decisions, those two notable directed acquittals would have been more obviously representative of judicial censure of the prosecution. Yet under the 'reasonable prospects of conviction' test, which focuses attention instead upon jury verdicts, the directed acquittal element can easily be overlooked.

A POSTSCRIPT ON THE CRITERIA FOR FILTERING OUT

A prerequisite for a revised test which turns upon half-time submissions is that greater discretion than that currently permitted under *Galbraith* should be allowed to the judges to accede to them. Would any more of the submissions in the sample of cases have succeeded under such a regime? The question may be unanswerable, because of the lack of consistency in the manner in which *Galbraith* is currently interpreted by Stipendiary Magistrates and judges. But Case 3 may provide some insight, for in this instance there can be little doubt that the prospects of a successful submission would have been greater before *Galbraith*. The testimony of witness H, that the defendant had 'confessed' to the murder of his wife, was dubious, as was his motivation to give this evidence. As defence counsel put it, 'lies by this witness can support the prosecution's case, but not create one'. But, H's evidence may ultimately have been important in that the jury convicted of murder despite the pathologist's statement that he 'could not exclude suicide'. Did the defendant's 'confession' to H assist the jury to resolve the doubt left by the pathologist? Before *Galbraith*, the judge would have weighed the *quality* of the evidence of both witness H and the pathologist, and either none or all of the evidence would have gone to the jury. Of course, judicial antipathy towards H's testimony (as 'unsafe') might also have prevented the pathologist's evidence from going to the jury, as a result of a directed acquittal. Alternatively, judicial confidence in the pathologist's evidence may have resulted in H's evidence going to the jury as well. Clearly, there would have been a decision for the judge to reach. Under *Galbraith*, the existence of a *quantity* of evidence, even where weak, resulted in rejection of the submission.

The defence case

Assuming that there has not been a successful submission of no case, the defence will then present their version of events. In contrast with the restrictions on the presentation of the prosecution case, for example the rules on disclosure, the defence enjoys considerable flexibility.

This derives from several sources. First, the comparatively low burden of proof required from the defence. Except in those cases where the defence have to establish proof on a balance of probabilities, for example where they rely on a statutory defence as distinct from a common law defence (*R. v. Edward* [1975] QB 27); and in those cases where statute specifically imposes a legal burden of proof on the defence (such as cases involving diminished responsibility, offensive weapons, or corruption charges), the defence only have to create a 'reasonable doubt' in order to gain an acquittal. Furthermore, with the advantages of going second, the defence only has to contest the prosecution's case as it emerged *in evidence*. As already indicated, a good deal of their work may have been done for them when inadequacies emerge in the prosecution's case even though those were insufficient for a successful submission of 'no case'. Secondly, with the exception of the restrictions on the use of alibis,[41] the defence have the considerable advantage of being able to reserve the nature of their defence. Third, many rules of evidence have evolved primarily for the protection of the accused, and these provide the defence with considerable scope for exploitation; additionally, where disputes arise as to the manner of interpretation of a rule, they will normally be resolved in the defendant's favour. Finally, the defence case is, to the defence and defendant at least, largely predictable in that in the majority of cases the principal witness for the defence will be the defendant – who can usually be relied upon to be motivated to give evidence in his own favour.

There is, however, one major countervailing difficulty for the defence. In general, the accused gives evidence before any other defence witnesses. As Emmins (1983) points out, this is done for two reasons: first, the accused is usually the person best able to give the defence case, and secondly, his going first prevents suspicions that his evidence has been tailored to that of the other defence witnesses. It does not, of course, prevent the defendant from tailoring his version of events to that given by the prosecution witnesses – such 'brinkmanship' defences will be discussed in detail later; nor does it prevent co-defendants seemingly confirming one another's story, despite the technical non-corroborative value of so doing.[42] The difficulty is that in giving evidence from the box on his own behalf the defendant subjects himself to cross-examination – like any other witness. For a defendant of previous good character (for example, like all police officers who find themselves in the dock) this may not be too important since he can afford to put his character in issue. Where, however, the defendant has previous convictions he has an invidious choice. He can refrain from casting aspersions on the character of prosecution witnesses or challenging the voluntariness of confession evidence or 'verbal' admissions – both potentially effective defence strategies – and thereby protect himself from questions in cross-examination designed to discredit him. Alternatively he can challenge the prosecution witnesses and risk the potentially damaging impact on the jury of the revelation of his own character.

The only other alternative is for the defendant not to give evidence on his own behalf.[43] This only occurred in two of this sample of cases. In Case 3, the accused was charged with the murder of his wife – who drowned in the bath. The defence closed on the basis of suicide with some additional reference to the possibility of an accident. The defendant was regarded by the police and DPP as both a pathetic figure and a pathological liar. According to defence counsel he did not give evidence on the assumption that the prosecution would 'run rings around him'. Following an unsuccessful half-time submission the defence called no further evidence; the defendant was unanimously convicted after two hours. Defendant A in Case 5 did not give evidence either, and similar considerations may have applied (an interpreter was required throughout the case). The defendant was convicted.

DEFENCE STRATEGIES

For the purposes of the following discussion the defences adopted in the sample of cases studied may be characterized as falling into two categories: brinkmanship defences and denial defences (see

Table 3). Brinkmanship defences may be characterized by the manner in which the defendant accepts a large part of the prosecution's evidence but places a different emphasis on it – thus, 'I was there, it did happen, but it wasn't *quite* like that'. They may be further subdivided: first, into those where the defence reinterprets an act as lawful, for example in cases of self-defence or consensual intercourse; secondly, into those where the defendant disputes having the necessary or sufficient *mens rea*. In such cases the events themselves are hardly contestable, so a 'successful' defence might then be defined in terms of a conviction, but of a lesser offence than those charged on the indictment. Denial defences may similarly be subdivided: first, flat denials or alibi defences, and secondly, those cases where the defendant agrees that he was present at the incident but denies playing the part alleged by the prosecution. It can be seen from *Table 3* that the two basic strategies were equally popular, with acquittals spread over the five subdivisions.[44]

TABLE 3
Individual case outcomes for the sample of eighteen cases showing principal defence strategy adopted

Case number	Verdict	Strategy
6	G	denial/alibi
7	NG	denial/alibi
5	G	denial/alibi
1	NG	denial but present
14	NG	denial but present
9	G (Mans)	denial but present
3	G	denial but present
12	NG	denial but present
18 (Def A)	G	denial but present
16	G	brinkmanship/no denial – MR
10	G (Mans)	brinkmanship/no denial – MR
2	NG (count 10 only)	brinkmanship/no denial – MR
13	NG	brinkmanship/no denial – MR/R
8	NG	brinkmanship/no denial – R
4	G	brinkmanship/no denial – R
15	NG	brinkmanship/no denial – R
17	NG	brinkmanship/no denial – R
18 (Def B & C)	G	brinkmanship/no denial – R
11	NG	denial and brinkmanship

Key
NG – not guilty   G – guilty   G (Mans) – guilty of manslaughter
R – reinterpretation of facts   MR – *mens rea*

THE PROCESS OF PROSECUTION 159

However, it should be stressed that in the attempt to understand why convictions or acquittals result, such a distinction may be artificial. It cannot be known whether the particular defence strategy adopted was successful, or whether the verdict resulted from some weakness in the prosecution's case, or from some other feature of the case associated with the defendant, or whether it was the circumstances of the offence which swayed the jury. This fact, that even with hindsight there can be no certainty about the basis of juries' decisions, combined with the many and varied strategies open to the defence to establish a reasonable doubt, creates difficulties for the prosecutor keen to apply the reasonable prospects test (see *Table 4*). Unlike the prosecution, the defence can confidently run several strategies concurrently, in the knowledge that such an approach may be sufficient to establish the kinds of nagging doubts which in turn create a reasonable doubt about guilt. Yet routinely the prosecutor will not know what line the defence will take; he may therefore be able neither to prepare a proper challenge to it, nor to assess how persuasive it will be to the jury. Finally, the defence may exploit the advantageous position it derives from the adversarial system – both legitimately and through the use of tactics that may not fully serve the wider public interest. This topic will be discussed last.

(i) *Brinkmanship defences* These defences are probably most successfully run by defendants who either have the benefit of good and/or early legal advice or who are themselves reasonably articulate, intelligent, or 'sophisticated'. This is because such defences routinely require considerable 'explanation' by the defendant to the court.

'Sophistication' may be attained either as a result of previous experience as a defendant or through experience of the process. For example, police officer defendants have the double 'blue serge' advantage: they are both reasonably well appraised of the 'tricks of the trade' and have an unblemished character with high credibility. Although obtaining convictions against police officers is notoriously difficult in cases where the principal prosecution witnesses/complainants are themselves not of good character, prosecutions are more readily brought where other police officers are prepared to give evidence. Even under these circumstances the brinkmanship defence can be very successful. A classic illustration occurred in Case 8, the police officer charged with common assault on a woman skinhead. The charge was based on a 'punch in the stomach' given by the defendant *after* she had been subdued by two other officers;

TABLE 4
A check-list for prosecutors of potential pitfalls exploitable by the defence emerging from the sample of eighteen cases

Prosecution failure

1. establish facts – intent
2. rebut defences
3. moral culpability this defendant
4. moral culpability in contrast co-defendants
5. moral culpability in contrast possible co-offenders
6. switching strategy
7. witness failure
8. interrogation tactics
9. trials within trials

Nagging doubts

10. defence opening
11. many early versions given to the police
12. identification
13. confusion/muddying of the evidence
14. experts – testimony not sufficiently predictable

Defendant factors

15. motivation
16. intelligent/articulate/sophisticated
17. good character
18. 'blue serge' (police officers)
19. lower expectation as witness – no confidence
20. co-defendants listen throughout – mutual corroboration
21. witness involvement
    – character
    – relationship with defendant

'Sporting theory'/defence ethics

22. early legal advice
23. exculpatory statement
24. advice for co-defendants
25. abuse of privilege (lawyer – client)
26. reserved defence – 'defence by ambush'
27. exploiting gaps
28. exploiting rules
29. low burden of proof to satisfy

this was corroborated by statements from those other police officers. The defendant had originally denied doing more than simply restraining her, but at trial a careful trading of ambiguities and semantics enabled him to elaborate on this. His explanation of events changed, with the admission that he had given her 'a quick chip [sic] in the stomach' to calm her down. Under cross-examination he claimed that the controlled use of violence was sometimes a tool of the trade and that in police parlance 'restraint' could well have included a punch in the stomach. This was tantamount to an admission of the prosecution's case, but was placed in the context of a 'lawful blow' (Criminal Law Act 1967, Section 3). To explain his initial denials he stated that at *that* stage he had not consulted his solicitor and therefore did not appreciate that police parlance diverged from legal niceties. He also claimed that he made the admissions to the solicitor; such a conversation is privileged and therefore cannot be explored by the prosecution.

A similar strategy was adopted by defendant B, also a police officer, in Case 17, in that he admitted all the objective elements of the prosecution's case – except that he claimed the victim was 'making groping movements down his body' when he shot him – but ran a defence based partly on this evidential dispute, which reinterpreted his acts as lawful. During both his interrogation and at trial he stated that his intention was, if necessary, to kill the man despite the fact that he had at that stage not seen a gun. His explanation of his behaviour was that he 'feared for his life and those of his two colleagues'; this defence of self-defence was subsequently assisted by the judge's bold ruling that a defendant's belief in the necessity to use force need not be reasonable.[45] One of the principal advantages of the brinkmanship defence, and to a lesser extent, a defence of 'I was there, but I didn't do it', is that, since the accused accepts a substantial proportion of the prosecution case, the points in dispute are comparatively limited. The defence can thus concentrate its efforts on raising doubts in relation to these issues. Similarly, the prosecution case loses some of its accusatorial impact and the defendant appears more 'reasonable'. Case 11 illustrates this. It concerned a police sergeant accused of multiple rape, indecent assault, and unlawful sexual intercourse with his German foster daughter. The victim explained her lack of complaint over the course of several years on the grounds that her foster father had told her that no one would believe her if she complained *because* he was a policeman. When she eventually made her allegations, the defendant admitted during interrogation that he had had intercourse with her from the time when she was about 14½; he himself subsequently wrote a statement under caution of eight pages giving details of these admissions. A further written statement, made in the privacy of his own home and handed to the police over a week later, amounted to a partial retraction of some of his earlier admissions. But even this later statement was unclear on the question of whether he had first had intercourse with her before her sixteenth birthday (somewhat surprising for someone acquainted with the law). At trial, the admissibility of his confession was unsuccessfully contested on the grounds of oppression and inducement. Since the judge did not even call upon the prosecution to reply to the defence submission, it was apparent to all, except the jury who were of course not present, that the judge considered the submission spurious.[46] The defence case was that consensual intercourse had taken place, but not until after her sixteenth birthday. This amounted to 'I was there, I did do it, but not *when* the prosecution allege and therefore it is not an offence'. This strategy made the victim's knowledge of certain distinguishing features of the defendant's penis, which would have been damning if he had denied intercourse altogether, unproblematic. Despite the jury having access to the written confessions of the defendant, which contradicted his evidence from the box, he was acquitted on all charges. This highly unusual result[47] is a testament to the persuasiveness of 'blue serge', particularly when run in combination with a brinkmanship defence; persuading the jury of the existence of a reasonable doubt is by no means impossible if some predisposed doubt exists before the case has even started.

Another area where the brinkmanship approach may be successful, despite overwhelming factual support for the prosecution's case, is in defences involving disputes over *mens rea*. The potential difficulties which brinkmanship defences pose for juries by obfuscating the issues (unlike simple denials) may be amplified where the case concerns issues that are hard to establish in themselves – like provocation or intent. In Case 16, the defence was one of diminished responsibility; it should of course be borne in mind that in such cases the burden on the defence increases from raising a reasonable doubt to establishing the defence on a balance of probabilities. The defendant did not dispute the facts of the prosecution's case – indeed, the events were hardly contestable – but only his state of mind at the time of the death of his victims. Two defence psychiatric experts were called to testify to his 'severe personality disorder', but they failed to agree on a label for its specific form.[48] A prosecution psychiatric expert was called to rebut their evidence, claiming that he had found no significant evidence of any of the symptoms to which the defence had referred. Given that the defence, in this kind of case, has to satisfy the higher standard of proof, the persuasive impact of this brinkmanship defence on at least some of the jurors can be gauged from the fact that it took over twelve hours to return verdicts of guilty of murder.

Case 15 was similar to Case 17 in that a brinkmanship defence of self-defence was argued. However, the acquittal might be characterized as more clearly derived from prosecutorial failure than from the success of 'brinkmanship'. The case originally concerned four defendants involved in the death of a drugs dealer. Two of them were charged with only minor drug offences and they subsequently refused, on the basis of legal advice from a solicitor whom they shared with the principal accused, to act as prosecution witnesses unless the major charges against defendant A were dropped. The other co-defendant, defendant B, – whom defendant A implicated as being largely responsible for the murder – was not committed for trial; his experienced criminal background may have made him more likely to refuse to make any admissions to the police or to co-operate in any way. Since defendant A had been committed separately, there was no *prima facie* case against defendant B at committal. At trial defendant A thus had the advantage of being able to accuse defendant B of the actual stabbing whilst admitting otherwise 'assaulting' the victim in self-defence. Furthermore, even in the prosecution's view he was not the most morally culpable of what could have been two defendants. From the jury's perspective, it was clear that there *should* have been two defendants.[49] A's early and partially exculpatory statement to the police, made when he and his solicitor volunteered themselves at the police station, created a credible framework for exploiting a doubt latent in the prosecution case. He was acquitted.

Thus, brinkmanship defences may attempt to reinterpret events, to explain the reasonableness of a defendant's appreciation of a situation, or to elucidate that which may be incapable of clarification with any certainty, namely, the state of mind of the defendant at the time of the offence; all are aimed at interpreting the defendant's actions as lawful, or at least considerably less culpable than the prosecution would assert.

(ii) *Denial defences* The defendant in Case 1 employed a denial defence of 'I was there, but I didn't do it', in combination with counsel's effective presentation of a growing catalogue of 'nagging doubts' to the jury. The defendant was charged with murder. The victim's death resulted from a stab wound. Some of the prosecution witnesses were implicated to a greater or lesser extent in the prelude to the stabbing (which occurred in a shebeen) and their credibility was consistently eroded by defence counsel in relation to minor details. Whether the prosecution can afford to take the risk of using an involved and possibly morally culpable individual as a witness may be a dilemma the prosecution cannot resolve to its own advantage; where 'witnesses' are not present in court (because of their very culpability) the defence can equally exploit their absence. The prosecution case was also weakened by a principal co-defendant having 'got out' at committal. As in Case 15, even if the jury did not believe the defendant's denial defence, they may have had considerable doubt that he was solely culpable for the incident. The defendant was acquitted.

In both Cases 14 and 9 the defendants had originally denied the offences, and then after lengthy interviews made limited admissions to the police; logically these should have weakened the persuasive value of their denial defences at trial. However, these lengthy interviews may in turn have been problematic for the prosecution, since they provided the defendants with an opportunity to raise doubts about the voluntariness of their admissions. It also resulted in several defence versions – a sequence of denial, limited admission, denial – being put to the jury by both the prosecution and the defence, thus creating a platform for the 'nagging doubts' approach. In both cases there were verdicts favourable to the defence.

Defendants able to produce alibi defences are the most likely to have a virtual guarantee both that their witnesses will come to court and that they will 'come up to proof'; this will be particularly true where defendants call upon their families or friends to sustain their alibis. Where both the content and credibility of defence witnesses holds up in court, their evidence may have considerable sway. If both the prosecution case and the defence case are credible and persuasive, then the jury's verdict should favour the defendant.

Finally, where denial, as opposed to brinkmanship, defences are adopted, the prosecution's task is made doubly difficult. Since so little may be admitted by the defence, the prosecution have to prove many more elements of their case. Added to this are the advantages that denial defences derive from the considerable uncertainty surrounding the identification issues and eyewitness testimony which such defences frequently entail.

THE 'SPORTING THEORY' OF JUSTICE AND DEFENCE ETHICS

Within an adversarial trial process it is open to the defence to exploit both the rules of evidence and gaps in the prosecution case in a largely unrestricted manner. This contrasts markedly with the position of the prosecution who are constrained by a series of precedents and principles to a kind of 'fair play'. Capitalization on lacunae in the field of defence ethics is a strategy most easily employed where the defendant receives early and comprehensive legal advice, which may in itself prevent a successful prosecution from being launched. The strategy was adopted in a refined form in Case 6, which concerned an ex-police officer charged with a series of offences including rape, attempted rape, and thirteen counts of dishonesty carried out while he was a serving officer. This was one of those cases where the sum of the evidence could be characterized as being greater than all of its parts. The first tactic the defence employed was to apply (successfully) to have the indictment severed, and the initial trial went ahead on the basis of attempted rape, indecent assault, and wounding. In a subsequent trial within a trial the defence challenged the admissibility of some 'verbals', partly on the grounds that ambiguity existed over whether they applied solely to the offences on the first indictment.[50] Following an 'unfavourable' intimation from the judge, prosecuting counsel agreed not to call part of that evidence. Thus, the strategy of applying for severance of the indictment had the effect of fragmenting and substantially weakening the prosecution case. The second tactic the defence employed was to serve notice of a late alibi – the mother of the accused gave evidence that he was in bed on the night of the attempted rape and that she had seen him 'asleep over his police manuals'. Although there was no mention of this in her statement to the police, she informed the court that she had told her son's solicitor; it was therefore privileged information (see p. 161). Defence counsel took 'personal responsibility' for the mistake of not notifying the court of this salient point sooner. The prosecution was thus placed in the position which Section 11 of the Criminal Law Act of 1967 was designed to prevent, namely, it had no opportunity to investigate the alibi properly. That the prosecution did not challenge this late submission or apply for an adjournment indicates that in practice rules do not always fulfil their intended purpose. Defence by ambush may still occur despite Section 11. A final tactic employed in Case 6 was to exploit the defendant's 'exemplary character'. This tactic would have had considerably less persuasive value had the indictment not been severed (the prosecution were alleging offences over a considerable period of time); and counsel may well have had his fingers crossed behind his back when he explicitly put the defendant's character to the jury. Despite this gamut of defence strategies, the defendant was found guilty of the indecent assault and wounding charges (although he was acquitted of the attempted rape). He subsequently pleaded guilty to all the other counts except one rape and one theft charge.

Case 12 also illustrates how the rules of evidence can be legitimately exploited by defence counsel. This concerned a man accused of murdering his wife's lover. The wife, who was present at the time of the offence, did not give evidence.[51] This left inexplicable gaps in the prosecution's case. The jury were instructed by the judge 'not to indulge in guesswork as to what she might or might not have said'. Defence counsel, however, *did* encourage the jury to speculate as to the wife's role in the incident, and asked them to consider why her husband had not killed her as well, and what was he going to do with her if he had just murdered her lover while she was still in the flat? The prosecution were unable to comment. The defendant was acquitted.

A final example of a lacuna in the law being exploited by the defence concerned the cross-examination of rape victims about their sexual experiences with persons other than the defendant. This is substantially restricted by Section 2 of the Sexual Offences (Amendment) Act 1976 in respect of rape charges, but such cross-examination may be allowed at the judge's discretion where an indecent assault charge is included on the indictment, as occurred, for example, in Case 4. Thus, the inclusion of indecent assault charges on an indictment for rape may negate the protection afforded the victim by Section 2 of the Act and allow the defence to blacken the victim's character. If this occurs, the effect cannot surely be confined solely to the indecent assault element of the case. Ironically, there may have been little need for defence counsel to exploit this lacuna, since in all of the other rape cases in the sample the judges exercised their discretion under Section 2 and allowed the cross-examination of the victims about their sexual experiences. These illustrations of the way in which the malleability of the rules of evidence generally favours defendants may be compared with a similar tendency regarding developments in the law arising out of novel judicial interpretations; those interpretations which disadvantage the accused may become subject to appeal, whereas those that do not may be less readily rectified.[52]

It is hard to assess the impact on the jury of the repeated endeavours to blacken the character of the victim in Case 18, but attempts by the defence to exploit the rules may occasionally rebound on defendants. In Case 4, although the judge warned the jury that inculpatory statements made by one defendant are not evidence against a co-defendant unless they are adopted in the witness-box, defence counsel for one of the co-defendants subsequently tried to undermine an inculpatory statement. Presumably he did it on the grounds that a warning from the judge is not sufficient to ensure that the evidence will be ignored by the jury. But, may the fact of his dwelling on the 'excluded evidence' (sic) actually have resulted in the statement being given unmerited attention by the jury?

Although during the trial stage of the adversarial system there may be scope for the defence to exploit situations where the prosecution's hands are tied and thus to enjoy some advantage, it may be regarded as a reversal of the defence's earlier handicap during the stages of investigation and pre-trial procedure. It has been asserted both that the police have the upper hand during these stages and that they exploit their privileged position (see for example the débâcle in Case 14, p. 120). Defendants who are well advised or otherwise advantaged at the early stages can thus gain the full benefit of the subsequent reversed imbalance.[53] The scope for the prosecution to rectify the effects of this double advantage may be limited. They are constrained by the rules on disclosure, and they do not enjoy many of the strategies open to the defence, namely the ability to run several strategies at once; to engage in 'defence by ambush'; and to indulge generally in the tactics of confusion. It might be concluded on the basis of this sample of cases that the prosecution could do more to put its own house in order; in more 'ordinary' cases, however, the balance could be more even throughout. A more rigorous assessment of the strength of the prosecution case, grounded on the basis of what the prosecution case is, rather than how it might turn out in front of the jury, could have proved worthwhile. Even so, by and large the prosecution's case only became weaker at trial; highlighting inadequacies in the defence case was not sufficient to tilt the balance back into 'beyond reasonable doubt'.

Closing speeches

After all the defence witnesses have been called, prosecuting and defence counsel will, in turn, make closing speeches. It is only in very unusual circumstances that prosecuting counsel does not have the right to make a closing speech.[54] Closing speeches for the prosecution generally satisfy Watkins, J.'s (*obiter dictum* in *R. v. Bryant and Oxley* [1978] 2 WLR 589) criterion of having the 'becoming hallmark of brevity': counsel takes the jury through the indictment, reminds them of the relevant parts of the prosecution case, and comments on any implausibilities in the defence case. It has been noted that prosecuting counsel should continue to regard themselves as 'ministers of justice', assisting in its administration, rather than as advocates (*R. v. Puddick* (1865) 4 F and F 497, and approved in *R. v. Banks* (1916) 2 KB 621); they are not, for instance, meant to comment on the failure of an accused to give evidence (Criminal Evidence Act 1898, S.1(b)).

In contrast, defence counsel enjoys a broad discretion to make any comments he considers desirable, not only about the evidence of his witnesses but also about the whole of the case (*R. v. Wainwright* (1895) 13 Cox 171). However, defence counsel may not attack the character of prosecution witnesses except to take up allegations already made in cross-examination; otherwise there is a risk that the defendant may be recalled for the purposes of cross-examination as to character.

Neither prosecuting nor defence counsel may allege as fact matters on which no evidence has been given. In practice, however, there are ways and means of circumventing this rule and again they seem to operate in favour of the defence.

CLOSING SPEECHES FOR THE PROSECUTION

Although it is obviously right that prosecuting counsel should not take on the role of persecutors, one tendency that emerged in the sample of cases was for prosecuting counsel to overcompensate and show signs of 'reluctance'. References to a 'domestic tragedy' (Case 10), a 'sad matter' (Case 17), and a 'sad world' (Case 14) were not uncommon, placing prosecuting counsel on a somewhat uneasy footing and underlining elements of moral doubt.

Prosecuting counsel has the ability to constrain jury decisions where it is felt that evidence on a particular charge has not been established beyond reasonable doubt. Thus, in Case 9, prosecuting counsel questioned the credibility of his own eyewitness and asserted to the jury that they may think that 'a verdict of murder is inappropriate because there must be a doubt'. Similarly, in Case 10, prosecuting counsel displayed some hesitancy as to whether he was seeking a verdict of murder or manslaughter (confirmed in interview subsequently when he remarked, 'I put it as strongly as I felt I could *not* for murder'). In Case 15, although prosecuting counsel was firm in his claim that the Crown had proved the absence of legitimate self-defence (and therefore a complete acquittal would not be justified on the evidence), he appeared at the same time not to be seeking a verdict of murder since in the absence of defendant B (the co-defendant not committed), it was hard to establish that defendant A had gone to the scene with 'murderous intent'. Instead, he asked the jury for a verdict of manslaughter on the grounds that defendant A had been party to a joint intention to assault, but that his partner had gone further than agreed, which resulted in the victim's death. Therefore defendant A was legally guilty of manslaughter. The jury, who acquitted altogether, obviously did not find this reasoning persuasive. There are then some prosecution doubts that manifest themselves to the jury in ways that they would find difficult to disregard, and other more subtle assessments that reflect a degree of prosecution 'distaste'. It is difficult to assess the impact on the jury of these objective and subjective devaluations of the case by prosecuting counsel; they may be comparable with the potential impact of directed acquittals in respect of some charges on a jury's assessment of the charges remaining for their consideration.

It is also apparent that where prosecuting counsel attempts to summarize conflicting evidence within the prosecution case, so that all possible interpretations would still support a finding of guilt, he may damage his credibility and provide grounds for ridicule by the defence. So deviation in the course of the prosecution cannot easily be rectified in a closing speech.

It is debatable whether, in a closing speech, prosecuting counsel can effectively pre-empt defence arguments. He is just as likely to give them spurious persuasive value through the simple process of repeating them. For example, in Case 7, counsel warned the jury that although there had been some confusion over the colour and ownership of a particular coat and whether the defendant was wearing it on the day of the attempted murder, all three eyewitnesses had seen him wearing the coat. The strategy proved unsuccessful; the defence discussed the discrepancies between the eyewitnesses' testimony, and built on these by asking the jury to pay attention to the poor quality rather than the quantity of the witnesses. The defendant was acquitted.

Finally, to what extent should the prosecutor attempt to 'spoon-feed' the jury, by simplifying those issues which he may legitimately expect the defence deliberately to confuse? In Case 12 counsel could have done more to point out that it would be logically inconsistent to return any verdict other than guilty of murder. By doing so he might have encouraged the jury to conclude that the standard of proof, beyond reasonable doubt, had been reached through a process of elimination of the other possible explanations. He did not.[55] This self-imposed censorship, drawing back from stretching the rules, is a testament to the admirable ethical stance adopted by prosecuting counsel in the majority of cases in the sample.

Prosecuting counsel cannot close his case with the expressed intention of securing a conviction. He can, however, ensure that the jury do not return convictions on certain counts.[56] Although he may attempt to rectify damage done to the credibility of the prosecution witnesses (by contrasting them with the implausibility of the defendant's version), he will only do so in the certain knowledge that defence counsel in his closing speech will reopen any wounds to which the prosecutor has effected temporary repairs. As such, brevity may not only be cost-effective, but also the only attractive option for prosecuting counsel.

CLOSING SPEECHES FOR THE DEFENCE

In stark contrast to the generally underplayed tone of prosecuting counsel's closing speech, defence counsel may employ the full scope of the 'Rumpolesque' technique – brevity is not a hallmark. Emotional appeals to the jury; running several strategies at the same time; highlighting inconsistencies, inadequacies, and particularly gaps in the prosecution's case; reinterpreting the defendant's actions; and even ridiculing the prosecution's closing speech, as for example in Case 10 where the defence counsel remarked to the jury that, unlike the hesitant closing speech made for the prosecution, 'I have no hesitation about what verdict I ask you for': these are all commonplace and often interweave a fascinating web of mutual support.

Emotional appeals range from attacking the quality of the prosecution's case through hyperbole – such as 'you wouldn't convict a cat on that evidence' (Case 18) – to highlighting the difficulties of the defence's role. Counsel may note both the ease with which allegations are made and the fact that 'once made they are almost impossible to refute' (Case 11). An emotional appeal may be used to overcome a logically damning piece of prosecution evidence. In Case 17 defence counsel quoted Cardinal Richelieu: 'Give me six lines by an honest man and I can find something in them to hang him on.' Defence counsel may also resort to emotional appeals to bolster a case founded on expert evidence: thus in Case 16, in spite of long expert psychiatric testimony, counsel asked the jury, 'Does not common sense cry out and does not common speech oblige one to say that the perpetrator of these killings must be out of his mind?' Counsel may also make a virtue out of necessity when their client's record is known to the jury, again through an emotional contrast: 'My client is a young rogue, he's no angel, but he's no sex offender' (Case 18). Finally, there are simple appeals based on the client's plight: 'I appeal to your common sense and humanity ... release him from his ten-month nightmare' (the period the defendants had spent awaiting trial in Case 17).

Logically, it might be assumed that if defence counsel closes a case by putting forward two interpretations of the evidence, each version would undermine the plausibility of the other. This, however, does not seem to be so, partly because, as is frequently pointed out by defence counsel, the defence does not have to prove its case – only introduce an element of doubt. Therefore, it may be an advantage to create confusion. The other principal advantage of closing a case on more than one basis concerns the risk that defendants run on a charge of, say, murder, if their defence of denial is unsuccessful. They then have no grounds for seeking a verdict of manslaughter (not to be preferred of course to an acquittal), which is still better than risking a mandatory life sentence on a conviction of murder. For example, in Case 1, despite the principal defence of denial, counsel still paid attention in his closing speech to the failure of the prosecution to establish that his client ever intended the victim serious harm.

Although neither side may allege as fact matters on which no evidence has been given, the defence, in highlighting gaps in the prosecution case, may come close to this by implication. Some of these 'gaps' may be deliberate red herrings. For example in Case 11, counsel made reference to the absence of any physical evidence on the victim of resistance to the rapes, mentioning the 'all a woman has to do is to keep her legs together' myth. Yet the prosecution case had been founded on a presumption of submission to an authority figure. Some of the 'gaps' to which the defence attempt to attach meaning may be more simply regarded (by the jury) as omissions in a witness's evidence: in Case 18 counsel asserted that the doctor's evidence of discoid bruising was *not* consistent with the victim's account, since she made no mention of having her legs held apart. Perhaps the saddest example of this strategy, and one which forcefully underlines society's interest in not only acquitting the innocent but also convicting the guilty, concerned Case 7. Counsel made great play of the prosecution's failure to produce evidence for any motive on the part of his client for the attempted murder; the defendant was acquitted. Only weeks later the defendant was charged, then later convicted, of the murder of another vagrant who had been locked up with him overnight in a police cell (*Guardian*, 7 June, 1984). During the investigation he admitted to police that he had killed nine times in the previous thirty years. Defence counsel would obviously not have known this, but whether his knowledge of his client's previous acquittal on a similar murder charge should have made him somewhat more reluctant to employ arguments about motive is open to question.

Finally, highlighting apparent inconsistencies in the prosecution's case, and drawing attention to elements which it may be very hard for the prosecution to establish with any certainty, are two further potentially successful and legitimate defence strategies. Less persuasively, counsel may insinuate that accepting the prosecution's case requires the jury to believe that the defendant acted in an illogical and irrational manner. The assumption that guilty parties must act rationally, whereas innocent behaviour is readily accepted to be apparently irrational, is somewhat ironic.

The imbalance between prosecution and defence in the latter stages of the criminal justice process has been reaffirmed by this brief analysis of closing speeches. The defence can have it any way they choose – and rightly so in the traditions of the adversarial system. Whether the reason why juries acquit is that they have accepted the defence attack on the prosecution, or have simply failed to be persuaded by the prosecution's own case, cannot be known.

Judicial discretion

The judge occupies a position of great power in the English criminal trial. He controls the conduct of the trial and the admissibility of evidence, to a considerable extent by the exercise of discretion rather than through rigid application of rules; and through his summing up he may exert considerable influence on the jury. Judges inevitably differ in their ability and in their approach to these tasks. The course taken by any particular case may thus depend upon which judge(s) deal(s) with it.

Before a trial starts, the judge might have to take a decision on severance; where there are two or more charges relating to a series of alleged offences, should they be taken together at a single trial or be tried separately? The question is inextricably connected with the admissibility on each charge of evidence of the other alleged offences, and that in turn affects the decision to prosecute. In Case 4, the DPP decided to prosecute some eight alleged rapes and indecent assaults, having formed the view that the allegations were sufficiently similar in detail to be cross-admissible (*DPP v. Boardman* (1974) 60 Cr. App. R. 165 H. L). When the case was passed to prosecuting counsel, she did not accept the DPP's judgment that all charges should be tried together, and acquiesced when the judge severed the indictment into three trials. The defence continued to press, unsuccessfully, for complete severance into eight trials. However, there were difficulties early in the first trial (one of the complainants could not be found, one juror was repeatedly late), and the judge took the opportunity to discharge the jury. He then stated that, on a closer reading of the case papers, he ought, on the authorities, to have severed the case further, into five trials, because it would otherwise be extremely difficult to sum up fairly to a jury.

The events in this case illustrate three points. First, the exercise of judicial discretion on matters such as severance and the admissibility of 'similar fact evidence' is complicated and demanding. Secondly, the prosecution's initial decision in such a case may, in effect, rest on the assumption about the way the judge will exercise his discretion. In this case it was accepted by prosecuting counsel, when the matter was put to her by one of the researchers after convictions in the first trial, that there were no longer reasonable prospects of conviction in respect of some remaining charges. The cases reached the standard if some were tried together, but not otherwise. Yet, thirdly, convictions did result on most charges – once again showing the naïvety and incompleteness of simply linking initial decisions to prosecute with ultimate outcomes in court, without looking at the route by which they are obtained. Ultimately and ironically, there were convictions in the first two trials and these led to pleas of guilty on most of the other charges.

During the course of a trial there are specific stages at which the judge may be called on to reach a decision: for example, on the admissibility of evidence at a trial within a trial and/or whether to uphold a submission of no case (see pp. 151–56). The judge may also control any undue loquacity or irrelevance by counsel. Judges occasionally intervene to put questions to a witness, and observation of trials suggests that on some occasions this attempt to 'help' nullified counsel's effort to develop the questioning subtly for another purpose. The 'help' offered by the judge to the jury in summing up also requires considerable sensitivity and skill. There can be no doubt that a judge is able to slant his summing up in one direction or another, although there is a saying at the Bar that one can safely sum up for an acquittal but not for a conviction. In virtually all the trials observed, the summing up was readily characterized by counsel and others on 'both sides' as favouring one side or another.

Thus, judges may reinterpret witnesses' credibility to the jury, going beyond even prosecuting counsel's characterizations, as in Case 9. Judges may also explain some legal issues in a manner favourable to the defence, for example in Case 17 directing the jury on the law that the defendants should be assessed on the facts as they mistakenly believed them to be.[57] Finally, judges sometimes misdirect the jury on some factual matters presumably regarded by counsel as so minor as not to require correction; but it is hard to assess their impact on the jury. In Case 17, for example, the judge stated that there had been no bleeding from the victim's head, despite evidence that there had been.

These few illustrations show how the judge's exercise of discretion and his general approach to the case may help to determine the fate of a prosecution. The extent to which judges in their summings up actually affect jury verdicts cannot be conclusively determined, but there is strong impressionistic evidence that the influence may be considerable, in some cases.

The verdict of the jury

For the prosecutor employing the reasonable prospects test the bases on which juries return convictions are of considerable interest. Yet little is known, beyond informed speculation, about the factors that influence juries. This dearth of knowledge results partly from the restrictions on undertaking research into jury decision-making. No one is allowed to record jury deliberations or to interview jurors (Section 8, Contempt of Court Act 1981). What little has been gleaned about jury decision-making from the use of shadow juries and simulated trials suggests that the subtleties of the legal distinctions over which the lawyers have agonized during the course of a prosecution may be neither understood nor acted upon by juries.[58] For example the rules of evidence, which require the judge to warn the jury of the desirability of corroboration in certain types of cases, may influence juries in unexpected ways – making a conviction more rather than less likely. Thus there is a tension between the bases on which juries make decisions and the legal criteria which, from the lawyer's perspective, they should be applying. The judicial direction that 'the law is for me (the judge) and the facts for you, members of the jury', is similarly somewhat at odds with the reality of the situation wherein the jury receive a barrage of implicit and explicit advice on the facts, right up to the moment that they retire. The jury are then truly 'on their own' with regard to the facts.[59] It could therefore be regarded as ironic that as cases are processed through the criminal justice system there is progressively more legal specialization at each stage, yet ultimately they are presented for a decision to complete amateurs. When convictions result, the jury's unique view of the facts and the law may be overturned on appeal; but any perverse interpretation which leads the jury to acquit may not. Or, as leading Treasury Counsel succinctly put it, such jury acquittals are 'between God and their conscience'.[60]

Speculation about the bases of jury decision-making is bound to increase with the extension of the reasonable prospects test through the Crown Prosecution System. Such speculation will inform prosecutors' decisions about whether cases should be brought in the first instance, and it is therefore clear that empirical inquiry into the role of the jury would be desirable. This study provides a possible way forward. Tracking cases through the criminal justice system and throughout their trial permits speculation about the factors that may have influenced the jury, speculation which can be based both on close observation of the juries, and on a contextual interpretation of jury notes to the judge. But these extrapolations necessarily remain at the level of speculation. Thus, this research was handicapped in its retrospective analysis, although it was not, of course, as disadvantaged as the prosecutor who had to speculate in advance.

BEYOND REASONABLE DOUBT – AN INCREMENTAL APPROACH TO CERTAINTY

Juries are sometimes presented with cases in which the 'experts' involved have been unable to reach a conclusion about the defendant's guilt or innocence. The prosecution may resolve the difficulty by recourse to the policy that, where there is a 'genuine point of balance', the case should go before the Court (Royal Commission on Criminal Procedure 1981: Appendix 25). If the jury, having heard the evidence, similarly come to a point of equilibrium they cannot pass the case to another tribunal; the presumption of innocence should therefore incline them to acquit. But juries were, in the sample of cases, able to resolve such doubts and convict. Case 3 is a good example. In this case the prosecution pathologist inclined to the view that the defendant had murdered his wife, but gave the defence its foundation of doubt in that he 'could not exclude suicide'. Yet the jury was unanimously sure of the defendant's guilt, presumably beyond reasonable doubt, after two hours of deliberation. How was the foundation of doubt dispelled? A civilian witness gave evidence of the defendant's virtual 'confession' to him; but his credibility was substantially impaired, both in chief and in cross-examination. Other witnesses gave testimony of the couple's turbulent and sometimes violent relationship, and of the defendant's lack of genuine grief after the victim's death. None of this testimony was necessarily inconsistent with the victim having committed suicide, and indeed some of it pointed to that conclusion. There was further independent medical evidence of her previous suicide attempts. The most damning evidence against the defendant was that the number and positioning of bruises on the corpse (including those on her ankles) were inconsistent with the 'rescue attempt' which he claimed to have made. Yet if he had admitted to assaulting her earlier in the day – which might have precipitated a suicide – the main plank of the prosecution case would have been substantially undermined. He did not. His denial of the violence necessary to produce the bruises was consistent with his failure to acknowledge previous (established) matrimonial violence. Was it this general picture that tipped the balance for the jury? Did the defendant's lies about a comparatively inconsequential matter result in the jury disbelieving his version of events in relation to his wife's death?

In reaching the point of certainty equivalent to beyond reasonable doubt, juries may be assisted by the judge. In Case 6 the evidence was primarily circumstantial, yet a conviction resulted. In his summing up the judge had employed the image of a rope in reference to the separate pieces of circumstantial evidence: the individual strands of evidence were insufficient to support a conviction but taken together they might. He distinguished the rope from a chain, where a weak or broken link would necessarily result in an acquittal. This latter approach has more relevance to the situation pertaining to eyewitness testimony[61] and makes Case 17 (acquittal on eyewitness testimony) an interesting contrast with Case 6 (conviction on circumstantial evidence). It seems that the route to 'beyond reasonable doubt' varies according to whether the evidence is circumstantial or reliant upon eyewitnesses.

In Case 4, the judge went still further in attempting to assist the jury. Having given them directions that they might reach a majority verdict, the judge subsequently exhorted them, when they failed to return with a verdict, to achieve some consensus, in so far as was consistent with the terms of their individual jurors' oaths, bearing in mind external factors such as public time and money.[62] Thus, the degree of certainty attained by the jury and implied by 'beyond reasonable doubt' may, in some cases, derive partly from the impact that the confident views of some members of the jury have on others. This, in turn, may have been enhanced by the judge's second set of directions.

Few of the cases in the sample are illustrative of a measured, incremental approach to decision-making, wherein residual doubts are progressively resolved in such a way that guilt is inexorably established. The bulk of the decisions are more evidently evocative of a 'broad brush' approach by the jury, which owes more to notions of common sense than to evidential formulae.[63] This arguably sits more comfortably with acquittals than convictions. Is it reasonable to assume, even allowing for the discrepancy between the respective burdens of proof on the prosecution and defence, that convictions reflect certainty on the part of the jury whereas acquittals do not?

THE 'BROAD BRUSH' APPROACH TO CERTAINTY

Numerous cases suggested that the jury adopted a 'broad brush' approach in reaching a decision. In some respects this may seem defensible. If cases exist where lawyers, with their technical expertise, cannot decide between guilt or innocence, how could one expect juries, if they took a similar approach, to do any better? This raises two questions. What limits, if any, should be set upon the jury's latitude? How far, if at all, should the prosecutor take account of it – if he thinks some *pattern* is discernible? Five such patterns are discussed below.

(i) *The 'pecking order' of relative guilt (co-defendants and witnesses)* One of the difficulties in Case 17 was that the case against defendant B was evidentially stronger, on paper, than against defendant A. B admitted an intent to kill, and so an attempted murder charge could be justified on the indictment; whereas A had made no such admission, so that the attempted murder charge against him was not so strong. Yet defendant A had precipitated the shooting incident; but for his actions, it appeared unlikely that defendant B would have opened fire on the victim. So was defendant B to be charged with a more serious offence than A, simply on the basis of what he said at interview, despite the obvious sequence of events? This appeared contrary to common sense and natural justice. One may speculate that the arguably greater moral culpability of defendant A contributed to the DPP's decision to bring an attempted murder charge against him (in order to ensure 'fairness' between the defendants – see Chapter 2, pp. 103–04 on public interest). Subsequently, in the submission of no case on this charge, legal questions of evidential sufficiency apparently gained primacy over moral questions of comparative culpability; a directed acquittal resulted. In turn the jury were then faced with defendant B, who was clearly morally less culpable than defendant A, but who still faced the more serious charge of attempted murder. Was their role in the decision-making sequence to allow moral assessments to trump evidential ones – contributing to the acquittal of both defendants A and B? Herein lies the problem for a legal process which mixes both moral and legal assessments, and lay and legal assessors. Lawyers may never know whether juries actively ignore the legal guidance they are given or simply fail to appreciate it. The same moral and public interest factors which contribute to a decision to bring charges, or to bring charges at a specific level, may later result in defendants' ultimate acquittals.

Similarly, in Case 4, defendant C, the youngest of the three defendants, had made admissions which were allowed in evidence after a trial within a trial. It was explained to the jury that these statements could inculpate defendant C but not defendants A or B, since they did not adopt any of his statements in evidence (see p. 167 above). Yet it was obvious, and accepted by all counsel and the judge, that defendant C was not only the 'baby' of the group, but a mere hanger-on. If the jury were impelled to convict him on the basis of his statements, as well as other evidence against him in common with the other two, it seemed extremely unlikely that his co-defendants would escape conviction – unless defendant C were to be penalized for his apparently greater honesty. Similar dilemmas may confront juries when attributing moral culpability if prosecution witnesses (for example Case 14) or absent parties (for example Cases 1 and 15) appear to the jury to be at least as responsible for the crime as the accused whose guilt they have to judge.

(ii) *'Rough justice'* In Case 5 only one of the two defendants charged with murder went into the witness-box. He twice gave clear evidence that three other Vietnamese, named on the indictment but only in respect of the associated affray charges, were involved in starting the fire. This underlined what had been apparent anyway: that only two of at least five culprits faced murder charges in respect of the fire. The two principal defendants were convicted none the less.

This finding may be contrasted with the acquittal in Case 1. Although the chain of causality in relation to death was less clear, in that the medical evidence as to just when the victim was stabbed was inconclusive, the defendant in Case 1 was accepted to have been involved in the mêlée preceding the victim's death. But it could not be ruled out that others were 'just as involved'. The jury acquitted. Had the jury attempted to achieve parity between the potential defendants: convicting all (of something of which they felt certain) in Case 5; and completely acquitting, by not attributing sole responsibility to one defendant about whom they could not be certain, in Case 1?

(iii) *Sympathy votes* Even aside from the Crown's difficulty over the comparative culpability between defendants A and B in Case 17, both were also beneficiaries of a complex appeal for public sympathy by the defence. In addition to their good characters (both were police officers with service commendations) the defendants were presented as being 'up against it' in respect of the allegedly extremely dangerous man they intended to arrest.[64] Since it was so readily accepted that the victim who had been mistaken for the fugitive should be treated for the purpose of the trial as if he were the wanted man, little countervailing sympathy was likely to arise. Similarly, in Case 8, the victim was a skinhead troublemaker. The jury may have seen her as being of dubious social worth, whereas the policeman was doing a difficult but necessary job, even if he did overstep the mark. Some of the jurors did not even stifle their yawns.

(iv) *A poor 'moral/legal fit' between facts and offences* Among those canvassed so far, this is perhaps not only the most widely recognized of the prosecution's difficulties in relation to the jury, but also the one in which some legitimate scope for reform exists – to improve the 'fit'.

In Case 14, a constituent element of the manslaughter charge against the defendant required that the prosecution establish his legal 'malice' towards his girlfriend. Technically, this was not problematic since the deliberate insertion into her body of the syringe containing a noxious substance satisfied this requirement (*R. v. Cato* (1976) 1 All ER 260 CA). However, the jury's note – raising the question of what amounted to 'maliciously' – suggested that they had not understood this point. The defendant was acquitted of the manslaughter charge.

Reform, to improve the fit between morals and the law, would necessarily involve drawing up finer offence gradations.[65] Until this happens the prosecution will continue to suffer the contradiction of having to indict, for example, for murder, in the knowledge that a case will only seriously be considered for manslaughter once the defence raises 'provocation' or 'lesser intent', as for example occurred in Cases 9 and 10. Such shifts in the prosecution case mid-trial may be damaging to the prosecution's prospects of any conviction.

(v) *The interaction between common sense and advocacy* That jurors are susceptible to the influence of counsel and the judge is not in dispute;[66] the question remains, can or should prosecuting counsel attempt to sustain the prosecutor's 'reasonable prospects of conviction' prediction once a case starts to go wrong at trial? Where a case ought to succeed but looks likely to fail, can counsel exploit his adversarial skills to 'put it back on course'? Again this sample of cases illustrates that prosecuting counsel's manoeuvrability is limited: he can influence the cases that ought to fail but are likely to succeed, but can do little to make a case succeed where it is likely to fail.

In enhancing what little manoeuvrability he has, the rapport that counsel strikes up with the jury may be important. There are numerous outward signs of juror capabilities which are obvious to experienced advocates even early on in the course of a trial. Counsel's expectations may range from the minimal ones that the jury should stay awake and pay attention, to the more ambitious hopes that they might take some form of notes, mark exhibits, even ask salient questions. As a general guiding principle, there seems no reason why counsel should not begin with an approach to the jury which assumes low expectations, then progressively step up his 'pitch' if it appears to be received as condescension.

In conclusion, does this analysis of jury verdicts lend further support to the argument that prosecutors ought to shift their focus away from the jury as a guide for their initial decisions about whether to proceed?

The issues which crystallize during the course of the trial for consideration by the jury at the end will necessarily differ from those canvassed in the initial decision whether to prosecute. Thus, the prosecutor is required to comply with a test that is, in itself, inaccessible. Even if the prosecutor is astute enough to anticipate how the case will evolve and sustains his approach through counsel, he remains handicapped if common sense trumps 'legal niceties' in the jury room. Lawyers may have their fair share of common sense but they are employed for their technical expertise. Once they depart from a technician's role, they are on dangerous ground. A possible example of this arose in the attempted murder charge in Case 2. This case could be described as one likely to succeed (because of the jury's common sense approach to individuals who shoot at policemen) but which ought to fail (technically the prosecution were liable to have difficulty in establishing the necessary *mens rea* for attempted murder). It is arguable that the prosecutor who made the initial decision to proceed in this case might have been distracted by his prospects of conviction before a jury.[67] Although estimating that a case has a reasonable prospect of conviction should necessitate the prosecutor establishing that he *will* be able to satisfy the technical legal requirements and get the case past 'half-time', does the lure of success sometimes undermine this more clinical assessment? Conversely, does the prospect of failure in front of a jury deter a prosecutor from proceeding where there may be good legal justifications for going ahead? If the prosecutor were to focus his attention not on the likelihood of obtaining a conviction from a jury, but rather on the need to avoid a directed acquittal, he might not only thereby ensure that he has the possibility of a reasonable prospect of conviction, but also avoid the probability of a reasonable prospect of a directed acquittal. Such an approach would also lessen the probability of 'letting off the guilty', since more cases which ought to succeed, but are likely to fail, will proceed.[68]

Should prosecutors be attempting to anticipate the common-sense assumptions of jurors? These may not be the best basis for decision-making. Common sense, at least in relation to identification and eyewitness testimony, is often plainly wrong (Yarmey and Tressillian-Jones 1983). Thus, for the DPP to take account of the dilemmas of the jury room might be to anticipate decision-making which would have been ill-founded had it been left to the jury. Anticipating ill-founded convictions and proceeding may be in contravention of the spirit of reasonable prospects; if the defendant's protection against such ill-founded decisions exists only in relation to his rights to appeal, this amounts to a poor protection even when it succeeds, since the process itself will have been punishing. Similarly, anticipating ill-founded acquittals and not proceeding lessens the protection society receives from 'convicting the guilty'.[69]

NOTES

1 Including the co-defendants in Cases 1 and 15 whom the examining magistrates did not commit for trial.

2 Criminal Law Revision Committee (1972) considered some of the evidential difficulties of obtaining convictions against 'professional' offenders.

3 An analysis of 149 cases of murder (a sub sample of the Central Criminal Court retrospective analysis – see Chapter 2) produced a complete acquittal rate of 21 per cent, with 13 defendants (9 per cent) being acquitted on the direction of the judge. These acquittal rates are substantially higher than those reported by Morris and Blom-Cooper (1979) for the period 1957–77, when an acquittal rate of 10 per cent was noted. The high proportion of directed acquittals may indicate that the DPP is prepared in very serious cases to proceed, where the evidence does not amount to more or much more than a bare *prima facie* case. Thus, the 'body' (corpse) factor results in the case becoming one of genuine doubt on a lower standard of evidence. But to avoid the risk of perverse convictions the judge may subsequently have to exercise his discretion not to allow a case to proceed, more widely than was urged in *Galbraith*.

4 Even these figures may be over-optimistic since of the 188 convicted defendants 70 pleaded guilty, bringing the contested conviction rate down to 72 per cent (118 of 165).

5 Although contested cases may not be representative, since the majority of offenders ultimately plead guilty, they are nevertheless important. In 1981, 62 per cent of Crown Court cases involved pleas of not guilty with subsequent acquittals in about half of these cases. HMSO, Cmnd 8668. See also for example Butler 1983.

6 The *Judges' Rules* are not rules of law (see Archbold 1982: 15–45). They are

shortly to be replaced by the Codes of Practice under the Police and Criminal Evidence Act 1984.

7 On the role of the defence, see p. 156.

8 See also Chambers and Millar (1983: 91–2).

9 The courts may be reluctant to permit the prosecutor to drop charges where a *prima facie* standard of evidence exists; indeed, in some circumstances they are obliged to allow a case to proceed when this standard is satisfied (see pp. 25, 129, 207). This dilemma for the prosecutor will be obviated in the Magistrates' Courts, by Section 23 of the Prosecution of Offences Act 1985 which concerns the power of the DPP to discontinue proceedings in the 'preliminary stages'.

10 Alternatively, the police might avoid such practices: they may be a false economy.

11 See, for example, the new code of practice in the Police and Criminal Evidence Act 1984, and the draft code issued by the Home Office (1984) for detention, treatment, questioning, and identification by the police; for the searching of premises and seizure of property; and for the exercise of powers of stop and search.

12 But not necessarily so. The first case involving a tape-recorded confession resulted in a jury acquittal of a defendant on rape charges (*Guardian*, 26 June, 1984).

13 These tensions are inherent in the adversarial system and are subtly reinforced by the trial process. See, for example, McBarnet (1981).

14 S.37 of the Sexual Offences Act 1956 prevents prosecutions from being commenced for the offence of unlawful sexual intercourse with a girl under 16, more than 12 months after the commission of the offence.

15 Yet this is precisely what the reasonable prospects test requires the prosecutor to do. On the grounds of a paper assessment of a witness's potential credibility he may go far beyond the discretion allowed to the judge by the decision in *Galbraith* (see Chapter 1).

16 Despite a directed acquittal on the attempted murder charge the defendant in Case 2 received a sentence of 25 years' imprisonment for his conviction on lesser charges. See also Shea (1974).

17 The converse of this position, where the law is clear but the quality of the evidence variable, occurred in Case 14, which only posed a problematic decision as to how to proceed once the seriousness of the circumstances (homicide) determined that there *would* be a prosecution. Again the difficulties of presentation, of which the DPP were aware from the start, deriving from the poor fit between the evidence and the law, may have contributed to the ultimate acquittal (see p. 180).

18 It was noted in Chapter 1 that some confusion exists over whether anticipating likely lines of defence is always regarded as a constituent part of the reasonable-prospects test: the empirical research served to confirm that such confusion exists.

19 The emergence of further forensic evidence reversed this decision, but ultimately an acquittal resulted. Whether this could be attributed to problems of presentation, or possibly more properly to the failure to commit his co-accused, is uncertain.

20 The vast majority of cases reach the Crown Court for trial by the 'paper committal' route – an essentially bureaucratic exercise discussed in Chapter 1.

21 These occurred in Cases 2, 3, and 5. In Case 2 only one count was tested; in Case 3, the DPP had vacillated over the charge and the committal was used partly as a vindication of the course chosen; and in Case 5 a committal was necessary because of the identification issues involved. See the guidelines on identification, *R*. v. *Turnbull and others* [1976] 3 WLR 445, and the Attorney General's guidelines on

identification given on 27 May, 1976 in the House of Commons (Hansard, Vol. 912, No. 115).

22 Although the prosecution may revive its original charges on indictment if defendants are committed on less serious ones, once a co-defendant is 'lost' the prosecution cannot be repaired (Emmins 1983: 46) except – exceptionally – through recourse to a Voluntary Bill of Indictment.

23 See Chapter 1, Note 3.

24 Although opening speeches for the defence are comparatively rare, and theoretically confined (Archbold 1982: 4–393) to cases where the defence evidence goes beyond that of the defendant, the two cases in the sample (11 and 12) where the defence made an opening speech resulted in acquittals. This may underline the importance of the initial blueprint theory – at least in those cases where the defence has a viable alternative to offer.

25 It may also be argued that it is undesirable if the jury needs too much spoonfeeding by counsel in order to reach a position where they are capable of understanding the situation. This would imply either that wholly different standards are being brought to bear on different sections of society or – at the other extreme – that 'trial by one's peers' is a spurious notion.

26 R. v. *Buckland* (1977) 2 NSWLR 452 at 470 (CCA). The latter part of this approach was confirmed in R. v. *Pearce* (1979) 69 Cr. App. R. 365, in which the Lord Chief Justice, Lord Lane, stated: 'It is the duty of the prosecution to present the case fairly to the jury; to exclude answers which are favourable to the accused while admitting those unfavourable would be misleading.' Although relating to a partially exculpatory statement, this principle may be equally applicable to the prosecution's choice of witness.

27 It would be wrong, however, to assume that the police always take statements reliably or accurately just because they are taken shortly after the event.

28 In *Dallison* v. *Caffery* [1965] 1 QB 348 Lord Denning, MR, noted, 'The duty of a prosecuting counsel or solicitor, as I have always understood it, is this: if he knows of a credible witness who can speak to material facts which tend to show the prisoner to be innocent, he must either call that witness himself or make his statement available to the defence.' Bates (1980) notes not only that this was a civil case and therefore of limited application, but also that Diplock, LJ, was critical of Lord Denning's approach.

29 Guidelines for the disclosure of 'unused material' to the defence in cases to be tried on indictment: [1982], All ER 734. These guidelines were issued by the Attorney-General in December, 1981. See also Archbold (1982: 8th Supplement 4–178).

30 For example the unused witness statements, the S.102 statements of those prosecution witnesses read over at committal, the S.9 statements of those witnesses the prosecution intend to read at trial and any depositions of witnesses called live at committal. See S.102, Magistrates' Courts Act 1980, S.9, Criminal Justice Act 1967.

31 The rationale for the Royal Commission's recommendation that the investigatorial and prosecutorial functions should be separated, namely that objectivity may be impugned where one individual undertakes both roles, may also be extended to the role of the police officer as witness. Defence challenges are partially based on the assumption that interrogating officers have an interest in obtaining confessions. Where this interest becomes overt the voluntariness of confessions may be challenged.

32 In Case 6, the judge did instruct the jury to ignore certain questions and

answers following a defence challenge, but one which was not contested by the prosecution.

33 It should be stressed that such differential appreciation of the evidence of police and civilian witnesses is not encouraged by the Court of Appeal. In *R.* v. *Fisher* [1983] Crim. LR 486, it was held that it was 'undesirable that police officers as witnesses should be put into any different category from any other witnesses'.

34 In Case 80 (see Chapter 2, p. 92) an experienced prosecution expert witness 'deferred' the evening before committal to a more eminent defence expert.

35 Yet if it subsequently emerges on appeal that the evidence was incomplete it is generally the expert whose reputation suffers, rather than the advocate who 'steered' his testimony (Goodwin-Jones 1984).

36 That witnesses' credibility remains vulnerable even after they have left the box may be compared with the way that it may be vulnerable *before* trial to accusations of collaboration.

37 An alternative possibility, that this witness was produced by the prosecution solely to discharge its duty to the jury of presenting all of the evidence capable of belief (but not believed by the prosecutor), does not reflect well on the ability of the prosecution initially to prove the murder charge and thereby satisfy the reasonable-prospects test.

38 The paper committal route may be better characterized as a conduit than a sifting exercise and therefore does not amount to a real check on the prosecutor's assessment that there is sufficient evidence to bring a case (see p. 17). See also later discussion of Case 17.

39 There was also another full-time direction here, attributable to technical error by the prosecution with regard to offence dates.

40 No systematic findings on whether *Galbraith* has caused or contributed to a waste of court time are offered, not only because no earlier work was conducted for the purposes of comparison, but also because of the difficulties of subdividing the time spent in legal argument on 'matters arising' whilst the jury is absent.

41 Under Section 11 of the Criminal Justice Act 1967, notice must be given within seven days of the close of committal proceedings – unless leave of the judge is granted for a late alibi.

42 *DPP* v. *Hester* (1973) 57 Cr. App. R. 212; *DPP* v. *Kilbourne* (1973) 57 Cr. App. R. 381. The Police and Criminal Evidence Act (1964) S.79 will require the defendant to give his evidence before other defence witnesses, if he wishes to testify.

43 The right to make an unsworn statement from the dock was abolished by S. 72 of the Criminal Justice Act 1982. Two defendants in this sample of cases would have made unsworn statements had that avenue still been open.

44 Whether some convicted defendants might have been better advised to run different defences is an open question. For example, it could be argued that in Case 3 the prosecution might have been less successful, or possibly not even taken place at all, had the defendant used brinkmanship rather than denial (see p. 176 on juries).

45 This was later confirmed by the Court of Appeal in *R.* v. *Williams (Gladstone)* [1984] Crim. LR 163.

46 It might be suggested that it is more difficult for a police officer to contest the voluntariness of confession since, in the words of the judge in Case 6, the defendant was 'no dumb johnnie', i.e. 'blue serge' had a rebound effect.

47 Baldwin and McConville (1980), in their study of defendants who had made written confessions, found that 90 per cent of London defendants pleaded guilty at trial and 76 per cent of Birmingham defendants pleaded guilty at trial. Of the 10–24 per cent who contested their cases only between 2.4 and 5.2 per cent were acquitted.

48 See the section on expert witness testimony for the potential impact of disagreement, pp. 145–49.

49 The failure in Case 15 to establish the defendant's sole moral responsibility may be contrasted with Case 3. Here the prosecution clearly failed to exclude all doubt on the grounds of the facts since even the prosecution's expert witness could not entirely discount suicide. But the prosecution did establish the defendant's moral culpability, whether he caused her death directly or indirectly by driving her to suicide.

50 On the face of it, this defence tactic was not 'unethical'. Yet it is notable that defence counsel had not indicated his intention to challenge evidence during the earlier discussion about severance.

51 At the time of the case the law was anomalous in that a wife was neither compellable nor competent as a witness for the prosecution where the accused was her husband (apart from exceptional cases, see Archbold 1982: 280–82), but was competent but not compellable for the defence. Indeed, the imbalance introduced by the rules on competence and compellability extended to the fact that the prosecution could not even comment on the failure of a spouse to give evidence for the defence. The law has recently been altered. The Police and Criminal Evidence Act 1984, S. 80 now makes a spouse generally competent as a prosecution witness and compellable under specified circumstances.

52 The Attorney General has the power to refer points of law to the Court of Appeal following aquittal on indictment (Criminal Appeal (Reference of Points of Law) Rules (SI 1973 No. 1114). Lord Widgery, CJ, in Attorney General's Reference (No. 1 of 1975) [1975] 3 WLR 11 at p. 13 hoped that the procedure would be 'used extensively for short but important points which require a quick ruling of this court before a potentially false decision of law has too wide a circulation in the courts'.

53 It is accepted that this tendency may well have been exaggerated in the sample of 'high class' cases studied (Criminal Law Revision Committee 1972).

54 Where the defendant is unrepresented and did not call evidence other than his own as to the facts, i.e. where an unrepresented defendant did not have the right to an opening speech (an eventuality of which the prosecuting counsel was apprehensive in Case 2).

55 It might be suggested that had he done so this would have amounted to expecting the jury to speculate about the missing spouse's evidence without explicitly asking them to do so – which he would have been prevented from doing by Section 1(b), Criminal Evidence Act 1898.

56 This can be achieved either by 'tilting' verdicts or, at an earlier stage, through resort to plea negotiation.

57 Only confirmed in a subsequent decision (*Williams (Gladstone)* [1984] Crim. LR 163).

58 See for example Cornish and Sealy (1973). For shadow jury research, as opposed to simulated trials, see McCabe and Purves (1972).

59 Ironically, the jury do not always appreciate their altered position. This was most graphically illustrated when the jury retired in Case 17 and returned almost immediately to ask for a copy of the judge's summing up! (It was largely available, published with extensive verbatim extracts in that day's edition of the *Daily Telegraph*).

60 Roy Amlot, in reference to the case of *Ponting*; (see the *Observer*, 10 February, 1985). See also the comments of Lord Devlin on the role of the jury in this case, in the discussion of public interest (p. 32).

61 The literature on probability theory (see Chapter 4) argues that a plurality of

eyewitness testimony will militate against findings of guilt. This is because, in theory at least, if the witnesses are not chronologically correlated, inconsistencies between them will increase the probability that they did not observe the same offender, and thereby potentially damage their credibility.

62 This was done in accordance with R. v. *Walhein* (1952) 36 Cr. App. R. 167 (although that case predated the introduction of majority verdicts by S. 13, Criminal Justice Act 1967).

63 Cornish and Sealy (1973) similarly note that juries are not as influenced as would be expected by the direction that proof be established 'beyond reasonable doubt' as opposed to 'on the balance of probabilities'.

64 This picture was partially created by the media and certainly sustained by prosecuting counsel in his opening wherein the fugitive was described at least twice as 'a very dangerous man'.

65 For example, along the lines recommended by the Criminal Law Revision Committee (1980).

66 See generally Mars-Jones for a fictional, but plausible account of how jurors may be led by the lawyers.

67 An alternative explanation in terms of public interest considerations for the prosecutorial approach in this case has already been advanced (see p. 154). The two are not necessarily mutually exclusive.

68 Williams (1985) similarly asserts that 'the prosecutor may properly act although experience shows that juries tend to be unreasonably unwilling to accept certain evidence (e.g. strong evidence of police culpability) or unable to understand it'. To apply the reasonable prospects test rigorously may in his view 'stifle perfectly justified charges against the police, sophisticated fraudsters, and others'. As an alternative, he suggests a rule of practice which includes the necessity for the prosecutor to consider 'whether a prosecution would have a fair chance of success (not necessarily a better than evens chance)'.

69 Such consequences were amply illustrated by Case 7. Had the prosecution not proceeded following the earlier 'hung jury', the outcome would not have altered (since the defendant was prosecuted and acquitted anyway), but the prosecution would have foregone the possibility of conviction, which might in turn have prevented the subsequent killing by the defendant.

CHAPTER 4

IS THE REASONABLE PROSPECTS TEST AN ATTAINABLE STANDARD FOR THE CROWN PROSECUTION SERVICE?

In Chapter 2 the extent to which prosecutors at the DPP adhere to the tenets of 'reasonable prospects' in their day-to-day decision-making was reviewed. Many prosecutorial decisions were characterized either as representing a 'corrupted' form of the reasonable prospects test or as failing to address explicitly the crucial differences between the *prima facie* approach and that required by the higher evidential standard. Thus, the more extensive filtering out of cases that might have been expected with the adoption of the reasonable prospects test was not manifest in the nature or number of the cases going forward for prosecution.

Chapter 3 followed a series of cases through the prosecution process and through trial to outcome. In charting the progress of these cases, a variety of factors was identified which may radically alter the prospects of obtaining a conviction in any particular case, once a decision to proceed has been made (and sometimes even before). Hence, that chapter showed that it would be inappropriate and artificial to attempt to assess the accuracy of prosecutors' reasonable prospects predictions (assuming that these are made) in terms of the outcome of cases at trial.

This chapter draws on those two empirical chapters to provide a comprehensive review of why the reasonable prospects test may represent an idealized rather than an attainable standard. In essence, this amounts to a theoretical critique of the assumptions on which the reasonable prospects test is founded, and an exposition of the practical difficulties entailed in actually applying the test. Thus, the factors that undermine the prosecutor's reasonable prospects predictions, and thereby make assessment in terms of outcome invalid, also negate the foundation upon which those initial predictions are based. In this sense the argument comes full circle, for the prosecutor who looks to his case outcomes to justify his initial decisions is, in terms of the reasonable prospects test, as likely to be disappointed as not. His enthusiasm for any future rigorous application of the test may consequently be eroded.

Discussion of the reasonable prospects test within the first half of this chapter is concerned with what prosecutors *ought* to do to satisfy such a test: it adopts Twining's (1983) 'expository' approach to the law. Such legal formalism focuses on the rules, aligning itself with a rationalistic and aspirational approach at the expense of an empirical analysis. In contrast, the second half of the chapter broadens the conception of decision-making. It adopts Twining's 'contextual' approach – setting the rules in the context of the legal and social processes within which they operate and focusing on *how* prosecutors behave. It is grounded in empirical reality and attempts to 'get behind the simple verdict the legal system usually demands of its decision-makers to see precisely how a complex reality is compressed into such simple terms' (Hawkins 1983: 21–2). This is why it has been insisted that any assessment of whether the reasonable prospects test is satisfied must be made within the context of the broader concerns of public interest implied in the reasonable prospects approach.

I THE EXPOSITORY APPROACH

The reasonable prospects test: the theoretical assumptions

The DPP's approach requires the prosecutor to assess, first, whether he has a reasonable prospect of proving the case beyond reasonable doubt in front of an impartial jury properly directed in accordance with the law; and, secondly, whether a prosecution is in the public interest. In satisfying the reasonable prospects *test* the prosecutor is engaged in the identification of good risks to filter into the system rather than bad risks to filter out.[1] This will involve him in an exercise which is essentially forward-looking. In contrast with the *prima facie* approach he will have to predict, at a minimum, the likely credibility and persuasiveness of the prosecution's witnesses as perceived by a jury. The need to predict a series of factors which, by their very nature, are either unpredictable or difficult to predict with any accuracy, creates an unsound basis for the prosecutor's decisions. Moreover, the justification for this becomes even more questionable when each element of the reasonable prospects test ('beyond reasonable doubt', 'impartial jury', etc.) is examined, since these factors are similarly uncertain. Each factor will be reviewed separately here. It is accepted that for the experienced prosecutor this may amount to an artificial exercise; the elements may be mutually dependent, with the assessment of any individual case being more of an intuitive appreciation than such an objective 'unpacking' of the test might suggest. However, 'intuition' cannot easily be imported into the Crown prosecution system. Hence, it is necessary to formulate guidance for prosecutors.

PROVING A CASE BEYOND REASONABLE DOUBT

Even if the much publicized '51 per cent chance of conviction' signifies a statistical 'red herring', what prosecutors mean when they talk about a reasonable prospect is 'whether a conviction is more likely than an acquittal' (Attorney General 1983). However, there appears to be a contradiction between this prediction and – implicit in the 'conviction' element of the reasonable prospects test – whether the case can be proved beyond reasonable doubt. This persuasive burden implies a degree of certainty far beyond a balance of probabilities (the standard more logically evoked by talk of 'better than evens chance' in relation to the reasonable prospects test). At face value, it indicates an extremely stringent test for the prosecutor to satisfy; but closer analysis reveals alternative meanings, more consistent with the requirements of criminal trials. Three interpretations suggest themselves:

(i) the prosecutor only has to establish that he has a reasonable prospect (a better than evens chance) of demonstrating that this case will be *one of those* (out of all those cases which he considers) where proof beyond reasonable doubt may be established;
(ii) the prosecutor only has to prove *his* case beyond reasonable doubt and does not have to predict the erosive effects of the defence case or take them into account;
(iii) proof beyond reasonable doubt is a convenient legal fiction that defies either legal or mathematical quantification.[2]

The first problem facing the prosecutor concerns how to determine whether the quality of evidence he has will satisfy a 'reasonable jury'. Whether the evidence will satisfy the prosecutor beyond reasonable doubt is not a sufficient guide. Jurors are not 'case-hardened'. They may be satisfied by a quite different level of probability than that required to exclude all reasonable doubt for the professional decision-maker.[3] Where may the prosecutor derive insight as to the subjective level of probability required to satisfy the reasonable juror?

There have been numerous attempts by the judiciary to define what should amount to reasonable doubt for the reasonable juror, but they have been subject to criticism by the higher courts and have fallen from common usage (Eggleston 1983). Even the currently preferred formula 'certain so that you feel sure', indicative of the way in which the arguments have gone full circle, patently fails to provide any guidance for the would-be prosecutor. If there is no objectively agreed legal standard and no guidance as to how it is subjectively applied by jurors, what problems might confound its attainment?

Glanville Williams (1977), writing pre-*Galbraith*, noted the distinction between the persuasive burden (the burden of proof) and the evidential burden (that of introducing sufficient evidence to be placed before a tribunal of fact; that is, to avoid a successful submission of no case). In relation to the evidential burden the judge acts as a censor so that where the prosecution do not adduce sufficient evidence to satisfy it, the case will not be left to the jury (one safeguard against perverse jury convictions). Similarly, where there is an evidential burden on the defence, the judge may prevent specious defences going to the jury (a safeguard against perverse jury acquittals). However, the test that the judge applies varies according to the nature of the defence. For certain so-called defences (for example, provocation, self-defence, duress) the persuasive burden remains with the prosecution, so that all the defendant has to do is to lay a foundation of doubt – adduce a modicum of evidence that might raise a reasonable doubt in the jury's mind; the judge may be correspondingly easily satisfied of this. However, in the case of most statutory defences (for example diminished responsibility, those arising in relation to certain corruption charges, and offensive weapons charges) the persuasive burden is generally borne by the defendant who has to establish his defence to the satisfaction of the jury on a balance of probabilities. Thus, although the evidential burden on the prosecution technically remains the same, the stringency of the persuasive burden required can be lessened where specific kinds of offences and defences are involved; whether the prosecutor is working to models (i) or (ii) above may affect the way in which the reasonable prospects test is satisfied. Thus, even if an objective definition of 'beyond reasonable doubt' could be formulated the burden placed on the prosecution would vary on the basis of the nature of the likely defence.

It would not be a single standard within the existing legal process.

In much the same way, the (subjective) application of the (varying objective) test may vary depending on the nature of the case. Walls (1971) notes that in more serious offences (with more serious consequences following a conviction) juries may require a subjectively higher standard of proof than they require for trivial offences. Similarly, with the exception of offences of strict liability, the onus is principally on the prosecution to establish *mens rea*; proving intent is notoriously difficult for certain charges where the offence is very serious and the facts primarily limited to the defendant's knowledge (for example, proving an intent to kill in an attempted murder charge). Normally the defendant's intent will have to be inferred from observable events – his actions, words, and the surrounding circumstances; with notable exceptions such as recklessness the law provides little guidance as to how these mental elements may be established.[4] In addition, establishing that an event did *not* happen, or did not happen to a sufficient degree (for example where the prosecution has to rebut self-defence or provocation to a beyond reasonable doubt standard), may be inherently more difficult for the prosecution than establishing a positive case.

If the law provides little guidance, can science help in relation to quantifying what amounts to proof beyond reasonable doubt? As yet, mathematical analyses seem to have confused rather than clarified the issue (see, for example, Tribe 1971). Indeed it is likely that such approaches will fundamentally contradict the 'common-sense' assumptions of the existing legal process. For instance, the prosecutor has to predict the persuasive totality of a case made up of a series of witnesses who may be of varying credibility. The mathematics of probability theory would suggest that one can neither be satisfied beyond reasonable doubt of the truth of an inference drawn from facts about the existence of which one is in doubt; nor will a series of witnesses who satisfy the balance of probabilities criterion 'summate' to satisfy the beyond reasonable doubt criterion (Eggleston 1983). However, on the basis of their experience with juries, many prosecutors seem to believe that the latter approach is what occurs in practice: shaky testimonies may provide mutual corroboration, along the lines that 'they can't all be lying'. Can prosecutors legitimately follow their noses in the face of what mathematics tells them?

Certainly, that the criminal justice system permits majority verdicts suggests toleration of degrees of doubt – given the questionable assumption that each of the persuaded individuals has reached the 'beyond reasonable doubt' criterion. It might be suggested that to define mathematically for individuals what amounts to a reasonable doubt would involve explicit recognition of the fact that society imposes its sanctions in the light of a quantitatively immeasurable yet recognized doubt – i.e. where that doubt does not quite become a quantifiable 'reasonable doubt'.[5] Thus, although it remains open to the defence to exploit mathematically the concept of reasonable doubt (Williams 1979) the prosecution can neither determine the degree of probability that the law counts as a virtual certainty (since there is a lack of objective consensus and no potential mathematical analysis of its *subjective* application by individual jurors), nor invite the jury to convict on the basis of doubt.

Finally, the requirement on the prosecution in relation to the reasonable prospects test is not only to establish the inherent credibility of events, but also to be satisfied that the jury will find them persuasive. It is a mammoth leap from believing that (objectively) something *might* have happened to believing (subjectively) that it *did* happen. Glanville Williams pertinently reverses Thomas Hardy's aphorism to make the point that 'though nothing is too strange to have happened, a good deal is too strange to be believed' (1979: 352). In practice, the prosecutor may only have to be persuaded, not convinced, of the appropriateness of proceeding. Indeed, the decision-making criteria may tolerate some degree of doubt, in that the Attorney General's *Criteria* advise placing the case before the court where doubts cannot be resolved.[6]

In stark contrast, the jury have to be *convinced* of guilt beyond reasonable doubt; when in doubt their duty is to acquit. Since there are rarely any blinding moments of truth in criminal trials, only greater or lesser degrees of uncertainty, it is not surprising that a doubt which does not inhibit a prosecutor from prosecuting may impel a jury to acquit. Finally, these potentially opposing perspectives may be accentuated in practice by the different manners in which the prosecutor and the jury reach decisions. Generally speaking, the prosecution controls its own pace, allowing itself time to resolve doubts if possible. If that is not possible the case goes on to trial. There the case proceeds at a pace determined by experienced professionals, so the ability of the jury to check and double-check is limited. For the jury, doubts may persist which the prosecutor has been able to resolve to his own satisfaction; similarly, the prosecutor may anticipate that the jury will resolve doubts that he either has or has not been able to resolve. Either way, it may be easier for the prosecutor to assume that the jury will reach a decision beyond reasonable doubt, than it is for the jury to achieve that decision.

Thus, lawyers may be justified in avoiding too close an inspection of what amounts to proof beyond reasonable doubt, since its attractiveness seems to lie in its very fuzziness. If the reasonable prospects test is to be adopted within the Crown prosecution system, lawyers will have to be tolerant of the application of a test that is pitched at an amorphous goal.

THE CONCEPT OF AN IMPARTIAL JURY

To what extent do prosecutors apply the concept of *impartiality*? There is evidence that in practice prosecutors concede that the impartial jury is a 'legal fiction'. This has received implicit recognition in Northern Ireland where trials without juries are the currently accepted mode for certain categories of case (the scheduled offences) in which perverse verdicts are both anticipated and intolerable. In England and Wales the procedures for jury vetting,[7] the prosecution's right to stand by jurors and challenge for cause, the provisions for disqualification and majority verdicts, and the practical measures adopted at the Central Criminal Court to inhibit 'jury nobbling', all indicate that the concept of an impartial jury is, at the least, fragile. The Attorney General's exposition of the factors that may be taken into account when assessing the public interest similarly recognizes the concept of perverse jury verdicts. Furthermore, if in practice the DPP wishes to avoid the unfortunate effects of acquittals, for example in obscene publications cases which attract considerable publicity, he must similarly recognize that juries' subjective assessments of cases will vary on demographical, geographical, and cultural grounds.

The DPP might maintain that prosecutors take account of jury verdicts twice, once *impartially* in relation to the reasonable prospects test and once *partially*, that is taking account of possible juror bias, in relation to the public interest test. But this would amount to asking prosecutors to suspend judgment on the one test until the other had been satisfied – which would be another example of the 'intellectual acrobatics' sometimes required by English criminal procedure (per Lord Lane, CJ, in *Watts I.* (1983) Cr. App. R. 126). It also results in the dilemma for prosecutors of what to do with cases which ought to succeed but are likely to fail, and cases which ought to fail but are likely to succeed: a number of practical examples were given in the preceding chapters. Thus, prosecutors prosecute in the real world, East End juries and all. The concept of an impartial jury is abstract in practice and erodable in theory.[8]

PROPERLY DIRECTED IN ACCORDANCE WITH THE LAW

Can the prosecutor be confident that judges will exercise their legitimate roles in a predictable fashion? The cynic's view that they frequently cannot might be supported by the assertion in Archbold (1982) that 'the most common ground of appeal is some form of misdirection or non direction', thereby highlighting the fallibility of judges as opposed to jurors.

Similarly, the judiciary do not always behave in the fashion that might be predicted from the guidance issuing from the Court of Appeal. Judges may fail to exercise their discretion, in contradiction to the prosecutor's legitimate anticipations, and they may occasionally abuse their discretion in respect of their role in plea negotiation and during the summing up.[9] In defence of this aspect of the judicial role, it should perhaps be noted that in an analogous field, that of sentencing, guidance issuing from the Court of Appeal has been criticized as contradictory and therefore often unhelpful (Ashworth 1983; for the judicial view, see Ashworth *et al.* 1984).

THE 'COMPOUND' TEST — REASONABLE PROSPECTS AND PUBLIC INTEREST COMBINED

Having satisfied himself that all of the elements of the reasonable prospects test can be satisfied, the prosecutor should then, in theory, address the question of whether a prosecution is in the public interest. The theoretical difficulties raised by this sequential model of decision-making have already been extensively discussed (see Chapter 1). Briefly, these difficulties were anticipated as being likely to result in a practical overlap between evidential assessments and consideration of the public-interest element. Such an overlap was indeed encountered: in practice the prosecutor anticipates the impact of the public-interest element when deciding whether or not he has a reasonable prospect of conviction. Thus, the operation of the reasonable prospects approach did not reflect the attractive simplicity of the theoretical two-stage model. This finding lends support to the contextual analysis developed in the second half of this chapter; the public interest element of the two-stage model becomes one part of a complex context within which prosecutors make real-life legal decisions. In contrast, the expository analysis attributes explanatory pre-eminence to the content of the rules rather than their application. The finding that there is interaction between the two stages does not lie so comfortably with an expository analysis as with the contextual analysis.

The reasonable prospect test: can it be applied?

If the essence of the reasonable prospects test is predictive, do prosecutors have access to the appropriate information to enable them to make prediction decisions with accuracy? The discussion in this section is divided into three parts: the quantity and quality of information the prosecutor is provided with in respect of individual cases; his previous experience of the way similar cases turned out; the accumulated experience of prosecutors which the conviction statistics may (or may not) represent.

PAPER DECISIONS

When applying the reasonable prospects test the prosecutor has to focus his mind not only on whether there is sufficient evidence that is not manifestly unreliable to prove each element of the prosecution case (that is, establish a technical *prima facie* case) but also on whether that evidence is inherently credible (capable of being believed) and persuasive (likely to be believed). The prosecutor can use his technical legal skills to establish both whether a *prima facie* case is made out on the papers and whether the evidence is credible, by looking for inconsistencies both within and between witness statements, by establishing their credibility in the light of what is known about the defendant's version of events, and by looking for gaps in the evidence. However, even this apparently straightforward assessment of the quantity of evidence may be problematic. In many 'straightforward' cases referred by the police on the 'short-form' basis, the information the prosecutor receives may amount to little more than a brief statement of facts.[10] How is the prosecutor to make a reasonable prospects assessment – apart from merely anticipating a guilty plea – on this quantity of information? The converse dilemma arises in more complex cases where the police, in collecting evidence, typically adopt what may be characterized as a 'blunderbuss' approach. They should not necessarily be criticized for this, but the result is that the prosecutor routinely sees a considerably greater amount of information than that presented to the court – the volume of 'non-tendered' bundles testifies to this. The prosecutor filters out information on the grounds of inadmissibility and irrelevance to the specific charges brought. He may also exclude information that may become admissible, for example the participants' antecedents, but which at an early stage is recognized to have greater prejudicial than probative effect. Later on, witnesses may fail to 'come up to proof' in a trial setting which does not set out to elicit information in the same ways that investigating police officers have done. Although it may be argued that the skilful prosecutor has the technical competence to predict the quantity of evidence that will emerge, it is possible that in some cases his judgment on the admissible evidence will be coloured by his knowledge of other evidence that will remain inadmissible. Furthermore, in respect of the quality of the evidence, the prosecutor making paper-based assessments of persuasiveness will be at a greater disadvantage. He can make some general predictions as to *credibility* dependent on his knowledge of whether the witnesses have previous convictions, or are serving police officers, or are otherwise experienced witnesses. Indeed, he may well have first-hand experience of how a particular police officer or expert witness is likely to 'perform' in the witness-box. However, in relation to assessing the *persuasiveness* of civilian witnesses, and making an assessment of the extent to which they may be relied upon, the prosecutor is heavily dependent on the investigating police officer's assessments. Unfortunately, police officers, who may have limited experience or appreciation of the subtleties of the trial process, may not be in the best position to make reliable witness assessments. Furthermore, officers may allow their involvement in the investigation to bias their assessments towards an overly favourable view of the witness's potential.[11] When witness statements 'come alive' at court their contribution may become more or less persuasive than it seemed on paper; but they are unlikely to remain constant. Once again, the way in which witnesses' accounts are elicited differs in police questioning and at trial. So the inarticulate witness who cannot be led by counsel may be less lucid, and perhaps therefore less credible, than he or she was in a dialogue with a helpful interviewing officer. Even if this were not so, the prosecutor is reliant on the police view; the jury's appreciation of the witnesses is more likely to be coloured by the judge and counsel.

In addition, although witnesses may be given the facility to refresh their memories from their statements immediately before their appearance at trial, it remains an anathema to prosecutors actively to rehearse their witnesses. When the prosecutor does have the opportunity to meet witnesses on a face-to-face basis before trial, for example police officers and expert witnesses, he rarely examines them in a manner equivalent to cross-examination. The prosecutor's legal training and professional code may discourage such practices unless they can be justified in terms of clarifying inconsistencies. Thus, witnesses' persuasiveness is left untested. This is particularly unfortunate in relation to expert witnesses who have something of a 'head start' in terms of persuasiveness. The prosecution may be as easily impressed by scientific evidence as lay jurors, and therefore their initial assessments may be more in keeping with the likely reactions of jurors. However, the tendency of experts to draw conclusions in their statements, without including the necessary preceding thought processes and scientific detail, may serve to mislead prosecutors. Lack of attention to legal niceties and the possibility of expert evidence being undermined by cross-examination, compounded by the lack of force with which experts' views are often expressed in court, may all contribute to the failure of a prosecution case launched primarily on the basis of expert evidence.

Finally, of course, the defence case will provide additional information which may give the case an entirely different complexion. The process of presenting the evidence in court may be likened to a Chinese whisper: each stage the information passes through alters the nature of that information. It is thus apparent that at trial the jury will often see a case in a different shape and context from the prosecutor: this highlights the precarious nature of his paper-based predictions.

The prosecutor is in an unenviable position: he is asked to place himself in the shoes of the reasonable juror — or perhaps the twenty-four shoes of the entire jury! To achieve this he should not only divest himself of his prosecuting experience — the daily grind of criminality — but also set aside his knowledge of facts that will be inadmissible in front of the jury. Otherwise the case as a whole is unlikely to make the same impression upon him as it will upon the jury.[12] It would be problematic to assume that laymen exactly share a lawyer's interpretation of the facts which constitute the legal elements of a case, and, furthermore, naïve to expect lawyers and laymen to agree on the extent of their persuasiveness. Finally, given the defence case and experience of prosecution witnesses at first hand, the jury has to decide beyond reasonable doubt – a different standard from reasonable prospects. Yet, despite all these handicaps, the prosecutor has to reach a decision.

THE PROSECUTOR'S EXPERIENCE

To what extent is the prosecutor helped by his, or his colleagues', previous experience? In practice the usefulness of such experience may be limited. First, at the DPP the prosecutor's experience of juries may be limited. The majority of consent cases are left to local prosecutors and the remaining categories of DPP cases are principally prosecuted in the Crown Courts, so they are handled by counsel. In addition, few prosecutors sit through the course of trials of their cases. Thus the information they receive as to why cases succeed or fail comes to them second-hand through counsel or the court clerk. Unfortunately, this process not only results in a loss of information, but the quality of the feedback prosecutors receive may fail to address the pertinent considerations that led to the initial decision to prosecute. The complexity of the decision-making process is not matched by the information prosecutors receive about the intricacies of the trial. The court clerk's report addresses questions *he* finds salient arising from the trial; these may differ, however subtly, from those originally in the mind of the professional officer – and because the differences are subtle they are easily submerged. Furthermore, the time-lag between the decision to prosecute and the outcome of cases – especially those that go to appeal – may make what limited feedback there is of questionable value; the prosecutor may have lost his intimate knowledge of the thinking behind the decision to prosecute (and may also have shifted divisions and thereby lost responsibility for the case).

Secondly, for those cases prosecuted in the Magistrates' Court, where the prosecutor is involved through to conviction, his experience may also be misleading. Although the vast majority of all prosecutions are dealt with in the lower courts (95 per cent in 1983), prosecutors should not build these experiences into their assessment of the reasonable prospects test precisely because this test relates to convictions by an *impartial jury*. The willingness of case-hardened magistrates to return convictions may be a pressing direct experience for the prosecutor; but if that experience is taken into account in future prosecution decisions then the reasonable prospects test will contribute to a twin-track system of criminal justice, in that it will fail to raise the standard of prosecutions in the

Magistrates' Courts. Experience with magistrates acting in their capacity as examining justices would also be inappropriate: the *prima facie* test is the relevant standard to be satisfied for a committal, not the reasonable-prospects standard.

Similarly, impressions received from colleagues may be misleading, unless the recipient is fully informed of the relevant strategic considerations that formed a part of the decision; the widely held misconception that it is extremely difficult to obtain convictions against police officers (only true for some categories of cases such as assault) illustrates this difficulty. Misconceptions may be amplified where there are ensuing jury trials.[13]

As a postscript it is worth noting that some of these difficulties may be attenuated for local prosecutors applying the reasonable-prospects test. Generally speaking, local prosecutors deal with large numbers of less serious cases, whereas the DPP deals with a small number of very serious cases.[14] The local prosecutor will more frequently conduct his own cases at court. Local prosecutors tend to have a closer working relationship with the police than does the DPP and this is likely to continue even after they have obtained theoretical independence from the police. This may have the advantage of improving the quality of information for the prosecutor, for example in respect of assessments of witnesses' credibility, but the disadvantage of increasing the scope for the police to influence prosecution decisions. Furthermore, there are significant variations in local organizational arrangements – from centralized departments, which tend to be remote from investigating police officers, to departments which are 'divisionalized' along police lines, where working relationships with the police are close. Such organizational differences may additionally affect the various constraints on prosecutors' decision-making capacities. Finally, there is some danger, with the scope for inconsistency in prosecution decisions which the reasonable prospects test permits, that extension of the test through the Crown prosecution system may magnify its weaknesses without necessarily maintaining the DPP's principled stances, in relation to plea negotiations for example. Thus, the research findings cannot simply be generalized at a local level.

CONVICTION STATISTICS

Prosecutors pay some attention to the conviction statistics. But in order for the statistics to provide a valid guide, the prosecutor has to be aware of the prosecution strategy that was adopted in respect of any particular conviction. Thus, at the *general* level, prosecutions are brought by the DPP only where both stages of the prosecutorial model are satisfied, i.e. reasonable prospects plus public interest. Similarly, jury convictions, not being open to investigation, may be based on either or both of these factors; if it is impossible to separate the influence of the weight of the evidence from the 'merit factor' in jury decisions, conviction statistics cannot validly be regarded as a reliable guide as to whether or not the reasonable prospects test was satisfied for the jury.

Similarly, at the *particular* level there exist what may be termed defensible departures from the test. These are cases in which the prosecutor knowingly applies reasonable prospects in a less than rigorous fashion. The first departure concerns very serious offences; in these cases the prosecutor feels reluctant to filter out cases which fall between the *prima facie* and the reasonable prospects standard because the consequences of an inappropriate decision to filter out may be worse than leaving the decision to the court (and risking a judicially determined acquittal). Thus, the prosecutor allows the case to go to court because he regards the responsibility of deciding not to prosecute as too onerous. For instance, it is the policy of the DPP to put *prima facie* cases of infanticide to the court. Whether this amounts to a 'corruption' of the evidential standard, or is due to the effects of a public interest/reasonable prospects interaction is irrelevant for the purposes of this argument; in those cases the conviction statistics may mislead the would-be prosecutor. Similarly, the DPP has followed the Attorney General's policy of pursuing 'race relations' cases under certain sections of the Public Order Act on evidence that, as prosecutors are aware, does not satisfy the reasonable prospects test. Finally, many cases of homicide are launched on a murder basis in the full recognition that they are likely to result in manslaughter verdicts on the grounds of diminished responsibility or provocation. It is not, of course, open to the prosecutor to charge manslaughter in these cases on the assumption that such a defence will be raised and might be successful. The prosecutor has no alternative but to charge with murder since diminished responsibility and provocation are only defences to a murder charge. Hence, the prosecution has initially to be conducted on a murder footing.

Another critical factor which makes the conviction statistics an inappropriate guide for the would-be prosecutor derives from the fact that the majority of convictions are not obtained as a result of a judicially based examination of the prosecution case, but are based on guilty pleas. It is conceivable that a number of these guilty pleas are based on mere *prima facie* evidence. Where the prosecutor has an early indication of a guilty plea, it is somewhat artificial to ask him to fulfil the exercise of applying the reasonable prospects test: there is a patent prospect of conviction. But, if the defendant does not indicate that he intends to plead guilty, the evidence has to be tested in court and the prosecutor may be readily satisfied that he has sufficient evidence to satisfy the reasonable prospects test. Similarly, if the defendant pleads not guilty and challenges the validity of any confession he may have made, the prosecution may have some difficulty in satisfying the beyond reasonable doubt criterion in a trial within a trial (particularly where the defendant has no previous convictions). Vennard (1982) noted the strong influence of confession evidence on a finding of guilty, but it is also true that where defendants plead guilty, the bulk of the evidence against them often consists mainly of their own confession. It is not suggested that these individuals are innocent, but if the evidence is never tested the total conviction statistics may be misleading. Were more defence solicitors to advise their clients to plead not guilty – on the grounds that they may then receive the benefit of the prosecutor's personal doubt as to his ability to satisfy the reasonable prospects test – then the conviction statistics might present a more realistic picture.[15] At present, they fail to reflect the complexities of prosecutorial decision-making; analysis of them would serve to confuse rather than clarify.

II THE CONTEXTUAL APPROACH

The prosecutor's decision: applying 'reasonable prospects' in real cases

Discussion so far has concentrated on the elements of the reasonable prospects test to which the prosecutor's attention should *by definition* be drawn and on his ability to comply with those requirements given the nature of the information in his possession and his acquired prosecutorial skills and experience. It now shifts from this artificially pure world of hypothetical cases to an examination of how prosecutors apply the reasonable prospects test in real cases. This will show that they routinely fail to achieve the test's objectives.[16]

The discussion will involve, first, an examination of the complexity of the decision: the recognition that it would be false to regard the choice to prosecute as consisting of a single decision. The process can more properly be regarded as a series of subdecisions: whether to prosecute, whom to prosecute, and for what offence to prosecute, combine to generate many permutations. Once this sequential nature of the prosecutor's decision-making is spelt out, the vulnerability of the 'reasonable prospects' test becomes apparent. This vulnerability forms the second focus of the analysis. Where the prosecutor's subdecisions combine to produce an overall decision to proceed it is implicit, by virtue of that combination, that the subdecisions are interdependent. Yet as the case moves forward to trial the separable parts of the prosecutor's decision – and their concomitant prosecution strategies – are differentially vulnerable to other dynamic forces within the criminal justice system, but outside the prosecutor's control. The fact that the prosecutor retains only limited control over a case once the decision to proceed has been reached means that other participants in the prosecution process may radically alter the prospects of obtaining a conviction in any particular case. The roles of these other participants will be briefly reviewed. Finally, prosecutors reach decisions in the real world in the knowledge that others will have a hand in whether or not a conviction is secured. This may, in turn, influence their preparedness to proceed in respect of specific charges. This has been termed the 'delegation' effect.

SUBDECISIONS WITHIN THE DECISION TO PROSECUTE

(i) *Multiple defendants and multiple charges* The formula for the reasonable prospects test apparently assumes the existence of a single defendant on a single charge. A substantial minority of cases in practice involve more than one defendant or more than one charge.[17] Can it be assumed that the test operates in the same way for complex cases as it does in respect of simple ones?

The likelihood of successful prosecution on any specific charge may be dependent on other charges or on whether other defendants are on the same indictment. To assume that the prosecutor satisfies the reasonable prospects test in relation to every charge brought would be to assume that he operates in an ideal world. He does not. Where the evidence against each of several defendants is interdependent it follows that the prospects of securing a conviction against each of them will also be interdependent. For such cases the test has to be operated in an 'impure' form. An example might arise out of a joint act of murder by two people where there is only a *prima facie* case against one of them and a reasonable prospect of convicting the other – but only if they are tried jointly. Otherwise the defendant against whom there is a strong case could attempt to shift the blame on to the participant who was not prosecuted because the case against him was weak. In this event, there would be no reasonable prospect of convicting either of them. Similarly, in relation to charges, the prospects of conviction against a defendant on one charge may be enhanced as a result of other evidence against him in respect of another charge. This mutual dependency of evidence between charges is referred to by lawyers as 'getting it in by a side wind'. Looked at in isolation, the strength of the evidence may not satisfy the reasonable prospects test in respect of each defendant on each charge; taken together it may do so. To operate the reasonable prospects test on any other assumption might result in no proceedings being brought.

But there are costs associated with applying the reasonable prospects test in this 'impure' form. Where a carefully balanced indictment is disturbed by, say, the subsequent decision of a judge to split it (*R. v. McGlinchey* (1984) 78 Cr. App. R. 282), or the refusal of the magistrates to commit certain defendants at all or on certain charges only, the range of convictions and acquittals ultimately returned may not reflect the prosecutor's assessment of whether a reasonable prospect of conviction existed in relation to any specific charge.

In making this series of complex decisions the prosecutor also has to weigh against one another the competing and conflicting guidelines issuing from the Court of Appeal. For instance, the principle that the prosecutor should not pursue every trivial charge that he can prove, since the ordinary man 'does not like the book being thrown at someone' (*Ambrose* (1973) 57 Cr. App. R. 538), does not lie easily with the duty of the prosecutor to charge to the highest the evidence will support (*Beresford* (1952) 36 Cr. App. R. 1). Furthermore, does the latter imply a *prima facie* or a reasonable prospects standard of evidence in respect of each charge brought, or in respect of a conviction for *an* offence? Similarly, the prosecutor has to resolve the competing and conflicting demands deriving from concern about his 'level of success' – the number of convictions against each defendant – versus 'success at what level' – the recognition that gaining convictions against some defendants on some charges may only be achieved at the 'cost' of acquittals in relation to other charges and/or other defendants.

Thus, although it is bad policy and bad practice to overload an indictment with a view to securing a plea to a lesser offence, the realistic prosecutor will be aware that defendants both plead and make plea bargains (see for example McCabe and Purves (1972); Baldwin and McConville (1977)). The prosecutor who is aware that his most serious charge is being pursued on grounds of public interest may wish to add an alternative charge, not to invite a plea, but in order to have some 'safety net' if the court rejects the principal charge. It can also be argued that the proper application of the more stringent reasonable prospects test makes plea negotiation a more attractive option for the defendant. Through a plea to a lesser offence he avoids a conviction on a more serious charge where the prosecutor would have had a reasonable prospect of securing a conviction. Prosecutors using the reasonable prospects test will need to be aware of the implications of such consequences — both for defendants and for their own decision-making strategies.

Finally, the prosecutor may have to resolve competing and conflicting public interest considerations. Such dilemmas occur in their most crystallized form in decisions about whether to use peripheral participants in a crime as prosecution witnesses. When applying and satisfying the reasonable prospects test it becomes perfectly respectable to use as a witness an individual against whom it would have been possible to establish a bare *prima facie* case. The possibility of offering immunity (now largely frowned on) does not necessarily arise where, in the prosecutor's assessment, the potential witness never meets the stricter criterion necessary if he is to become a potential defendant. However, his testimony may substantially enhance the case against another possibly more culpable individual, so the quality of evidence against that person is raised from the *prima facie* standard to the reasonable prospects criterion and he can legitimately be placed in the dock. Dock/box decisions are in practice rarely so straightforward. Often the prosecutor has to weigh the likelihood of a potential co-defendant co-operating as a Crown witness if he is not prosecuted, against his reduced credibility as a witness if it can be alleged by the defence that he has a motive for giving evidence for the prosecution. Often, the best strategy may be to prosecute the co-defendant on the basis of whatever charges may properly be brought *before* seeking his co-operation as a witness. But even this approach may jeopardize a successful prosecution against a more serious offender; or subtly encourage the prosecutor to be more lenient in his handling of the potential witness.[18]

(ii) *The Level of Tribunal*   Another decision that the prosecutor will have to make which will affect his prospect of gaining a conviction concerns whether charges are brought at a summary or indictable level.[19] This decision should be governed by considerations other than simply the prospect of success, such as the seriousness of the behaviour, the appropriateness of the charge, and the principle that a defendant should not be deprived of trial by jury by being undercharged. Yet, if the prospects of obtaining a conviction on identical evidence were greater in front of the magistrates than before a jury, applying the test in its most rigorous form would mean prosecutors having to carry out an artificial exercise in taking cases that are *only* appropriate for summary trial. Indeed, the prosecutor might finally have to decide that there was 'insufficient evidence' in cases where both he and the police were aware that convictions would routinely be returned by the magistrates, had the reasonable prospects assessment not been made. It seems unlikely that in the real world prosecutors routinely take their decisions in this way, and still more unlikely that they always allow the 'prospects of a conviction' element to outweigh other factors in their decision about the choice of tribunal. None the less prosecutors may increase the prospects of conviction by choosing their tribunal carefully.

That such practices occur and cause subsequent problems for the prosecutor is substantiated by the divided opinion, both between police forces and within the DPP, over whether cases should proceed even if the defendant elects for trial in respect of either-way offences such as theft. Where summary trial or a summary plea is anticipated, and the strength of the evidence is borderline in respect of the prosecutor's reasonable prospects assessment, the defendant's decision to elect trial by jury may tilt the case back into the category where the reasonable prospects assessment cannot be sustained, assuming that juries are more likely to acquit than magistrates given the same evidence. That prosecutors recognize a difference between the prospects of obtaining convictions in the Magistrates' Courts and in the Crown Courts is highlighted by the practice of attempting as often as possible to keep the amount of damage alleged in criminal damage charges below £400. This prevents the defendant from electing for trial by jury.[20]

THE REASONABLE PROSPECTS ASSESSMENT – ITS SEQUENTIAL VULNERABILITY TO OTHER ACTORS

The prosecutor's general dependence on the police for information in a sufficient quantity and of a sufficient quality to satisfy the reasonable prospects test has already been reviewed.[21] It is also the case that the decisions which the police make about whether to bring proceedings, whom to charge, and with what, may constrain the prosecutor to proceed along predetermined lines. Similarly, the prosecutor is even more likely to be constrained where the police take statements from witnesses whom the prosecutor – with the benefit of hindsight – might prefer to regard as potential defendants; in such cases it may be too late to charge participants who have been treated as witnesses. In addition, the prosecution's case against the main participants may be weakened where the defence is able to implicate the prosecution witnesses.

These decisions by the police may constrain the prosecutor in his construction of a 'package' of charges against defendants. They may also create difficulties for the prosecutor in his dealings with the magistrates where charges have been preferred by the police working to a *prima facie* standard. Where the prosecutor wishes to exercise the discretion not to proceed, because the higher evidential standard cannot be satisfied, the magistrates may incline to the view that such cases should be decided by the court rather than allowing the prosecution to offer no evidence or to withdraw the case.[22]

Similarly, although the magistrates commit the majority of indictable cases for trial without consideration of the evidence (under Section 6(2) of the Magistrates' Court Act 1980), in a small proportion of cases the defendant or prosecutor may opt for an 'old-style committal' – under Section 6(1) of the Act – to examine the sufficiency of all, or part, of the evidence. Here, the magistrates are obliged to commit where a *prima facie* case exists. This may prevent the prosecutor from dropping cases where, as a result of seeing his witnesses giving their evidence, he recognizes that he has no reasonable prospects of conviction.[23] Although the prosecutor has some subsequent room for manoeuvre, by altering the way in which the indictment is drawn – for example, he is not bound to proceed on precisely the same charges as those upon which the case was committed – this may not wholly obviate the problem.

The activities of counsel at the trial stages of a case may also radically affect whether or not the prosecutor realizes his prospects of conviction. One obvious area is that of 'plea negotiation'. Although the DPP attempts to maintain control by either ruling this out in advance, or requiring consultation if it is raised, the practicalities of achieving day-to-day control over cases 'the conduct of which is a matter for counsel and the court' are considerable. Indeed, counsel may exercise his discretion in more subtle and hence less easily regulated ways. For instance, in his opening and closing speeches counsel may signal his view of the strength of the evidence to the jury and so may tilt them against returning convictions on certain counts on the indictment. Sometimes this even becomes explicit. Thus, a 'nod and a wink' may result in a similar outcome to that which might have resulted from an earlier plea negotiation, had it been allowed to take place. In such cases the prosecutor may not even recognize why his prospects of conviction predictions were not realized.

The impact that judges may have on the prosecutor's prospects of conviction through their decisions on severance has already been mentioned. At all stages in the subsequent trial the judge continues to exercise considerable discretion. His ruling on the admissibility of evidence and the emphasis which he gives to the various testimonies in summing up may affect the prospect of conviction. Finally, although any circumstances in a trial which show judicial bias in favour of the prosecution may provide the defence with grounds for appeal, no reciprocal right is available to the prosecution to remedy any apparent bias in favour of the defence. Not only is the prosecutor unable to anticipate the effects of judicial discretion on his prospects of conviction but also, if an acquittal results, he cannot know how far the jury were influenced by the judge's view of the evidence, or whether they acquitted irrespective of his view.

In relation to the prosecutor's prediction of the prospects of conviction, jury acquittals may take two forms. First, those where the jury finds the evidence insufficiently persuasive: cases where the prosecutor's assessment of the prospects of conviction was wrong. Secondly, those where the jury share the prosecutor's view of the persuasiveness of the evidence but acquit on other grounds: cases where the prosecutor 'got it right' but the jury returned a perverse verdict against the weight of the evidence. The prosecutor has no means of knowing into which of these two categories an acquittal falls.[24] Thus, in their role as 'ultimate acquitters', the jury may choose to acquit on grounds over which the prosecutor can have little control. It might be argued that in this respect they mirror the actions of the prosecutor, who may depart from a rigid adherence to an evidential standard on grounds of public interest.

THE 'DELEGATION EFFECT'

It has already been suggested that a split between the advisory and advocacy roles that prosecutors undertake, as for instance happens in Northern Ireland, may contribute to what has been termed a 'prosecution momentum'. Prosecutors often say that nothing concentrates the mind like having to get up on one's hind legs and prosecute a case in court. In certain categories of case the DPP routinely advises local prosecutors or the police on prosecutions without actually undertaking them. When delegation of responsibility for a case is anticipated, in that it is known that it will be left to the police, the prosecutor has little direct incentive to apply the reasonable prospects test rigorously in relation to the decision to bring proceedings. The analysis of the consent sample indicates that these cases sometimes received less extensive consideration than those which the DPP undertakes through to trial.[25]

Similarly, when cases are taken on indictment, they are delegated to counsel. It is hard to determine whether prosecutors are knowingly less rigorous in their approach to these cases, with the result that counsel indulge in the 'nod and wink' strategies referred to earlier; or whether cases either genuinely weaken during their progress, requiring counsel to rectify the damage; or whether some counsel are simply not imbued with the reasonable prospects ethos. The fact remains that prosecutors at the DPP do not routinely 'see their cases through'; whether and how the knowledge of this influences them is uncertain.

Should the reasonable prospects assessment be a 'once for all' or an 'ongoing' filter on prosecutorial practice?

BALANCE WITHIN THE ADVERSARY SYSTEM

The specific difficulties of sustaining a 'reasonable prospects' prediction within a criminal justice system where participants other than the prosecutor may work to a different evidential standard have been reviewed. However, there is one further overriding difficulty which may make it unrealistic to sustain reasonable prospects – namely, that the balance of advantage shifts from the prosecution to the defence as a case proceeds.

In the initial stages of the prosecution process the advantage lies with the Crown, both because of its greater investigatorial resources, and because it determines the nature and shape of the case to be brought against the defendant. As a result of these advantages the decision to prosecute is taken as a case reaches its 'high-water mark', and before there is any erosion of the evidence. After this point the balance shifts, so that the remainder of the prosecution is an uphill process. Rules of procedure and evidence combine with the greater tactical and ethical latitude allowed to the defence to ensure some sort of fair play. Thus, the defendant is compensated for his earlier handicap. Once the extent of this shift is appreciated it becomes clear that it would be unrealistic to expect the prosecutor or his agents to go on employing a series of reasonable prospects assessments in order to keep the prosecution decision under intermittent review. Otherwise, substantially more cases would never reach the jury, including many that now result in convictions or 'come good'. A prosecution witness may, for example, fail to impress the lawyers in court by his level of *competence* in giving evidence; nevertheless the lay jury may be persuaded by the witness's *sincerity*. Discrepancies between different prosecution witnesses' versions of events may point up an ostensibly weak case or, on the other hand, may convince the jury that no collaboration has occurred between them.

INFORMATION VERSUS CONTROL

Once it is recognized that it would be unrealistic to expect the prosecutor to attempt to withdraw a case from the court at any stage when it falls evidentially below the standard required by the reasonable prospects test, a further irony emerges. The closer the case comes to the verdict, the greater are the prosecutor's prospects of making accurate reasonable prospects predictions, because the quality of his information improves. At the same time, however, his ability to determine the course of the prosecution and hence to validate his reasonable prospects prediction is correspondingly lessened.

It has been noted that the stage at which effective decisions are made as to whether and how cases proceed is not necessarily always the same. In some prosecutions the critical decision is taken very early, when the case papers are received, but for others the prosecutor, operating the reasonable prospects test, may 'reserve judgment' pending advice from counsel or even an old-style committal. This strategy, intended to delay any final decision until more – or perhaps better – information emerges, is questionable. In the process of delaying his decisions, the prosecutor may lose effective control over the case to the courts, since, once committed, cases cannot be dropped without the judge's permission. Indeed, since it is generally recognized that cases tend to acquire momentum as they move through the prosecution process, the prosecutor who is induced to delay his decision on whether to proceed may contribute to this momentum. Certainly, delay will do nothing to restrain it.

It has already been concluded that it would be unrealistic to assess reasonable prospects predictions in terms of the outcome of cases. In addition, it would also be unrealistic to expect prosecutors to improve their predictions by reassessing their decisions in the light of improved information. Similarly, expecting them to maintain control over the case or over other participants in the process is equally unrealistic.

Set against the contextual analysis such conclusions are dispiriting, in that they suggest that changing the rules without altering the process is unlikely to have much impact on the realities of prosecutorial decision-making. However, changing the rules may influence the prosecutor's perception of the context within which he has to reach decisions. Instead of trying to extend the prosecutor's influence through the process and thereby improving his accuracy by bringing him closer to his goal, the goal should be moved closer to the prosecutor. This proposal is discussed in detail in the last chapter.

NOTES

1 In Chapter 1 it was noted that, in respect of the public-interest element, the Attorney General's criteria identify factors that may enable the prosecutor *not* to proceed in the public interest, i.e. the criteria facilitate filtering cases away from the courts.

2 It should be noted that interpretations (i) and (iii) are not mutually exclusive.

3 It might be argued that over a two- or three-week period of attending court, jurors may become 'case hardened'.

4 Even in this area, despite comparative clarity, there are inconsistencies in the guidance offered: for example, according to whether the statute uses the word 'recklessly': *Elliott* v. *C* [1983] 2 All ER 1005 (DC); *Caldwell* [1982] AC 841 (HL); or 'maliciously': *Woodward* v. *Dolbey* [1983] CLR 681 (DC); *Grimshaw* [1984] Crim. LR 108. The position is different again for rape cases: *Breckenridge* [1984] Crim. LR 174.

5 The application of beyond reasonable doubt has been described thus: 'a subtle compromise between the knowledge, on the one hand, that we cannot realistically insist on an acquittal whenever guilt is less than absolutely certain, and the realisation, on the other hand, that the cost of spelling that out explicitly and with calculated precision in the trial itself would be too high' (Tribe 1971: 1375).

6 This proposition clearly draws upon principles of public accountability and may be bolstered by one of the tenets of the adversarial system – that 'the truth will

out': a somewhat doubtful assertion in the light of the observations arising out of this research.

7 The Attorney General's guidelines (1981) 72 Cr. App. R. 14 (published 1 August, 1980) on jury vetting permit the DPP on the authority of the Attorney General to make certain checks on potential jurors. Those checks may go beyond the investigation of criminal records. 'Jury vetting' is only permitted in certain exceptional types of case of public importance, for which the provisions as to majority verdicts and the disqualification of jurors may not be sufficient to ensure the proper administration of justice.

8 The difficulties arising out of the requirement that the prosecutor apply a compound test (namely, reasonable prospects followed by public interest) are dealt with in detail later.

9 For example, guidance from the Court of Appeal (*Dix* (1982) 74 Cr. App. R. 306 and *Vernage* (1982) 74 Cr. App. R. 232) suggests that where the medical evidence of diminished responsibility is uncontradicted the judge should accept a plea of manslaughter: the judge's decision in R. v. *Sutcliffe* to leave the issue of diminished responsibility to the jury went against this. Similarly, evidence of pressure from the judge on the prosecutor to accept a plea was noted in this study – see Case 85, Chapter 2, p. 94. Finally, judges have not been immune from making improper comments during their summings up, which have resulted in convictions being quashed; see R. v. *Mutch* (1972) 57 Cr. App. R. 196, and R. v. *Gilbert* (1977) 66 Cr. App. R. 237.

10 If the reasonable prospects test is to be made to work in respect of the bulk of these cases, the police may well have to reconsider their use of the 'short-form' procedure. Thus, the resource implications of adopting reasonable prospects may, for the police at least, be considerable; they will either have to provide the prosecutor with fuller written reports or maintain close contact on individual cases to ensure that the prosecutor has the necessary background information to make reasonable prospects assessments.

11 Unlike the Scottish system of precognitions where the prosecutor theoretically has the opportunity to assess his witnesses first-hand, it is only in rare cases that the prosecutor will meet his witnesses at a stage where he retains the ability not to proceed with the case. Old-style committals are advantageous here, but they are comparatively infrequent and tend to occur only in the marginal cases; and unless the prosecutor stands his ground when his witnesses fail to impress him, he may find the case committed.

12 See Williams (1985). Williams asserts that the appropriate test of whether a case should proceed ought to be the prosecutor's belief in the suspect's guilt and not his belief that a jury will more likely than not convict. He states that 'if prosecutors make a practice of bringing charges in which they do not themselves believe, they greatly increase the risk that innocent persons will be convicted, and therefore should refrain from charging in these cases'. The empirical research, in stark contrast, demonstrates that prosecutors, being both 'case-hardened' and routinely having access to more information than will be available to the jury, are more likely to be convinced of a suspect's guilt than the jury. Therefore, it is a rare occasion when a prosecutor prosecutes an individual whom he does not believe to be guilty. Making the prosecutor's belief in the suspect's guilt the initial criterion in the decision to prosecute, may, in practice, result in too many cases going forward which will ultimately fail.

13 The perceived difficulty of satisfying the evidential requirement in relation to cases brought against police officers is capable of substantiation; police officers

make convincing defendants. The Crown's witnesses, in cases where they are not other police officers, are often individuals of questionable character (e.g. individuals in a police station at the time of an alleged assault). Thus, the balance of the evidence is weighted in favour of the defendant. In order to satisfy the reasonable prospects test fewer prosecutions are brought. Whether this departure amounts to a real departure from the test (i.e. a *very* reasonable prospect of conviction is required when compared with the weight of evidence required to prosecute a civilian) or whether it results from the prosecutor making an assumption that a reasonable juror would be more likely to believe a policeman/defendant than a 'criminal'/witness and therefore the persuasive element of the reasonable prospects test cannot be satisfied, depends largely on the correctness of the prosecutor's assumption. If juries are prepared to convict in cases that the prosecutor filters out, then a very reasonable prospect test is being applied. See also Williams (1985).

14 This may make the local prosecutor more vulnerable to the problems arising out of a quantitative lack of evidence, rather than the variable quality of excessive information (see pp. 196–97).

15 Will a rigorous application of the reasonable prospects test result in more not guilty pleas, to test the reasonable prospects standard; or more cases being filtered out of the criminal justice system where the defendant may have been willing to plead guilty?

16 Directed acquittals may be taken to be illustrative of such failure. The directed acquittals in the sample were attributed to the way in which public interest considerations *overrode* strict adherence to satisfying the reasonable prospects test. The paradoxical outcome was that directed acquittals resulted from either failure to exercise the discretion *not to* prosecute under the reasonable prospects test, or conversely, an exercise of discretion to prosecute arising out of the public interest element of the approach. They are thus symptomatic of the scope for prosecutorial discretion under the reasonable prospects approach.

17 For example Moody and Tombs note that 29 per cent of cases in their Scottish census involved multiple charges (1982: 146).

18 It should of course be remembered that these dock/box dilemmas only arise in a minority of cases. The general observation, that the reasonable prospects test does not necessarily operate in the same way for complex cases as it does in relation to simple ones, remains valid.

19 The DPP, the Attorney General, and the Solicitor General are in the exceptional position of being able to withhold consent to a summary trial (Magistrates' Courts Act 1980, S.25(3)).

20 R. v. *Canterbury and St. Augustine Justices, ex parte Klisiak* [1981] Crim. LR 253 and R. v. *Ramsgate Justices, ex parte Warren and others* [1981] Crim. LR. It has also been suggested (see Brown 1984) that women protesters from the Greenham Common peace camp have had criminal damage charges against them dropped by the prosecution where the cost of the damage alleged would have given the accused the right to elect trial by jury.

21 One such difficulty, already referred to in Chapter 1, may arise out of the evidential constraints imposed on the police by the judges' rules; Rule 3 in combination with principle (d) of the judges' rules requires that interrogation of suspects should cease and they should be charged once a *prima facie* case has been disclosed. Yet if the police adhere to this practice they are disadvantaged in the cases which they have to put up to the DPP. If they want to enable the prosecution to satisfy the persuasive burden, the police may find themselves in the position of having to breach the judges' rules. These rules will be superseded by the Codes of

Practice for the detention, treatment, questioning, and identification of persons by the police (currently available in draft form: Home Office (1985)). It none the less remains unclear as to precisely which standard of evidence (*prima facie* or reasonable prospects) the police should be working in their investigations.

22 In the case of *Littlewood* (1983) the prosecuting solicitor for the Metropolitan Police sought to offer no evidence; the judge at the Inner London Crown Court insisted that the case proceed to trial; a conviction resulted. It was quashed on appeal, although principally on the grounds of a defective summing up. The issue of whether the prosecutor should have been allowed to drop the case was not addressed in the judgment (unreported case No. 3172/C/83 Court of Appeal Criminal Division, 4 November, 1983). Similar conflict occurs in the Magistrates' Courts, e.g. the case of *Matthews* (*The Times*, 12 November, 1980, p. 1).

23 This situation may occur where the prosecutor has previously 'reserved judgment' on his prospects of conviction until he has the opportunity to see the witnesses (see p. 210).

24 Similar difficulties arise in respect of interpreting the basis on which juries convict, except that these may be clarified at appeal if the defendant exercises that right.

25 The failure to make a rigorous application of the reasonable prospects test may be partially attributable to the quality of information the DPP receives in consent cases which primarily come to the DPP in a 'short-form' format. Thus, likely lines of defence may not be readily apparent. The prosecutor may be deceived into believing he has satisfied the reasonable prospects test.

CHAPTER 5
CONCLUSIONS

The fundamental problem in the field of prosecutions, and therefore for this research, centres upon prediction. If the accuracy of prosecutors' predictions about the outcome of criminal cases could be guaranteed, it would theoretically be possible to dispense with the subsequent trial process altogether. Of course, it cannot. This chapter considers what may reasonably be attempted.

If the reasonable prospects approach were to form the basis of a reformed prosecution system, according to the findings of this study this would amount to substituting a less than adequate prosecutorial standard for the *prima facie* one, which is clearly inadequate. In the form expressed in the Attorney General's *Criteria*, 'reasonable prospects' provides little guidance in respect of a series of crucial prosecutorial issues – amongst others the choice of charge, the choice of tribunal, and whether or not to accept a plea to a lesser offence. The criteria leave considerable uncertainty over whether a prosecution would be brought in various sets of circumstances; there is thus an unpredictable element within 'reasonable prospects'. The standard it replaces, the *prima facie* test, may similarly be criticized on the grounds that it does little to prevent the bringing of dubious prosecutions. This may involve an abuse of both human and public resources. It can be argued that the *prima facie* test achieves consistency in much the same way that paper committals do – namely by a *laissez-faire* approach which largely moves inconsistency to a later stage in the prosecution process. Under the *prima facie* test prosecutions are brought even where it has not been predicted that they are likely to succeed.

Throughout this book prosecutorial responsibility has been divided into two stages, between the decision as to whether to prosecute and the decision as to how to prosecute. At a theoretical level, the philosophy behind the reasonable prospects approach has retained its value in relation to both stages, that is as a check on instituting proceedings and as a potential brake on prosecution momentum. However, at an empirical level, the research has confirmed the view that the theory is not necessarily followed in practice and has highlighted that, at least for prosecutors at the

DPP, the emphasis tends to be on how a prosecution should proceed rather than on whether it should proceed. This is because the seriousness of many of their cases reduces effective prosecutorial discretion to proceed by alternative means, for instance through use of a caution. The prosecutor is thus in some difficulty: in practice the reasonable prospects test is a guide for 'whether' to proceed, and does not enlighten him as to the manner of proceeding. However, if the overall approach is characterized as 'getting it right' – only putting a person on trial when it is more likely than not that a conviction will be returned – where correct initial decisions as to whether to prosecute are made, appropriate 'how' decisions should follow. This is because a correct decision as to whether to proceed under reasonable prospects necessarily implies a justifiable conviction on a predetermined charge. In this respect 'whether' and 'how' are inextricably linked at a theoretical level. However, the research conducted has shown the complexity of their relationship at a practical level. To link the 'whether' and 'how' of prosecutions in practice requires the rules to be more realistically aligned with what it is possible to achieve. It is therefore suggested that changing the rules, that is revising the standard for prosecution, could operate to minimize unjust prosecutions; it could replace poor predictions about the 'correctness' of prosecutions with better predictions about whether prosecutions should be launched; improving the ability to answer the question 'whether' should in practice improve the consequential task of answering 'how'.

The research indicates that there are three principal issues which require review. Each will be addressed in this chapter. First, the reasonable prospects test as an evidential criterion should be revised. Secondly, the public interest element in the reasonable prospects approach should be restructured. Clearly, the two reforms proposed in this chapter should not be separated. However, of themselves, they are considered insufficient, and the third issue reviewed concerns the question of accountability. The general tenor of this book has been that a revised prosecution system should neither rely on 'good chap theory' nor ignore the views of 'good chaps'. The decision-making model at the DPP is to be commended in that it capitalizes on the pressure that may be brought to bear informally on prosecutors by their peers. Cases observed there illustrated the extent to which the decision-making structure would impel prosecutors to consider, then reconsider, cases, to avoid the risk of 'perverse' convictions. However, the need for measures of accountability beyond those of the prosecutor's peers is heightened as the prosecutor's independence is enhanced. That the reforms proposed here will, it is hoped, assist in achieving accountability is to their advantage. None the less, since the prosecutor's discretion is to be expanded, the question of accountability remains crucial whatever the final form of the prosecutorial test.

THE CRITIQUE OF THE REASONABLE PROSPECTS TEST

The analysis in Chapter 4 raised doubts about the practicality of the reasonable prospects test, most fundamentally because it requires the prosecutor to predict the largely unpredictable. In practice, prosecutors employing the reasonable-prospects test neither necessarily succeed in filtering out weak cases – one of the principal justifications for the wider application of the reasonable prospects test – nor achieve any substantial degree of consistency in their application of the test.[1] In view of the formidable range of practical difficulties for the prosecutor using the reasonable prospects test, it is not surprising that the research identified some 'defensible' departures from a rigid adherence to it, as a means of making the test work 'in the real world'. However, such practical concessions contribute to the creation of an environment in which still greater flexibility may occur.

It might be argued that there was a certain inevitability about this finding. Consistency in decision-making does not usually accompany the widening of discretion which 'reasonable prospects' allows. The test is predicated on subjective prosecutorial judgments. So inconsistency in decision-making is unsurprising. If the 'letter' of the reasonable prospects test remains, it is likely that prosecutors will remain unable to reconcile the Royal Commission's aims of consistency, fairness, and the avoidance of 'unnecessary' prosecutions.

Might some alternative formula for the exercise of the prosecutor's discretion permit discrimination in his decision-making yet avoid inconsistency in approach by reducing the subjective and predictive elements inherent in the reasonable prospects test? In the absence of a real-world 'legal science', total objectivity will remain illusory, and any form of words may be criticized given a sufficiently rigorous analysis. Nevertheless, it may be possible to design a test which reduces to a minimum the subjective element in the prosecutor's decision. It is suggested that the revised evidential test presented below represents such an attempt. However, it must be assessed in the context of the subsequent recommendations concerning the public interest and accountability. It is readily accepted that a 'form of words' could never be sufficient as a guide to good prosecuting.

The revised evidential test: the advantages of drawing the prosecutor's sights back to 'half-time'

The basis for such a revised test was briefly described in Chapter 1. In the consideration of whether there is any available model for another prosecutorial standard which could strike the appropriate balance in prosecutions, attention was drawn to another of the Royal Commission's original concerns: the rate of directed acquittals.[2] As an existing filter on weak cases, this judicial decision offers a ready-made 'cue' which might be adopted by prosecutors. There would be eight principal advantages for the prosecutor in a test which required him to satisfy himself that there was no reasonable prospect of a directed acquittal on the charges on which he intended to proceed.

First, the prosecutor would only need to attempt to assess the strength of the prosecution side of the case, since defence submissions of 'no case to answer', which may result in directed acquittals, follow the close of the prosecution case at trial. The 'totality' approach to decision-making canvassed in the Fisher Report (1977), which recommends that the prosecutor consider not only his own case but also that of the defence as fully as possible, is somewhat idealized because there are severe practical limitations on the extent to which it can be achieved. Unless a duty to disclose its case is imposed on the defence, it is unrealistic to expect the prosecutor to take a genuinely inquisitorial stance within the context of an adversarial criminal justice system. Indeed, such an approach might result in the prosecutor's pursuit of the truth being at the expense of the acquittal of some of the guilty.[3] Obviously the revised test would not make it completely unnecessary for the prosecutor to consider likely lines of defence; indeed, clear lines of defence which the prosecution will have to rebut, such as self-defence, have to be taken into consideration when assessing the strength of the prosecution's case. However, the formidable additional difficulties of assessing the likely impact of unknown defences, and possibly (in the examples of 'defence by ambush') unknowable defences would be avoided.

Secondly, the subjective elements within the decision to prosecute will be reduced since the prosecutor only has to anticipate how another 'professional' will view his case rather than how lay jurors will regard it. Magistrates and judges, whether through experience or training, are more 'case-hardened' than jurors who are new to the task of deciding cases. As a result, these professionals may be regarded as less likely than the jury to take a view of the case which diverges from that of the prosecutor. Thus, the alternative test will draw on the prosecutor's objective technical legal skills in assessing whether there is a *prima facie* case, supplemented by the exercise of his individual judgment as a case-hardened prosecutor as to whether he finds the evidence inherently credible (i.e. capable of bearing, and likely to bear, the weight necessary to return a conviction); and likely to be similarly persuasive to other case-hardened decision-makers.[4] The prosecutor only has to speculate about the evidence that other professional case-hardened lawyers would find reasonable; he does, however, have to be certain in his own mind that the evidence is capable of being believed. This 'belief' criterion should be distinguished from that advanced by Glanville Williams (1985; for further discussion of the belief criterion, see p. 198 (n.12)). The belief element within the revised test is critically pitched between the prosecutor's own belief in the defendant's guilt (about which he may be too easily convinced) and his belief that the jury will convict (about which he is as likely as not to be wrong). Although Williams moderates his 'belief' criterion with the proviso that the prosecutor must also believe that he has a *fair* chance of success, the belief criterion within the revised test avoids this subjective (and hence inherently flexible) element. By focusing the prosecutor's attention on the need to persuade another case-hardened decision-maker of the strength of the *provable* case, the revised test allows the prosecutor to proceed in cases where he personally may experience some doubt and would not necessarily, were he the fact-finder, convict the accused at that stage. Furthermore, with the revised test the prosecutor does not have to predict how a non-case-hardened jury – the interaction of twelve jurors – will assess persuasiveness. Indeed, the jury are given more than a symbolic role; assessing actual persuasiveness remains their province. This would represent a reaffirmation of the role of the jury in the criminal justice system. Hence, prosecutors would be asked to employ forethought rather than foresight in their decisions.

Third, reasons for directed acquittals are more clearly discernible than is the reasoning behind jury decisions which remains largely a matter for speculation. Thus, if the prosecutor were to focus on directed acquittals, he should gain an insight into what went wrong in the cases that fail at that stage. Such feedback is more likely to serve an effective educative function than looking to jury verdicts as interpreted by counsel, or, more routinely, court clerks, neither of whom necessarily share the prosecutor's initial view as to precisely why the decision to proceed was made.

Fourth, structuring a revised evidential test around the directed-acquittal stage may further assist the prosecutor by providing him with a body of legal principle and practice which have already evolved around the justification for these decisions. The present test requires the prosecutor to import artificial notions of how a higher court might decide a case which is actually for summary hearing. In so far as judges and magistrates operate to much the same evidential standard in directing acquittals, the prosecutor applying the revised test does not have to consider which level of tribunal will deal with his case in deciding whether to proceed.[5] Under the revised test, cases triable either way where the defendant unexpectedly elects Crown Court trial should present no special difficulty. Although magistrates and judges may differ in their decision-making skills, the main source of duality in the reasonable prospects test, that between magistrates and jurors, would be obviated since the revised test bites *before* cases go for consideration by the jury. Hence, adoption of the revised test may help to iron out a tendency towards 'twin-track' decision-making by either the prosecutor or the courts.

Fifth, with respect to the problems created for the prosecutor compiling a 'package' of charges against two or more defendants, application of the revised test would probably make these finely balanced decisions less vulnerable to the actions of others – for example, the judge's decision to sever the indictment. Under the present test, where the interdependent parts of a 'prosecution package' are separated, some no longer enjoy reasonable prospects. Application of the revised test should focus the prosecutor's attention on the need to avoid a directed acquittal in the case of *each* individual defendant; and thereby avoid the 'woolliness' of thinking about sufficiency of evidence across defendants which the reasonable prospects test facilitates. Since mutual dependency between charges and defendants routinely increases the actual persuasiveness of the case to a jury rather than the strength of the evidence against any individual defendant, the revised test should reduce the prosecutor's vulnerability in respect of making 'wrong' decisions. This is because the standard by which he would initially be judged would be whether or not a directed acquittal had been avoided. Similarly, where these acquittals occurred they would necessarily entail the prosecutor's censure, whereas jury acquittals do not necessarily have this effect if all parties concerned conveniently define them as 'perverse' or beyond comprehension.

In relation to multiple defendants there is, however, a question about the appropriate allocation of potential defendants between the dock and the witness-box. The empirical research demonstrated a tendency under reasonable prospects to 'fudge' questions of evidential sufficiency when the public interest in securing a conviction against a specific defendant was considered overwhelming. By clarifying the evidential standard, any decision by the prosecutor not to pursue charges against potential co-defendants, but rather to use them as prosecution witnesses, would become exposed for what it is – a public interest decision.[6] Such explicit treatment of positive public interest criteria has already been advocated as a general principle; in specific cases it may have a further advantage in that, if the prosecution is open about its decision-making strategies, it may be correspondingly harder for the defence to damage the Crown's case by alleging its witnesses are 'escapees' from the dock.

Sixth, in respect of multiple charges, although the problems arising out of plea negotiation will remain, they should not be expected to increase. This contrasts with the position under the reasonable prospects test, where defendants may be more likely to take the initiative in seeking a plea negotiation, because they perceive the prosecution to have a reasonable prospect of conviction on the major charge against them if the case proceeds to trial.

Seventh, adoption of the revised test would reduce any tension that might occur between the prosecutor and the courts because of the greater discretion allowed to the prosecutor to assess the strength of the evidence, not available to the courts following *Galbraith*. Working to the revised test, the prosecutor would be more closely aligned with the courts. Their approach would not of course be exactly the same since the prosecutor would still employ public interest criteria to structure his decision-making, whereas the courts would be confined to evidential questions.

Lastly, the revised test would also serve to distinguish more clearly the evidential stage of the decision-making model from questions concerning the public interest. These criteria would no longer be partly subsumed in the evidential limb of the reasonable prospects test in the way that they are when the prosecutor has to predict whether a given jury are likely to convict. Similarly, the need for positive public interest criteria to 'drag up' evidentially questionable cases – questionable within the confines of the reasonable prospects test – would be obviated. Since jury behaviour would no longer form part of the prediction there would be no need to justify proceeding in cases where pessimistic jury predictions had been reached. The evidential merits of the case as perceived by the prosecutor would determine whether it proceeded. Drawing a clear demarcation between questions of evidential sufficiency and public interest would have the further advantage that the latter criteria would have to become more explicit. This is not only desirable *per se*, but would also help to facilitate the review of emergent public-interest criteria.

The revised evidential test: problems with a 'half-time' test

The exact scope of the courts' powers following *Galbraith* raises a possible practical complication for the revised test. In relation to a submission of 'no case', the scope for judicial discretion has been narrowed in such a way that, if adopted by the prosecutor as the core of the revised test, it would entail a lowering of prosecutorial standards, to a point where he might no longer be able to maintain the spirit of the reasonable prospects approach. It is submitted that the *Galbraith* judgment is out of keeping with the spirit of the times, as reflected first by the Royal Commission and now by the Government. The proposed Crown Prosecution Service is modelled on the DPP, who seeks to prevent cases coming before juries where it would be unsafe for them to convict. Following *Galbraith*, judges can no longer withdraw cases from juries on this basis. Is it not anomalous that the judiciary is prevented from exercising a discretion which is being widely extended to prosecutors? In practice the divergence may not be so great, since the research showed that there is some uncertainty in the trial courts as to how strictly *Galbraith* should be interpreted. But, as a basis for a revised prosecutorial test, the principles enunciated within *Galbraith* are clearly inappropriate, since they address questions of the quantity of evidence at the expense of looking at its quality.

If *Galbraith* represents an unsatisfactorily low standard for the prosecutor, are there any alternative models that might be adopted? The 'unsafe or unsatisfactory' approach adopted by the Court of

Appeal for weighing evidence against the verdict was considered in Chapter 1. It has little obvious relevance for the prosecutor since the unsafe-unsatisfactory case law is predominantly concerned with elements introduced into the case once it reaches court – principally where the exercise of judicial discretion may have prejudiced the defendant. Some possible hints for the prosecutor are, however, suggested by the case law. For example, *R.* v. *Turner and others* (1975) (61 Cr. App. R. 67) suggests circumspection where the only evidence is the uncorroborated evidence of an accomplice and there is 'nothing approaching supporting evidence'; *R.* v. *Thorne and others* (1977) says that in similar circumstances the Court (at least) will 'examine the villain's evidence with care to see whether there are any weaknesses in it' (66 Cr. App. R. 6 (per Lawton, LJ, at p. 16); and *R.* v. *Ballie-Smith* (1976) 64 Cr. App. R. 76) apparently militates against the prosecution strategy of letting evidence in 'by a side wind'. These are fascinating titbits for the conscientious prosecutor, but they hardly amount to a coherent prosecution philosophy. Indeed, the Court avoids anything more concrete than the amorphous notion of 'lurking doubts . . . such doubts are resolved not . . . by rules of thumb and not by arithmetic, but . . . largely by the experience of the judges . . . and the feel which the case has for them' (Lord Widgery, CJ, in *R.* v. *Lake* (1976) Cr. App. R. 172 at p. 177). It should not, of course, come as any surprise or disappointment that the Court of Appeal does not provide guidance for the prosecutor; it considers only convictions, retrospectively, whereas the prosecutor is also concerned with potential acquittals, and in all cases prospectively. Similarly, the Court of Appeal is dependent on action being taken by the defence and therefore its ambit is somewhat constrained. Finally, its capacity to provide consistent and relevant guidance on matters of policy has, in the analogous field of sentencing, been questioned (Ashworth 1983).

The test for magistrates can be found in the 1962 Practice Note, 'Considerations for guidance on submissions of no case to answer'. This may be more relevant. Lord Parker, CJ, urged, as a matter of *practice* (not principle), that such submissions are only properly made, and should therefore only be upheld, where there is insufficient evidence or 'when the evidence adduced by the prosecution has been so discredited as a result of cross-examination or is so *manifestly unreliable* that no reasonable tribunal could safely convict on it' (Practice Note [1962] 1 All E R 448; emphasis added). The latter part of the proposition is helpful to the prosecutor since it implicitly shows some tentative weighing of the evidence and approves the attendant concept of 'safety'.

Precisely what model *should* be adopted is not resolved here. As a general principle it would be preferable if prosecutors, judges, and magistrates worked to similar standards at the different stages – prosecution, directed acquittal, conviction overturned on appeal – at which cases are filtered out of the system. This would not only reduce tension between different actors involved in the process but also ensure that the case the defence has to meet could clearly be established irrespective of the route taken by the case. The precepts of justice would correspondingly be enhanced.

A watering-down of standards?

Perhaps a more fundamental criticism of the revised test advocated here concerns the possibility that focusing the prosecutor's attention on getting cases past 'half-time', by avoidance of directed acquittals, would suggest a lowering of standards. If the revised test is characterized as falling between *prima facie* and reasonable prospects, it may be argued that a higher proportion of cases would be prosecuted than if the reasonable prospects test were adhered to. At a superficial level the prosecutor could claim to have 'got it right' once he got his case past half-time, irrespective of the ultimate acquittal rates. A superficial response to this – but one which might have real political ramifications – is that some local prosecutors are reckoned to have too close an interest in convictions already. If Crown prosecutors are to be weaned away from this perspective, averting their eyes from the end of the trial might not seem unhealthy.

More critically, this research suggests that in practice the reasonable prospects test is applied in a less than rigorous fashion. Not only do jury acquittals regularly occur, suggesting that the test does not necessarily identify 'good risks', but also directed acquittals are not completely avoided, further suggesting that it fails even to identify the 'bad risks'. Focusing the prosecutor's attention more closely on the stage of directed acquittals may result in a more thorough assessment of the strengths and weaknesses of the prosecution case. This should reduce the actual numbers of directed acquittals. Standards may thus be raised *above* the routine practice of reasonable prospects. Thus, substitution of an attainable but ostensibly less ambitious 'half-time' prosecution standard should represent a net gain, in terms of avoidable prosecutions, over the attempt to sustain a rigid adherence to the 'full-time' jury standard which, this research shows, may jeopardize consistency. Furthermore, the revised evidential test should still result in a similar pool of individuals not being prosecuted, albeit through a different route of reasoning, since public interest criteria would remain operative. Those individuals currently prosecuted when public interest criteria 'drag up' evidentially problematic cases would instead fail to satisfy the 'lower', but more consistently operable, evidential standard and thus would not be subject to prosecution. Those advantages claimed for, but in practice unattained by, reasonable prospects may actually accrue to the arguably lower 'revised test' proposed here. The revised test would substitute the existing requirement of a 'belief in the impossible' with the 'art of the possible'; the prosecutor would have to work with the 'here and now' and not with the 'hereafter'.

RESTRUCTURING THE PUBLIC INTEREST ELEMENT OF THE REASONABLE PROSPECTS APPROACH

Of the advantages already detailed as likely to result from adoption of the revised evidential test, the last concerned clarification of the public interest element of the reasonable prospects approach. If prosecutors are to enjoy the awesome responsibility of making decisions 'in the public interest', it is clearly desirable, if an equitable and consistent application of such criteria is to be attained, that these public interest criteria should be spelt out (Editorial, *Criminal Law Review* 1985 (January): 2). This will necessarily entail recognition not only of competing and conflicting public interest criteria, but also of the role that 'positive' public interest criteria can play, given the satisfaction of an agreed evidential standard. Thus, public interest criteria will be considerably widened beyond their present narrow expression – essentially as criteria for not prosecuting – within the Attorney General's *Criteria*.

Redrawing the boundaries of the evidential test – so as to narrow them – in combination with an expansion of the boundaries of public interest, may represent a return to the model of decision-making advanced by Lord Shawcross which was discussed in Chapter 1. In that discussion it was maintained that through the process of elucidating the way in which the DPP had used his discretionary decision-making powers, there has been a subtle departure from this model, wherein public interest is the 'dominant consideration'. It was noted that in this respect the two-stage model of decision-making advanced in the current Attorney General's *Criteria* can be problematic. How should the prosecutor resolve the dilemma which arises when he believes on the evidence that a conviction ought to result, but also believes that a jury is likely to acquit (see also Williams 1985)? Should the prosecutor ignore his uncomfortable prediction about the strength of the evidence and proceed, in the public interest, on the grounds that the damage caused by a potential acquittal would be less than the certain damage resulting from a decision not to proceed?

One solution to this dilemma, if a two-stage model of decision-making is to be retained, was proposed by a previous Attorney General, Sam Silkin (*Guardian*, 21 April, 1980). He recognized the convenience of a twin test which negated the necessity of examining the public interest where evidential sufficiency was not satisfied. But, like Lord Shawcross, Silkin believed that the two-limbed test in fact embodied a single principle: that a prosecution should only be brought when it is in the public interest. He noted: 'it is rarely in the public interest to prosecute unless the chances of conviction outweigh those of acquittal. But the case sometimes arises where there is a clear *prima facie* case but the jury is more likely than not to acquit.' If the basic principle of public interest is to be paramount, then decisions to proceed should be permissible even where the characteristics of a defendant or of witnesses would be likely to motivate a jury to acquit. Silkin concluded: 'if the DPP's equation does not allow for this, his arithmetic will provide an unsatisfactory answer.' The solution advanced by Silkin was that it should be assumed that the 'likelihood of conviction test' applies only to the legal strength of the evidence. Then the assessment of the prediction of the weight that will be attached to the evidence, as influenced by a series of potentially extraneous variables, can comprise part of the other aspect of the decision, namely the evaluation of the public interest.

The two limbs thus remain distinct, but the balance between them shifts with the contraction of the evidential limb and the expansion of the public interest limb. This parallels the solution advanced here, with its replacement of the jury-based evidential standard, with all its concomitant vagaries, by a standard more closely aligned to a judicially based evaluation of the evidence.

Silkin's proposal, in combination with the evidential revisions proposed here, is attractive in that it incorporates an element of a jury-based definition of public interest (otherwise known as public opinion) without allowing that 'public interest' factor to outweigh all others. By distinguishing those aspects of jury decision-making from the traditional legal arena of evidential assessments, both the prosecutor and the jury may make a contribution to the decision about whether a prosecution should be brought. The jury would retain a role in defining the public interest – both through predictions of how they *will* decide a case and through their continuing role as actual decision-makers – with the ability to return 'perverse acquittals'. But, such 'perversity' would not necessarily outweigh the potentially more reflective, more considered, more objective, and wider-ranging assessment of the public interest reached by the prosecutor. It is to this assessment that the discussion now turns.

On the basis of the empirical findings it is clear that prosecutors at the DPP are capable of applying a more sophisticated cost-benefit analysis of public interest criteria than that advocated in the Attorney General's *Criteria*. For example, in respect of the DPP's consent caseload, the extremities of different types of costs and benefits are usually fairly clear – at least in the abstract – even if they are not constantly employed in practice. In Section 5(2) cases, the cost of an individual wasting police time is weighed against the cost of discouraging even 'dubious' complaints from others in the future – especially from sensitive complainants such as rape victims. Although this trade-off between an actual waste of time and the potential general deterrent effect on the reporting of real crime may be dubious, at least there is some recognition that public interest involves 'net interest'. Similarly, cases arose where the public interest costs and benefits of taking or refraining from a course of action were spelt out. An example of this arose in Case 83 (see Chapter 2) where the public interest assessment made by the police conflicted with that made by the DPP. The police took the view that a husband should not be prosecuted for drug importation because this would make his wife unlikely to give evidence against his associates who kidnapped her in response to his 'double dealing'. The contrary view taken by the DPP was that the husband should be prosecuted, on the grounds that the public interest in prosecuting an individual accused of a serious drug offence outweighed the possibility of endangering the strength of the evidence on the kidnapping charge. Thus, both the costs and benefits of action or inaction against the husband were considered.[7]

However, the parameters of public interest were not routinely explored in this manner. In the absence of any explicit or relevant public interest policy addressing particular problems encountered by the prosecutor, it was common for a more one-sided approach to the public interest to prevail. An illustration of this arose in the attempted murder charge in Case 2 (Chapter 3) which concerned the shooting of a police officer. The public interest argument was all too clear: people who go around shooting at policemen should expect to be charged with attempted murder. Although, subsequently, there was a directed acquittal on this charge on account of evidential insufficiency, the judge remarked that the defendant had 'no right to complain'. The implication was clearly that criminals should be deterred from shooting at the police; herein lay the 'greater good' public interest argument. But what logical consequences flow from acting upon it? The defendant could not explicitly be punished for that 'offence'. Furthermore the totality of charges against the defendant were such that the attempted murder charge, even if it had succeeded, was unlikely to make any appreciable difference to sentence over and above the alternative – and more realistic – Section 18 count. Thus neither retributive aims nor individual deterrence could underlie the public interest assessment. Similarly, the seriousness of the other charges facing the defendant meant that a long trial following a lengthy remand was inevitable. Therefore, even individual deterrence would anyway have accrued to the defendant through the penalizing nature of the prosecution process. Both by elimination and by inference, a general deterrence aim on the part of the prosecution was plain. Yet the ramifications of deploying charges in an endeavour to achieve general deterrent effects were not explored in the round. Had they been, an alternative course might have resulted. First, the criminological literature clearly questions the efficacy of general deterrence (see for example Cook 1980); the practical net impact of the prosecution's chosen course may have been minimal. Secondly, there are public interest counter-arguments. Would not a directed acquittal, as widely publicized as the original charge, negate or undermine the pursuit of general deterrence? Similarly, what impact was there likely to be on the jury's confidence in the Crown case, when its leading charge was thrown out shortly after the case began? Might this not have had a 'knock on' effect on the prospects in relation to the other counts, and so be harmful to the public interest?

What discussion of this case also shows is that where there is a strong 'interest' from the public, the prosecutor may alight on the obvious public interest angle without looking further afield. Although defensible in isolation, this single (public interest) justification may subsequently be challenged. In his defence, the busy prosecutor might argue that it is only necessary to record his predominant public interest consideration; the alternatives are there between the lines. But this represents the slippery slope to sloppy thinking. How can it be known what these alternative considerations are and indeed, what, if any, weight they bear? How can the prosecutor's public interest decisions be monitored if they are not spelt out? How are other prosecutors to learn from the experiences of those who have employed the reasonable prospects approach? Since the DPP does contemplate 'unintended consequences' in reaching some prosecution decisions, public interest considerations are capable of being explored 'in the round'. An example of this would be where circumspection is shown over bringing perjury proceedings which might cast doubt on some previous conviction. But it appears that this rounded consideration occurs largely where a public interest policy has evolved for that category of offence. Although arguably a chicken and egg problem, there can be little hope of developing comparable public interest approaches to issues which permeate many cases, rather than being confined to a specific category, unless public interest costs and benefits are articulated in individual cases, regardless of their attributed importance.

Three recommendations are thus made in respect of the public interest limb of the reasonable prospects approach. First, 'positive' public interest criteria should be acknowledged; this would be necessary even with a revised evidential test, but imperative if the existing test is maintained. Secondly, public interest considerations need to be canvassed in relation to the wider human and economic costs and benefits of prosecution as against non-prosecution. Specifying a number of leading criteria should bring the policy more into the open; at present, cases where proceedings are not brought despite evidential sufficiency receive inadequate attention. By specifying criteria, practitioners may build up a body of public interest decisions in the same way as they have done with legal precedent. Spelling out these points may also help to shift the balance of presumption: from a position where proceedings are taken unless there are compelling reasons *against* doing so, to a position where proceedings are not taken unless there are sound public interest reasons *for* doing so. Third, in order to achieve consistency in decision-making it is recommended that there should be proper monitoring of cases where proceedings are not brought, as well as those examined by the courts where proceedings ensue. This is discussed further in the section on accountability.

ACCOUNTABILITY

The issue of accountability may be divided into two parts. First, to whom is the prosecutor to be accountable and by what means? Secondly, how is accountability to be secured: what pressures are likely to be brought to bear on the exercise of the prosecutor's discretion? Informal pressure by other participants in the criminal justice process has already been characterized as desirable in itself, but insufficient. Formal pressure, in the mode of guidelines to facilitate consistency in the prosecutor's decision-making, may also make 'calling the prosecutor to account' a less onerous task.

Why prosecution accountability is important

The centrality of the prosecutor's role, as a fulcrum within the criminal justice process, maximizes not only the range of pressures that are likely to be brought to bear on the exercise of his discretion, but also the impact which his decisions are in turn likely to have on other participants in the process. Hence, it has been asserted that the establishment of the Crown Prosecution Service will enhance the accountability of the police, since submitting their cases to the prosecutor will make them 'accountable to him for the quality of their evidence and thereby the effectiveness of their policing' (Waddington 1983). Similarly, the prosecutor's decisions as to which cases will go forward to trial will critically affect the court's ambit.

This combination of the centrality of the prosecutor's role with his new-found independence makes the question of his accountability crucially important. Enhancing the prosecutor's discretion to make decisions in the public interest correspondingly enhances the need for those decisions to be reviewable. If the prosecutor is not only expected to apply his technical legal skills but also to act as a socio-legal pundit, using the ill-defined public interest criteria that the reasonable prospects approach currently entails, a potential for capriciousness in this private exercise of discretion clearly exists. Knowledge about the nature of the policies being adopted and the manner of their implementation may be regarded as the price the prosecutor has to pay for exercising his discretion 'behind closed doors'. The adequacy of the mechanism presently proposed through which he is to be called to account for his actions is open to question. This was reviewed in Chapter 1, but will be summarized again here.

Means of accountability

The Royal Commission recommended that a locally based prosecution system should be answerable to a locally elected police prosecutions committee, which would also be responsible for administering the prosecutor's budget. However, the Government's Working Party on Prosecution Arrangements, which reviewed the Royal Commission's recommendations, was concerned that a locally based system might not achieve satisfactory consistency in prosecuting policy. This did not mean that the aim was to bring about a uniform policy. Appropriate account was to be taken of relevant variations in local circumstances but improper influence was to be avoided. Despite any safeguard which the Working Party could devise the risk of interference with the prosecution function by a local supervisory body remained appreciable.[8] Yet the report of the Working Party did not spell out the practical differences arising out of the terms it used, such as between 'improper influence' and 'responsiveness' to local circumstances (Home Office 1983). Neither was it clear what influence would be deemed proper. Perhaps these semantic niceties were overtaken once the conclusion was reached that 'he who pays the piper calls the tune'.[9]

The Government in their White Paper, *An Independent Prosecution Service for England and Wales*, followed the Working Party's advice, opting for a centralized national prosecution service. However, this was not necessarily for the same reasons as those previously advanced. Central–local relations in Government were a particularly sensitive and controversial topic at that time. Against this background, it is not surprising that the Government should have been sensitive to any suggestions that, had they adopted a locally based system, it might have been subject to local interference.

Problems with the proposed means of accountability

PROCESS

What about the model of accountability chosen – namely, Parliamentary democracy? The Attorney General is to be answerable to Parliament for issues of general prosecution policy rather than for the intrinsic merits of specific cases prosecuted. The only exceptions will be cases in which either the Attorney General or the DPP intervene, when the Attorney will be answerable for specific decisions. This is simply an extension of the present arrangement wherein the Attorney General is responsible for the actions of the DPP. The difficulty with this system is that the Attorney General will only be answerable for a tiny proportion of all prosecutions. Furthermore, these cases primarily concern special questions of policy (the very justification for having them prosecuted by the DPP); therefore, artificial distinctions will be drawn between these cases and decisions in those which make up the vast bulk of prosecutions. It is surely the latter which should attract the *de facto* description of 'a prosecution policy'.

Which cases should then be subject to scrutiny? Those which proceed to trial may be of less pressing concern – first, because it has been suggested that clarifying the evidential limb of the prosecutorial test will result in fewer weak cases proceeding to trial; and secondly, because for those cases that do proceed, the trial process will continue to act as a check on prosecutors' decisions. But, what of those cases where prosecutions do not result? Uglow (1984: 239) has suggested that it is these cases to which public criticism has most recently been directed. Under the revised test the prosecutor's discretion to filter out what he deems to be 'weak' cases will not be lessened. It is apparent that some check will be required on cases which do not proceed on grounds of lack of either evidential sufficiency or public interest.[10] Otherwise the unconscientious 'non-prosecutor' may relegate his non-prosecuted, 'no merit' cases to the category of 'insufficient evidence', or vice versa, to avoid the risk of being called to account. Currently, no mechanism to counter such a tendency is proposed.

Thus the proposed system of Parliamentary accountability does not appear likely to provide an effective check on prosecutors' day-to-day decision-making. Although 'top-ended' accountability may work in relation to flagrant abuses of power, even the adequacy of this can be questioned.[11] Certainly, it will do little to maintain a policy for *not* prosecuting; like an iceberg, 90 per cent of prosecution policy may lie underneath the visible tip and never attract the public's gaze.

Furthermore, although the bulk of prosecutors' decisions will be informed by centrally provided guidelines, of which the Attorney General's *Criteria* are the first example, there should be significant reservations about placing too much confidence in this course. There are obvious problems in implying that the prosecutor is the person to be held solely accountable. Although a central figure in the prosecution process, he does not necessarily enjoy full control over the cases brought to trial. The research has demonstrated some significant departures by counsel once cases come to trial from strategies preferred at an earlier stage by the DPP.[12] In addition, counsel is face to face with the judge. If there is pressure on him to deviate from how the prosecutor wanted him to present the case, much will depend upon counsel's view of the case at that time. Furthermore, since the reasonable prospects of conviction test allows such scope for subjectivity by the decision-maker it cannot safely be assumed that counsel will view a case in just the same way as the independent prosecutor who prepared the case, regardless of any pressures brought to bear on him at trial. At the DPP the difficulty is kept within certain limitations through use of the Treasury Counsel system, the small team of barristers retained by the DPP. Unless some equivalent scheme is introduced locally – and none has been canvassed so far for the new national system – it cannot be assumed that counsel will be *ad idem* with the new Crown Prosecutors. In addition, since the independence of the Bar is to be preserved, through the maxim that 'the conduct of the case is for counsel', the line of accountability apparently stops short. One obvious way in which it might have been extended was to issue the Attorney General's *Criteria* to all members of the Bar. This has not been done, although the Attorney has a clear *locus standi* in that he is titular head of the Bar. The overall impact may be that not only will different actors in the criminal justice system look to varying evidential standards, but they will also be accountable in different ways for prosecutions: the police to local police committees and informally to the prosecutor; the prosecutor to the Attorney General and informally to the courts; counsel apparently to no one; and the judiciary to the Court of Appeal.[13]

STANDARDS

This leaves the more fundamental difficulty: according to what standards is the prosecutor to be held accountable? In this sense focusing on the adequacy of the mechanisms for accountability may be premature – considering means before ends – in that no machinery can operate satisfactorily until there is a clear programme to be enforced.

The inadequacies of the DPP's prosecution criteria have been documented at length, yet the research has also highlighted aspects of the DPP's prosecution principles and practices which merit wider application. One rationale for offering a revised basis for prosecution decisions may be that the spirit of the reasonable prospects approach is captured, whilst some of its practical pitfalls are avoided.

The revised test represents a balance between *prima facie*, which relegates accountability and control to the courts by proceeding where there is sufficient technical evidence to make a case out (without assessments of credibility, persuasiveness, or merit in prosecutions), and reasonable prospects, which locates greater effective decision-making with the prosecutor. The revised test also represents an attainable prosecution standard. In terms of accountability it offers both a legitimate measure of performance and a potential tool for establishing whether prosecutors need to be called to account for particular decisions. Furthermore, given that it is proposed that public interest should be 'hived off' from evidential assessments, public interest considerations should become more amenable to scrutiny.

It has become axiomatic that the exercise of judgment regarding evidential sufficiency should shift from the police to the prosecutor, and that the prosecutor should not be subject to unwarranted pressure from the courts in respect of evidential questions. The argument regarding public interest questions is less clear cut. The recommended restructuring of the public interest limb of the prosecutor's decision does not substantially alter the prosecutor's discretion. Pressures may well be brought to bear on the prosecutor in respect of this element of his decision. Such pressures may be of mixed value. Prosecutors may be criticized for being too remote from the public and while the police may be criticized for being too committed to their recommended course of action, it must be recognized that the police may be better positioned to lay a 'finger on the pulse' of local public opinion. In the informal arena of police–prosecutor relationships, the prosecutor may benefit from being aware of the views of the police about the 'public interest' without those views merging into interference. In contrast, in the formal arena of prosecutor–court relationships, that distinction may be harder to maintain. Where judicial influence takes the form of public censure, as for example in the case of *R. v. Ronsley*,[14] the prosecutor may find it harder, after due consideration, to proceed fearlessly. Having clear lines of accountability and an agreed mechanism for achieving it may help the prosecutor to resist 'undue pressures'.

On the other hand, in exercising their discretionary powers, prosecutors will be, in some instances, the 'sole repository of justice'. [15] How are prosecutors to achieve the requisite standards within their decision-making which this demands? This returns to the question implicit at the start of the book. What are the qualities of a good prosecutor? The research has provided the answer that the qualities of good prosecutors can be determined if the definition is based not on some elusive feature of prosecutors' personalities, but on their working practices. Prosecutors require both workable criteria capable of consistent application and a code of practice that will enable them to resolve the kinds of day-to-day dilemmas they face. In the absence of such provisions, the distinction between whether prosecutors proceed by the rules or by 'rule of thumb' can too easily become blurred.

NOTES

1 In the absence of a controlled comparative study it cannot be ascertained whether, by employing the reasonable prospects test, prosecutors succeed in filtering out *more* weak cases than if they had merely used the *prima facie* standard; the number that did proceed to trial in this study might indicate this to be unlikely.

2 Since some cases weaken unforeseeably at trial not all directed acquittals may be used as an index of prosecutorial efficiency. In the context of the knowledge as to *why* cases proceed such criticism is legitimate.

3 Where the reasonable prospects approach invites the prosecutor to test the strength of the evidence in borderline cases by recourse to old-style committals – for as long as they continue to exist – this may jeopardize those cases' prospects of conviction at subsequent trial. This is because an adversarial criminal justice system places emphasis on witnesses' credibility through their performance in giving their testimonies; additional 'live' court hearings provide the defence with extra ammunition, namely the witnesses' depositions with which to impugn them – an extra hurdle for prosecution witnesses to jump.

4 It would be possible to push the test further and ask the prosecutor to ask himself whether he does find the case persuasive (i.e. whether he actually believes in the offender's guilt at that stage). This would mirror the test reportedly applied under the previous Director, Sir Norman Skelhorn's regime, namely not only can you prove your case, but are you personally convinced of the defendant's guilt? However, this reintroduces the danger of asking the prosecutor to speculate about the actual persuasiveness of witnesses he has neither seen nor heard, and may facilitate confusion in the prosecutor's mind between that which he knows about a case, and that which he knows he can prove. The former may impel him to prosecute where the latter may indicate a likely acquittal, and hence the desirability of proceeding cautiously, if at all.

5 The *Galbraith* judgment applies to examining magistrates at committals but probably not in summary trials where the position is governed by *Practice Note* [1962] 1 All ER 448 – broadly the same as the pre-*Galbraith* position.

6 That is, a positive reason for not prosecuting witness A to secure a prospect of conviction (positive public interest) against defendant B.

7 It will be recalled that the DPP's view prevailed and was vindicated. The wife

gave evidence on the kidnapping charges despite the husband's prosecution. The accused were convicted and received substantial sentences.

8 Furthermore, a local system would not provide a uniform career structure for members of the prosecution service.

9 The Working Party's report and the Government's White Paper did acknowledge that where individuals' career prospects, and money that is available to them, are controlled by a local body, that body is bound to be able to influence policy decisions made by those individuals.

10 It is likely that the Director's annual report to Parliament will contain information on the numbers of cases accepted and carried forward or dropped. This will permit questions to be raised about whether acceptance reviews are too lax or too severe.

11 In the case of *Ponting*, Mr John Morris (Shadow Attorney General) described the 'dead-pan statement and 19 lines calendar of events' given by Sir Michael Havers (Attorney General), about the decision to prosecute, as 'an insult to the House' (Hansard, House of Commons, 13 February, 1985).

12 It should be noted that in some cases brought in the Magistrates' Court, the prosecutor who made the decision to prosecute will, in fact, be on his feet presenting the case.

13 In earlier chapters the prosecutor's difficulty in relation to counsel has led naturally into discussion of the problems created for his predictions on case outcomes by the courts. It would, of course, be constitutionally improper to consider any extension of the line by accountability beyond the role of counsel, extending to the judiciary.

14 In the case of *R. v. Ronsley* (*The Times*, 18 November, 1983), which concerned a 77-year-old woman accused of stealing goods worth £30, the Recorder, Simon Goldstein, described the decision to prosecute as a public disgrace. He stated: 'If Woolworth's want the sadistic pleasure of prosecuting this woman they will pay for it. I have every intention of making sure they pay their own costs, and every penny of defence costs.' After the judge's remarks, the prosecution offered no evidence in the case. The Lord Chancellor subsequently rebuked Recorder Simon Goldstein for his remarks which he described as 'intemperate', further stating that they 'should not have been made' (*Guardian*, 5 January, 1984).

15 Uviller (1973: 1159), who also asserts that the prosecutor is *not* the 'sole repository of justice' when cases are put to the courts; he fails to address the question in respect of decisions not to prosecute.

BIBLIOGRAPHY

Archbold (1982) *Pleading, Evidence and Practice in Criminal Cases* 41st edn, ed. Stephen Mitchell. London: Sweet & Maxwell.

Ashworth, A. (1983) *Sentencing and Penal Policy*. London: Weidenfeld & Nicolson.

—— (1984) Prosecution, Police and Public: A Guide to Good Gatekeeping. *Howard Journal of Criminal Justice*.

Ashworth, A., Genders, E., Mansfield, G., Peay, J., and Player, E. (1984) *Sentencing in the Crown Court*. Occasional Paper No. 10. Oxford: Centre for Criminological Research.

Attorney General (1983) *Criteria for Prosecution*. Home Office Circular 26/1983, 11 February, 1983. London: HMSO.

Baldwin, J. and McConville, M. (1977) *Negotiated Justice*. Oxford: Martin Robertson.

—— (1980) *Confessions in Crown Court Trials*. Royal Commission on Criminal Procedure, Research Study No. 5. London: HMSO.

Barnes, P. (1975) The Office of the Director of Public Prosecutions. In *The Prosecution Process*. Birmingham: Institute of Judicial Administration, Faculty of Law, University of Birmingham.

Barry, B. (1967) The Public Interest. In A. Quinton (ed.) *Essays in Political Philosophy*. Oxford: Oxford University Press.

Bates, J. (1980) *The Prosecutor's Handbook*. London: Oyez.

Brown, P. (1984) The Forces that Keep CND out of the Jury Room. *Guardian*, 23 January, 1984.

Butler, S. (1983) *Acquittal Rates*. Home Office Research and Planning Unit Paper No. 16. London: HMSO.

Calabresi, G. (1982) *A Common Law for the Age of Statutes*. Oliver Wendell Holmes Lecture. Cambridge, Mass.: Harvard Law School.

Chambers, G. and Millar, A. (1983) *Investigating Sexual Assault*. Unpublished paper given at Centre for Criminological Research, Oxford.

Cohen, J. (1962) A Layman's View of the Public Interest. In C. J. Friedrich (ed.) *The Public Interest*. New York: Atherton Press.

Cook, P. J. (1980) Research in General Deterrence: Laying the Groundwork for a Second Decade. In N. Morris and M. Tonry (eds) *Crime and Justice: An Annual Review of Research*. Chicago: University of Chicago Press.

Cornish, W. and Sealy, P. (1973) Juries and the Rules of Evidence. LSE Jury Project. *Criminal Law Review*.

Criminal Law Revision Committee (1972) *11th Report. Evidence (General)*. Cmnd. 4991. London: HMSO.

—— (1980) *Offences against the Person*. Cmnd. 7844. London: HMSO.

Dell, S. (1983) *Murder into Manslaughter*. Institute of Psychiatry, Maudsley Monographs 27. Oxford: Oxford University Press.

de Smith, S. A. (1980) *Judicial Review of Administrative Action*. 4th edn. London: Stevens & Sons.

Devlin, Sir Patrick (1956) *Trial by Jury*. London: Stevens & Sons.

Devlin Report (1976) *Report to the Secretary of State for the Home Department of the Departmental Committee on Evidence of Identification in Criminal Cases*. HC 338. London: HMSO.

Douglass, J. J. (ed.) (1977) *Ethical Considerations in Prosecution*. Houston, Texas: National College of District Attorneys, College of Law, University of Houston.

Edwards, J. (1984) *The Attorney General, Politics and the Public Interest*. London: Sweet & Maxwell.

Eggleston, Sir Richard (1983) *Evidence, Proof and Probability*. 2nd edn. London: Weidenfeld & Nicolson. (1st edn. 1978.)

Emmins, C. J. (1983) *A Practical Approach to Criminal Procedure*. 2nd edn. London: Financial Training Publications.

Ericson, R. (1985) Policing Policy. Unpublished paper presented at a seminar at the Centre for Criminological Research, Oxford, 31 January, 1985.

Feeney, F. (1985) Advance Disclosure of the Prosecution Case. In D. Moxon (ed.) *Managing Criminal Justice*. London: HMSO.

Fisher Report (1977) *Report of an Inquiry by the Hon. Sir Henry Fisher into the Circumstances Leading to the Trial of Three Persons on Charges Arising out of the Death of Maxwell Confait and the Fire at 27, Doggett Road, London SE6*. London: HMSO.

Goodwin-Jones, C. (1984) Science in Harness? A Study of the Expert Witness in the Legal Construction of Reality. Unpublished Ph.D. thesis, Cambridge University.

Havers, Sir Michael (1984) The Problems of the Office of the Attorney General. Address to the Medico-Legal Society, 9 February, 1984.

Hawkins, K. (1983) Thinking about Legal Decision-Making. In J. Shapland (ed.) *Decision-Making in the Legal System*. Issues in

Criminological and Legal Psychology No. 5. London: British Psychological Society.

Hetherington, Sir Thomas (1980a) The Modern Relationship between the DPP and the Private Individual. Address to the Royal Naval College, Greenwich, 18 March, 1980.

—— (1980b) The Role of the DPP. Address to Moot, Grays Inn, 24 April, 1980.

Home Office (1964) *Judges Rules*. Home Office Circular 89/1978. 27 January, 1964. London: HMSO.

—— (1972) *Memorandum on the Control of Prosecutions by the Attorney General and the DPP*. London: HMSO.

—— (1981) *Criminal Statistics for England and Wales*. Cmnd. 8668. London: HMSO.

—— (1983) *An Independent Prosecution Service for England and Wales*. Cmnd. 9074. London: HMSO.

—— (1984) *Cautioning by the Police: A Consultative Document*. London: HMSO.

—— (1984a) *Police and Criminal Evidence Act*. (Section 66) Codes of Practice. London: HMSO.

House of Commons Select Committee (1980) *Deaths in Police Custody*. London: HMSO.

House of Lords (1984) *Prosecution of Offences Bill*. London: HMSO.

Irving, B. (1980) *Police Interrogation: A Case Study of Current Practice*. Royal Commission on Criminal Procedure, Research Study No. 2. London: HMSO.

Irving, B. and Hilgendorf, L. (1980) *Police Interrogation: The Psychological Approach*. Royal Commission on Criminal Procedure, Research Study No. 1. London: HMSO.

James Report (1975) *The Distribution of Criminal Business between the Crown Court and the Magistrates' Court*. Cmnd. 6323. London: HMSO.

Leys, W. A. R. (1962) The Relevance and Generality of the Public Interest. In C. S. Friedrich (ed.) *The Public Interest*. New York: Atherton Press.

Lund, Sir T. (1973) The Professional Conduct and Etiquette of Solicitors. 12th repr. *The Law Society* (1960).

McBarnet, D. (1981) *Conviction. The Law, The State and The Construction of Justice*. London: Macmillan.

McCabe, S. and Purves, R. (1972) *By-Passing the Jury*. Oxford Centre for Criminological Research Occasional Paper 3. Oxford: Blackwell.

—— *The Shadow Jury at Work*. Oxford University Penal Research Unit, Occasional Paper 8. Oxford: Blackwell.

McConville, M. and Baldwin, J. (1981) *Courts, Prosecution and Conviction*. Oxford: Clarendon Press.

Mars-Jones, A. (1982) *The Lantern Lectures*. London: Picador.

Moody, S. R. and Tombs, J. (1982) *Prosecution in the Public Interest*. Edinburgh: Scottish Academic Press.

—— (1983) Plea Negotiation in Scotland. *Criminal Law Review*: 297–308.

Morris, T. and Blom-Cooper, L. (1979) Murder in England and Wales since 1957. *Observer*. (Reprinted as pamphlet.)

Nash, W. (1982) The Psychologist as Expert Witness: A Solicitor's View. *Issues in Criminological and Legal Psychology 33*. British Psychological Society, St Andrew's House, 48 Princess St East, Leicester LE1 7DR.

Pattenden, R. (1982a) *The Judge, Discretion and the Criminal Trial*. Oxford: Oxford University Press.

—— (1982b) The Submission of No Case – Some Recent Developments. *Criminal Law Review*: 558–66.

Royal Commission on Criminal Procedure (1981a) *Report*. Cmnd. 8092-1. London: HMSO.

—— (1981b) *The Investigation and Prosecution of Criminal Offences in England and Wales: The Law and Procedure*. Cmnd. 8092-1. London: HMSO.

Sanders, A. W. (1985) Prosecution Decisions and the Attorney General's Guidelines. *Criminal Law Review* 4: 19.

Shea, M. A. (1974) A Study of the Effect of the Prosecutor's Choice on Magistrates' Sentencing Behaviour. *British Journal of Criminology* 14(3): 269–72.

Sheehan, A. V. (1975) *Criminal Procedure in Scotland and France*. Edinburgh: HMSO.

Skelhorn, Sir Norman (1981) *Public Prosecutor*. London: Harrap.

Sorauf, F. J. (1962) The Conceptual Muddle. In C. J. Friedrich (ed.) *The Public Interest*. New York: Atherton Press.

Steer, D. (1980) *Uncovering Crime*. Royal Commission on Criminal Procedure, Research Study No. 7. London: HMSO.

Tribe, L. H. (1971) Trial by Mathematics: Precision and Ritual in the Legal Process. *Harvard Law Review* 84(6): 1329–393.

Twining, W. (1983) Identification and Misidentification in Legal Processes: Redefining the Problem. In S. Lloyd Bostock and B. R. Clifford (eds) *Evaluating Witness Evidence*. Chichester: John Wiley & Sons.

Uglow, S. (1984) Independent Prosecutions. *Journal of Law and Society* 11(2): 239.
Uviller, R. (1973) Prosecutorial Ethics. *Michigan Law Review* 71: 1159.
Van Dijk, J. J. M. (1983) *The Use of Guidelines by Prosecutors in the Netherlands*. Paper presented at the Centre for Criminological Research, Oxford, 24 March, 1983.
Vennard, J. (1982) *Contested Trials in Magistrates' Courts*. Home Office Research Study No. 72. London: HMSO.
—— (1984) Disputes within Trials over the Admissibility and Accuracy of Incriminating Statements: Some Research Evidence. *Criminal Law Review*: 15–24.
Waddington, P. A. (1983) The Proper Way to Police Accountability. *Police* (June).
Walker, N. (1980) *Punishment, Danger and Stigma. The Morality of Criminal Justice*. Oxford: Blackwell.
Walls, H. J. (1971) What Is 'Reasonable Doubt'? A Forensic Scientist Looks at the Law. *Criminal Law Review*: 458–70.
Wells, C. and Lindsay, R. (1983) How Do People Infer the Accuracy of Eye Witness Memory? Studies of Performance and a Metamemory Analysis. In S. Lloyd-Bostock and B. Clifford (eds) *Evaluating Witness Evidence – Recent Psychological Research and New Perspectives*. Chichester: John Wiley & Sons.
Wilcox, A. (1972) *The Decision to Prosecute*. London: Butterworths.
Williams, Glanville (1963) *The Proof of Guilt. A Study of the English Criminal Trial*. 3rd edn. London: Stevens & Sons.
—— (1965) The Application for a Directed Verdict – I. *Criminal Law Review*: 343.
—— (1977) The Evidential Burden: Some Common Misapprehensions. *New Law Journal* (February): 156–84.
—— (1979) The Mathematics of Proof. *Criminal Law Review*: 297–308, 340–54.
—— (1985) Letting off the Guilty and Prosecuting the Innocent. *Criminal Law Review*: 115–22.
Wood, J. C. (1961) The Submission of No Case to Answer in Criminal Trials – The Quantum of Proof. *Law Quarterly Review* 77: 491.
Yarmey, A. and Tessillian-Jones, H. (1983) Is the Psychology of Eye Witness Identification a Matter of Common Sense? In S. Lloyd-Bostock and B. Clifford (eds) *Evaluating Witness Evidence – Recent Psychological Research and New Perspectives*. Chichester: John Wiley & Sons.

NAME INDEX

Note: Names associated with legal cases can be found in the *Subject index*.

Archbold 130, 132 (n.24), 137, 166 (n.51), 195
Ashworth, A. 27 (n.40), 38 (n.62), 55 (n.4), 80 (n.18), 195, 223
Ashworth, A., Genders, E., Mansfield, G., Peay, J., and Player, E. 195

Baldwin, J. and McConville, M. 36, 46, 162 (n.47), 205
Barnes, P. 10, 16, 34, 36, 144
Barry, B. 27
Brown, P. 206 (n.20)
Butler, S. 54 (n.77), 117 (n.5)

Calabresi, G. 29 (n.43)
Chambers, G. and Millar, A. 119 (n.8)
Cohen, J. 29 (n.44)
Compton, Mr Justice 55 (n.3)
Cook, P. J. 228
Cornish, W. and Sealy, P. 175 (n.58), 177 (n.63)

Dell, S. 93-4
Denning, Lord 137 (n.28)
de Smith, S. A. 32 (n.49)
Devlin, Lord 13 (n.22), 19, 32 (n.51), 175 (n.60)
Dilhorne, Viscount 31
Douglass, J. J. 1

Edwards, J. 7, 24 (n.35), 32 (n.48), 44, 64
Eggleston, Sir Richard 191, 192
Emmins, C. J. 133, 152, 156
Ericson, R. 118

Feeney, F. and Casale, S. 137
Fisher, Sir Henry 13, 218

Goodwin-Jones, C. 149 (n.35)

Havers, Sir Michael 35, 232 (n.11)
Hawkins, K. 189
Hetherington, Sir Thomas 7 (n.12), 13, 29, 34, 37 (n.60), 40

Irving, B. 116
Irving, B. and Hilgendorf, L. 117

Lane, Lord Chief Justice 18 (n.27), 20, 135 (n.26), 194
Lawton, Lord Justice 223
Leys, W. A. R. 29 (n.45)
Lund, Sir Thomas 6

McBarnet, D. 42 (n.66), 121 (n.13)
McCabe, S. and Purves, R. 151, 175 (n.58), 205
Mars-Jones, A. 180 (n.66)
Moody, S. and Tombs, J. 36, 39, 47, 203 (n.17)
Morris, J. 232 (n.11)
Morris, T. and Blom-Cooper, L. 113 (n.3)

Nash, W. 149

Parker, Lord 22, 223
Pattenden, R. 21, 135, 136

Sanders, A. 39, 47
Scarman, Lord 136
Shawcross, Lord 30-1, 34, 225, 226
Shea, M. 127 (n.16)
Sheenan, A. V. 40 (n.64)
Silkin, S. 37, 99 (n.24), 226
Skelhorn, Sir Norman 15, 53, 219 (n.4)
Sorauf, F. J. 41
Steer, D. 116

Tribe, L. H. 192, 193 (n.5)
Twining, W. 189

Uglow, S. 232
Uviller, R. 235 (n.15)

Van Dijk, J. 40 (n.65)
Vennard, J. 153, 202

Waddington, P. 230
Walker, N. 98
Walls, H. J. 192
Watkins, Lord Justice 168
Wells, C. and Lindsay, R. 142
Widgery, Lord 21, 167 (n.52), 223
Wilcox, A. 32
Williams, Glanville 21, 74 (n.9), 99 (n.23), 182 (n.68), 191, 193, 198 (n.12), 200 (n.13), 219, 226
Wood, J. C. 21

Yarmey, A. and Tessillian-Jones, H. 141, 182

SUBJECT INDEX

accountability 230–36
acquittals: by judge 5, 151, 152–54, 218; by jury 53; *see also* trial, jury verdict; prosecutor avoiding 16–17, 42, 54, 154–55; rates 53–4, 128
adversarial system: defence attitude 156–57, 170–72; defence 'by ambush' 129, 156, 166; reliant on self-interest 136; 'sporting theory of justice' 165–68; temporal imbalances 115, 130–33, 151, 167, 209–10
alternatives to prosecution cautions 38, 80; diversion 42–3; rarity 82, 216
Attorney General: criteria for prosecution 7, 71, 93, 124–25, 190, 193, 194, 225, 227, 232, 233; critique 29–40, 100–10, 215; guidelines for disclosure of prosecution evidence 137; guidelines for jury vetting 194 (n.7); supervision of Crown Prosecution Service 231–33; supervision of DPP 32, 232

bill of indictment 130 (n.22)

charges: achieving a balance 105, 204; alternative summons procedure 47; alternative 'insurance' charges 205; *see also* plea negotiations, multiple charges; effect on 'reasonable prospects' 204–05; overcharging 6, 19; retention of police powers 40, 119, 207; summary or indictable choice 206; undercharging 37; varying the indictment 207
committals 66; 'old style' 17, 43, 48–9, 69, 86, 91, 128–31, 152; *see also* prosecution, 'momentum'; 'paper' 17, 69, 152–53
confessions (admissions) 123, 134, 202; admissibility 120, 131–32, 139, 162 (n.47), 164–65; *see also* Judges' rules
consent cases 8–9, 70–83; Law Officers' role 8–9; public interest 28, 70–2, 75–9, 80, 82; *see also separate entry*; public policy considerations 9, 70–1; the 157 sample 66, 70–83; incest 80–1;

buggery and gross indecency 77–80; wasting police time 71–5; husband/wife thefts or damage 75–7
conviction: considered by prosecutor 15; levels of 158, 204–05; rates 15, 38, 113 (n.4); statistics 200–02; *see also* acquittals
counsel: arbiter where disagreement 84, 124; relationship with prosecutor 50–2, 64, 83, 91, 92, 115, 125–26, 207–08; Treasury Counsel 8, 51, 64, 233; Metropolitan Commissioner's list 51; trial influence, opening speeches 132–35, 208; trial influence, closing speeches 168–70, 208
Crown Prosecution Service 5, 44

Dallison v. *Caffery* 137 (n.28)
defence 156–65; *see also* trial
defence case: prosecution duty to consider 13, 218; whether considered by prosecution 127 (n.18), 190, 218; evidential burden, judicial discretion 191
defendant: previous character 157; multiple defendants, consequences of police interviews 88–90, 114; effect on 'reasonable prospects' 203–06; fair play between 103–05, 178; frequency 203 (n.17); 'minor defendants' as witnesses instead 35, 84–6, 114, 119, 126, 164, 179, 205; separate trials 90
Deputy Director: involvement in cases 64
discontinuance of proceedings 24–5
DPP office: caseload 7–10, 65; creation 7; internal organization 7 (n.13), 64–5, 199; advocacy experience 199, 209; specialisms 10
DPP Northern Ireland 46, 48, 53
DPP v.: *Kilbourne* 157; *Hester* 157; *Boardman* 173; *Brown and others* 25, 31

Elliott v. *C* 192 (n.4)
evidence: admissibility 11, 33, 120, 121; *see also* Judges' rules; between co-defendants 130, 167; between spouses 166; similar fact evidence 173;

243

evidence: – cont.
corroboration 175, 223;
credibility/persuasiveness 196;
excessive editing 135; identification
165, 169–70, 177 (n.61), 182;
malleability of rules 166–67;
persuasive/evidential burden 191;
Practice Note, 'no case' 223;
quality see committals, 'old-style';
reliability 12, 21, 24–6, 37–8;
sufficiency 4, 11, 21

gatekeeper, prosecutor's role as 2, 16
Goldsmith v. *Pressdram Ltd* 35

'half-time' submissions 1 (n.2); see
also trial

Judges' rules 117 (n.6), 120, 207
(n.21)
judicial discretion 17–23; see also
trial; curtailed by *R* v. *Galbraith*
17–21; Crown Courts 18–21;
Court of Appeal 21–2; Magistrates'
Court 22–3; see also *R* v.
Galbraith; demarcation with juries
19–21 (n.32), 191; examining
witnesses 136, 166–67, 174;
narrower than prosecutor's 24–6,
125 (n.15); public interest
considerations 31–3; sentencing 32;
see also separate entry; severance of
indictment 115, 125–26, 165, 173,
204, 208, 220; summing up 144,
146, 149–50, 153, 174, 177, 195,
208
judicial review: non-prosecution
decisions excluded 1 (n.1)
jury see also trial, verdict; 'beyond
reasonable doubt' 21, 164, 190–92;
'by-passing' 17–18; composition
132; Contempt of Court Act 1981
62; demarcation with judges
19–21; 'Diplock Courts' (N.
Ireland) 53, 194; 'impartiality
concept' 38, 53, 99, 194–95;
majority verdicts 192–93; moral
judgments 178–82; Official Secrets
Act cases 28 (n.42); 'perverse
convictions' 32; prosecutor's
assumptions 95, 106; public interest
considerations 32–3, 38, 99, 106;
reaffirmation of trial role 17; right
to trial by 18; 'second guessing' by
prosecutor 11, 12, 15, 98, 110, 114,
159; see also tribunal; selection and
vetting 194; 'shadow juries'
(simulated trials) 175; sympathy
with police 99, 123, 162, 179–80,
187 (n.68), 200 (n.13); verdicts
174–82

Law Officers 8–9; see also Attorney
General; prosecution criteria

mens rea 16, 127, 158, 162, 192;
assault 68, 126; attempted murder
67, 126

murder/manslaughter 93–4,
126–27, 168–69, 171, 180, 201

nolle prosequi 24

plea-negotiations 6, 36–7, 50–1, 94,
137, 195, 205, 207–08
Police Act 1964 s.49 (prosecution of
police officers) 10; evidence from
other officers 117–18, 122–23,
159–61; 'very reasonable prospect
of conviction' 15, 118, 200 (n.13)
police as prosecutors 3
police relationship with lawyer
46–50, 116–21; re: public interest
234; retention of power to charge
40, 50, 121; separation of
investigation from prosecution 45
prima facie 4, 12, 20, 215
Procurator Fiscals 47; see also Name
index, Moody and Tombs
proof see jury, verdicts; standards;
balance of probability 4, 156;
beyond reasonable doubt 21, 116, 176–82,
190–94; location of burden 69;
persuasive/evidential burden 191;
reasonable doubt (defence) 156
prosecuting solicitors' departments
45, 200; solicitor-client relationship
5, 46, 49
prosecution: accountability 29, 43–5;
alternatives to 12; see also separate
entry; Attorney General's *Criteria*
7, 71, 93, 124–25, 190, 193, 194,
225, 227, 232, 233; 'by-passing' the
jury 17–18, 151; consideration of
defence case 13–14, 22; consistency
44; counsel 6; 'delegation effect'
209; dependence on police 39–40,
45–50, 82, 87–91, 108, 109, 114,
116–21, 126, 128, 196 (n.10), 197,
234; deterrent effects 81, 107–08;
'incremental approach' 91–5, 125;
independence 3, 4–5, 6, 7, 24–5,
39–40, 45–52; information v.
control 94–5, 131, 200, 207 (n.23),
210–11; jury assumptions 95–100,
177–82; 'momentum' 4, 39–40,
42, 47–8, 87, 92, 95, 125, 211; see

SUBJECT INDEX

also committals; non-prosecution decisions, accountability 232, rarity 128; private prosecutions 9, 25, 47 (n.70); Prosecution of Offences Regulations 7
public interest *see* consent cases; criteria 4, 11–12; *see also* Attorney General's *Criteria*; critique 100–10; DPP as arbiter 26–41, 122; 'national interest' distinguished 28; 'public opinion' distinguished 33, 36, 38, 105–06; redrawing boundaries 41; restructuring 221–30; social reinterpretation of legal issues 110, 122, 126, 128, 154, 178–79; 'trumps' over evidential sufficiency 81–3, 126, 128, 154; witnesses/co-participants 178–79, 205; *see also* defendant, multiple defendants

R v.: *Ambrose* 84, 105, 204; *Aramah* 32 (n.52); *Ballie-Smith* 223; *Banks* 168; *Beresford* 84; *Breckenridge* 192 (n.4), *Broad* 24; *Bryant and Oxley* 168; *Buckland* 135 (n.26); *Caldwell* 192 (n.4); *Canterbury and St Augustine Justices, ex parte Klisiak* 37 (n.59), 206 (n.20); *Cato* 180; *Cooper* 21; *Derby Magistrates' Court, ex parte Brooks* 32 (n.50); *Dix* 195 (n.9); *Edward* 156; *Elliott* 9 (n.18); *Evans* 136; *Fisher* 146 (n.33); *Galbraith* 17, 19–21, 23, 42 (n.66), 113 (n.3), 125 (n.15), 129–30, 155–56, 200 (n.5), 221; *see also* trial, 'half-time' submissions; 'reasonable prospects': test of, problems posed for; *Gibson* 32 (n.54); *Gilbert* 195 (n.9); *Grimshaw* 192 (n.4); *Lake* 223; *Lawrence* 98; *Littlewood* 25, 207 (n.22); *Luciano Petrone, ex parte* 23; *McGlinchey* 204; *Matheson* 93; *Matthews* 207 (n.22); *Mirfield* 121; *Moloney* 93; *Mutch* 195 (n.9); *Pearce* 135 (n.26); *Ponting* 32 (n.51); *Puddick* 168; *Ramsgate Justices, ex parte Warren and others* 37 (n.59), 206 (n.20); *Richardson* 137; *Ronsley* 233 (n.14); *Seymour* 97; *Sutcliffe* 93, 195 (n.9); *Thorne and others* 223; *Turnbull and other.* 128 (n.21); *Turner and others* 223; *Venna* 68; *Vernage* 195 (n.9); *Vinagre* 93; *Wainwright* 168; *Walhein* 177 (n.62); *Watts* 194; *Williams (Gladstone)* 161 (n.45), 174 (n.57)

rape 132–35, 143, 147, 166–67, 171–72, 192 (n.4)
'reasonable prospects' 10–41; *see also* counsel; judicial discretion; jury; witnesses; 'test' of 4, 11, 30–1, 37; *see also* evidence, sufficiency; the 'approach' 4, 12, 30–1, 37; *see also* public interest; test/approach 'collapsed' or combined 99, 102, 195–96; critique 215–16; departures 85; endemic problems 95–100, 110–11; guilty pleas 201–02; Judges' rules *see separate entry*; problems posed for 20; morality and social worth 96–9; 'once-for-all' or sustained 180, 209–10; practical difficulties 202–11; quasi-judicial 22; quasi-juror 26; recourse to counsel (pre-trial) 84, 92; recourse to Magistrates' Court 84, 92; revised test *see separate entry*; subdecisions 203–06; *see also* charges; defendants, multiple; tribunal; systemic problems 87–95, 109, 110; variations of standard 14–16, 35–6, 39, 82–3, 113, 122, 128, 154, 201; *see also* tribunal
research methods 61–70, 114; the consent cases 67; the '85' sample 67–9; the '18' sample, trial cases 69, 113–82; the '285' sample, records 69–70
regulations cases 9–10
revised test 52–4; discussed 154–56; problems 222–25
Royal Commission on Criminal Procedure 3, 5–6, 12, 14, 26, 54, 86, 120, 136, 176, 217, 218, 222, 231

sentencing 32, 94, 195, 223; *see also* judicial discretion; mitigation 34, 104; prosecution influence 127
solicitor-client relationship *see* prosecuting solicitors' departments; privileged communications 161, 165;
standards for prosecution *see* Attorney General's *Criteria*; 'beyond reasonable doubt' 21, 190–94; *see also* proof; fairness, openness, accountability 5; judicial reference points *see* judicial discretion; level of tribunal for reference 13, 207; *see also* tribunal; police cases 10; *see also separate entry*; *prima facie* 4; *see also separate entry*; reasonable prospect of conviction 4; *see also separate entry*; variability 14–16

trial 131–82; closing speeches, prosecution 168–70, defence 170–72; defence case 156–65; defence strategies 157–65; 'half-time' submissions 151–55; judicial discretion 172–74; *see also separate entry*; jury verdict 174–82, 208; *see also* jury; opening speeches 131–35; 'trial within a trial' 139, 153, 165, 178; witnesses *see separate entry*

tribunal: -level *see* conviction; magistrates or jurors as prosecutor's reference group 13, 23, 36, 97–8, 199, 206; 'twin-track justice' 14, 42, 220

Turner v. *DPP* 24, 25

witnesses 114–15, 123, 125, 129–31, 135–51, 197–98; 'coming up to proof' 135; confidence 142–43; credibility 149–50; experts: pathologists 92, 110, 124, 145–49, 153, 176, 198; motivation 143; perception 141; predictions of performance 136–51; *see also* prosecution, dependence on police; previous convictions 137

Woodward v. *Dolbey* 192 (n.4)

Worley v. *Bentley* 137